St. Bartholomew's Church
in the City of New York

St. Bartholomew's Church in the City of New York

Christine Smith

New York • Oxford
Oxford University Press
1988

Photo Credits: Alinari: 19, 22, 23, 43, 50, 62, 63, 66, 68, 69, 71, 73, 75, 76, 81; Anderson: 70; Bruno Balestrini, courtesy of Electa Editrice: 42, 45, 53, 80; Raffaello Bencini: All color plates; 1, 2, 3, 17, 24, 30, 40, 47, 57, 60, 72; Bohm: 41, 48, 51, 52, 64, 78; British Architectural Library, RIBA: 36; Mario Carrieri: 67; Courtesy of the Cathedral Church of St. John the Divine, New York: 10, 26, 27, 28, 31, 32; From E. C. Chorley, *The Centennial History of St. Bartholomew's Church, 1835–1935*: 8; Courtauld Institute, The Conway Library: 35; Electa Editrice: 39; Keith Goldstein, courtesy of St. Bartholomew's Church: 16; From C. R. Morey, *Lost Mosaics and Frescoes of Rome of the Medieval Period*: 77; Museum of the City of New York: 11; National Academy of Sciences, Washington, D.C.: 13; Nebraska State Historical Society: 12; From R. Oliver, *Bertram Grosvenor Goodhue*: 38; Carra Ferguson O'Meara: 20; Orzi and Pedretti: 56; Royal Commission on the Historical Monuments of England: 33, 34, 37, 44, 49, 55; Courtesy of St. Bartholomew's Church: 4, 5, 6, 7, 14, 15, 18, 25, 54, 82; Courtesy of St. Thomas Church, New York: 9; San Diego Historical Society, Ticor Collection: 79; Christine Smith: 58, 59, 61; Courtesy of Trinity Church, Boston, Massachusetts: 29; Michael Zaccaria: 46

Oxford University Press

Oxford   New York   Toronto
Delhi   Bombay   Calcutta   Madras   Karachi
Petaling Jaya   Singapore   Hong Kong   Tokyo
Nairobi   Dar es Salaam   Cape Town
Melbourne   Auckland

and associated companies in
Berlin   Ibadan

Library of Congress Cataloging-in-Publication Data
Smith, Christine.
St. Bartholomew's Church in the City of New York / Christine Smith.
p.   cm. Bibliography: p.   Includes index.
ISBN 0-19-505406-7
1. Saint Bartholomew's Episcopal Church (New York, N.Y.)
2. Church architecture—New York (N.Y.).
3. Architecture, Modern—20th century—New York (N.Y.)
4. Ecclecticism in architecture—New York (N.Y.)
5. New York (N.Y.)—Buildings, structures, etc.
6. Goodhue, Bertram Grosvenor, 1869–1924—Criticism and interpretation.
I. Title. II. Title: Saint Bartholomew's Church in the City of New York.
NA5235.N6S37 1989
726'.5'097471—dc19   88-734   CIP

Printing (last digit): 9 8 7 6 5 4 3 2 1

Printed in Japan
on acid-free paper

ACKNOWLEDGMENTS

WHEN A HISTORIAN of medieval and Renaissance architecture decides to write about a twentieth-century American church, she needs help. With pleasure, I express my thanks to those who shared their knowledge with me. In the earliest stages, Richard Pommer, Sarah Landau, and Catha Rambush set my feet on the right path. Richard Oliver, whose own book on Bertram Grosvenor Goodhue was at press, directed me toward the Goodhue archive at Columbia University; I learned much from our discussions about the architect. Edwin Olsen, from the firm of Caine, Farrel and Bell, gave valuable technical information about the church. To Percy Preston, archivist of St. Bartholomew's, my sincere gratitude for help in locating the original documents and drawings published in this book and for his enthusiastic support of my project. With David Trovillian, former verger at St. Bartholomew's, I explored the upper, lower, and intermediate zones of the building; his love for the church made him generous with his time.

Some friends and colleagues helped correct my errors by discussing the project with me; I thank Sheila Schwartz, Raymond Grew, Sarah Landau, Chris Woods, and David Van Zanten. Others read preliminary or final drafts of the manuscript and offered their comments; I am grateful to Marvin Trachtenberg, Richard Pommer, Royden Davis, S.J., Elbrun Kimmelman, Percy Preston, and J. Sinclair Armstrong. Henry A. Millon read the manuscript for publication; the book has benefited from his extensive knowledge and fine critical sense.

The rector of St. Bartholomew's, the Reverend Thomas F. Bowers, was generous in granting permission to consult and reproduce material in the possession of the church. The Reverend Andrew Mullins encouraged my project from its inception. Reverend Bowers's secretary, Ruth Ferguson, aided me materially in my work. Permission to consult Goodhue's correspondence at the Avery Architectural and Fine Arts Library (Columbia University) was granted by Janet Parks, Curator of Drawings.

My family also shared in this project. My brother, Richard Smith, prepared photographs for study purposes and helped me come to know the churches of New York City. My parents, Richard and Henrietta Smith, who had the foresight to have me baptized at St. Bartholomew's, really stand at the beginning of the project.

I was assisted in my research by Elizabeth Wicks and Dwight V. Gast. Maria Grazia Zatti, Fiorella Superbi, Andrew Cullinan, Gertrude Buckman, Jaimee Uhlenbrock, Michael Zaccaria, and Anne Michelle McKenna aided me in the last stage of the project. With the help of J. Donald Freeze, provost of Georgetown University, I was able to transfer the text onto a computer for final corrections. I also want to thank my editors at Oxford University Press: Joyce Berry, Irene Pavitt, Karen Lundeen, and Joan Bossert. My book has benefited in important ways from their skill and experience, and I have enjoyed working with these fine people.

All this help notwithstanding, the book is really the result of a collaboration between Raffaello Bencini and me. In 1982, Mr. Bencini came to New York from Florence, Italy, in order to photograph the church; his beautiful work illustrates the book. Two generous gifts, made in the memory of Elbrun Russell-French, enabled Mr. Bencini to carry out his work and were crucial to the project. Publication was assisted by a gift from the Estate of Ruth M. Shellens to Oxford University Press in memory of the Shellens family. Miss Shellens was a devoted member of St. Bartholomew's Church for more than forty years and a supporter of the Committee to Oppose the Sale of St. Bartholomew's Church. J. Sinclair Armstrong, founder, chairman, and president of this committee, and its board of directors and advisory committees have taken a particular interest in my project and been helpful in its publication. My special gratitude goes to these donors and supporters.

Florence
March 1988

C. S.

CONTENTS

St. Bartholomew's Church
in the City of New York

1 · Goodhue. St. Bartholomew's
Church, New York (1917–19)

INTRODUCTION: THE CHURCH

Located on broad Park Avenue in midtown Manhattan, and set off from neighboring buildings by a garden and terrace, the church of St. Bartholomew's was designed to impress the passer-by with the grandeur and dignity of its exterior (fig. 1). The design has an extraordinary clarity and monumentality, due as much to its stylistic qualities as to its size. Contrast dramatizes the different characters of the exterior and interior, in accordance with their different functions. While the exterior aims to impress with its confident monumentality, the interior (pl. XIII) draws out the worshiper, inviting active participation in an experience of transcendent spirituality. In contrast to the flat planes of the exterior, which define pure geometric solids, the mural boundary of the interior is evasive, even illusory. The exterior is tangible, hard, and sharp; the interior is dematerialized and visionary.

The exterior may be considered in terms of three main design components: the west façade, the massing of the volumes, and the dome. The guiding principle of the west façade, as of the whole building, is contrast; the long, low, horizontal block of the projecting narthex is contrasted with the tall, vertical, pierced screen of the façade's upper part (pls. I, II, III). To emphasize this contrast as much as possible, the roof of the narthex is flat, eliminating the visual transition between the juxtaposed blocks. While the narthex is entirely of white limestone, the upper façade is mostly of darker brick. The upper edge of the narthex, devoid of sculpture, again affirms, almost brutally, its separateness from the upper portion of the building.

Yet these parts are also forcibly linked by their complementarity: as opposites of equal strength and definition, they maintain and reinforce each other's character. Their shared features also unite them. The arches of the portal are repeated on a larger scale in the single arch framing the west window. The frontal, motionless, full-length figures in niches at portal level are echoed in the four figures placed against the mullions of the west window. Although the upper part of the façade is mostly of brick, limestone frames and defines the window and buttresses. Both the lower and the upper portions give an impression of planarity, relieved by sculptural ornament and columnar arcades. At the portal zone, the free-standing and attached columns support a trabeation; at window level, the columns are within the plane of the wall itself; below the gable, the colonnettes, flush with the wall, form a screen behind which the wall recedes. This succession of columns—in front of the wall, at the wall, and in place of the wall—unites the parts of the façade and lightens the effect of the wall mass.

These masses dwindle in width and in solidity as they rise from the pavement. The narthex block establishes the maximum façade width (75 feet). At the next level, the main section is perhaps half that width, the rest of the space taken up by polygonal and rectangular buttresses. But the sturdy corner buttresses terminate abruptly (like the narthex) just below the dwarf gallery in the central section; the slender, vertical strip buttresses drop away at the height of the gallery; and, finally, the central portion itself diminishes to become a miniature pediment, or gable. This progressive narrowing is even more evident when the façade is viewed from the top downward. The relation of the triangular pediment, the final member of the façade composition, to the whole façade is disproportionate. It is absurdly small in relation to the height and width of the whole. Thus while the general impression of the façade is of two simple, pierced, and sculpted solids in juxtaposition, analysis reveals linkages between the parts and subtle adjustments to the members, providing a unified upward motion for the whole.

2 · St. Bartholomew's Church, view from the northwest.

3 · St. Bartholomew's Church, view from the southwest.

The four arms that make up the nave, transepts, and east end of the church are conceived as pure geometric forms, blocks at right angles to one another. The nave, with its large windows, shares something of the style of the west façade (fig. 2). Indeed, all the arms are visually linked to the facade by the continuous dwarf gallery that runs along their upper edges. The gables on each of the transept facades, reminiscent of that on the west facade, underline the implied centrality of the structure. The periphery of the building is divided into an upper and a lower zone, as is the west façade. On the north side, an atriumlike entrance to the transept flanks the body of the church; the lower part of the north transept facade projects over the mortuary chapel. To the south, the chapel forms a subsidiary volume along the body of the church; the lower part of the south transept would have formed the fourth side of a projected, but never executed, cloister (fig. 3). Thus the lower sections are differentiated according to their diverse functions (narthex, atrium, mortuary chapel, cloister, chapel), but also united by repeated motifs, such as sculpted window arches.

The upper sections have greater visual continuity from part to part, due to the congruence of their shapes, materials, handling, and linking devices. But the parts are differentiated: the north transept is blind, whereas the south transept is filled with a rose window; the nave has tall windows with three lights each and a semicircular tracery lunette, and the west façade repeats this form on a gigantic scale with five lights beneath the lunette.

At the meeting point of these volumes, a square base marks the area from which the great tower, the culminating feature of the exterior composition, would have risen. The tower would have doubled the height of the church and been far richer in windows, buttresses, and sculptural ornament than any other part of the exterior. The dome that was built in its stead was not the architect's design, and it performs an entirely different visual function. By capping rather than extending the exterior masses, the dome gives undue importance to the main body of the church. It concludes, rather than attenuates, the structure; it diffuses, rather than concentrates, the massive volumes of the lower parts so that the movement of the whole building is centrifugal, rather than centripetal. The inlaid marble and tile decoration on the dome's eight faces seems unrelated to the sculptural character of the lower parts of the building, and the dome's planarity repeats that of the lower parts rather than opposing it, as the architect wished. The underlying design principle of the exterior, as originally conceived, was contrast between the large features and continuity between the small ones. Broad was opposed to high, light to dark, planar to sculptural, cubic to cylindrical. Of all these contrasts, the most striking would have been that between the tower and its base, the body of the church.

Contrast, again, directs the spectator's experience as he enters the narthex (pl. x). The luminosity of the portal's stone gives way to the shimmering half-light of the vestibule, and the hard white limestone sculpture of the exterior is succeeded by the soft colors of veined marbles; the austerity of the assertive wall surfaces of the outside of the building is replaced by the rich sensuality of walls sheathed in marble. The visitor, impressed by the verticality of the church structure rising above the pavement, now is enfolded by a low, intimate space whose ceiling undulates in a succession of domical vaults.

Lulled by the warmth of the vestibule, the spectator is surprised on entering the church proper. The intimacy of the low, broad vestibule is shed, and high, majestic vaults define a vast, open space (pl. xiii). The splendid apse—the focus of the church—immediately captures the attention of the spectator, who is drawn forward. Although the church is good-sized (250 feet long, with a nave span of 44 feet), it appears much vaster than it is. This is due partly to the contrast established between the spaces of vestibule and church and partly to the near absence of divisions among the spatial parts, so that the spectator feels enclosed by a single, articulated space. The nave elevation of contrasted, superimposed arches (one low and broad, the other tall and narrow) between massive piers creates the illusion that the great mural boundary has been hollowed out in giant niches. In fact, though, side aisles and galleries run behind this plane, within the thickness of the piers. The size of the crossing, marked by four immense barrel vaults, also suggests ample space. Finally, the great width of the apse and its development as a giant niche open up to the level of the vaults suggest that the whole interior space is of monumental proportion.

The major elements that define the interior space—vaults, apse, piers, gallery arches—are on a monumental scale and uninterrupted in their planar extension. Hence they enclose a relatively simple and undifferentiated spatial volume, which is the aesthetic center of the design. It is a positive space intended to be lighted and colored, made to breathe as a palpable entity. The mural boundary is of secondary aesthetic interest. Although the piers are imposing, they do not call attention to themselves as sculptural or structural forms. The openings in their faces are designed less to enliven their forms than to catch pools of shadow, contrasting with the luminosity of the nave. The varying luminosities of nave, shadowed galleries, and dark pier openings activate the space of the whole interior. The point of transition from the solids that define the spatial periphery to the space itself is softened or rendered ambiguous. Slender colonnettes, little more than pale vertical lines trapping shadows behind them, mask the corners of the piers; the gallery walls are opened with windows and tracery; and the marble sheathing of the lower walls foreseen in the original design would have rendered indeterminate the plane of the wall.

The dark color of the dome, much lower than the tower originally designed, contributes to the somewhat eerie quality of the uppermost spatial zone that the architect envisioned. The enclosed volume attains an almost palpable atmospheric density, as though divinity had taken form and hovered, immaterial yet visible, at its core. The great cross in the marble wall revetment of the apse is seen through this veil of light (pl. xiv).

Much of the effect of the interior depends on color, texture, and luminosity. The character of the space is defined by the treatment of the mural boundary as much as by its proportions. For this reason, the architect used a wide variety of materials with different aesthetic properties: white limestone, brown acoustic tile, colored marbles, gold and colored tiles. The splendid effects that he contemplated for the interior were best realized in the apse and chancel, where the stones capture and radiate light.

The building reconciles the potentially conflicting roles of public monument and sacred space through the contrasting character of exterior and interior. The exterior—razor-sharp, aggressively self-confident—projects an image of leadership and of no-nonsense efficiency. But the voluptuous sensuality of the interior—with its great, vaporous spatial volumes, in which the air trembles with a more-than-human living force—invites the spectator to experience an inner mystery.

4 · Leighton Parks.

1 · THE PATRONS

THE PARISH OF St. Bartholomew's, as a corporative institution, is not old in the history of Western civilization, but it is of respectable age in American history. When the parish was organized, in 1835, only fifty-nine years had passed since the United States had become a nation, and forty-six since the Protestant Episcopal church had been established.[1] The early parish was modest in its aims: we know little more than that "a number of gentlemen residing in the Bowery and vicinity deemed it expedient to establish a new Episcopal congregation." Until the latter part of the century, these gentlemen—well-to-do business and professional men—attended their church quietly, making little impact on the community at large.

The St. Bartholomew's built in 1835, on Lafayette Place and Great Jones Street, was described by a contemporary source as "very plain and destitute of architectural beauty" (fig. 5). And this was a fair assessment. The church was a vaguely Neoclassic meeting hall, looking rather like a Greek Doric temple with a Gothic or Regency spire on top. It cost $33,000 to build.

St. Bartholomew's II, on Madison Avenue and Forty-fourth Street, was more ambitious (fig. 6). The land for the building, owned by the New York and Harlem Railroad, was offered to the church at an advantageous price through the offices of a parishioner, William H. Vanderbilt. The choice of the architectural firm, Renwick and Sands, was made by a vestryman, Edward Matthews. The church, completed in 1872, was described in the *Evening Post* as the "Pisan-Romanesque or Lombardic style prevailing in the north of Italy;—a style which finds its highest development in the celebrated Cathedral of Pisa." The cost of the church was $228,584.

We do not know by what process James Renwick, who later built the neo-Gothic St. Patrick's Cathedral in New York, arrived at the choice of "Romanesque" for St. Bartholomew's II. He may have thought the style avant-garde, and in line with recommendations for church building made by such figures as John Ruskin. However, this church made (and could make) no claim to historical accuracy. Beyond a dwarf gallery (placed, however, at the triforium level), a columnar arcade with striped masonry, and a bell tower (campanile), the exterior had a most un-Romanesque as-

5 · St. Bartholomew's Church I (1835).

6 · Renwick and Sands. St. Bartholomew's Church II (1872).

pect. It interests us primarily because Bertram Goodhue's design for the west facade of St. Bartholomew's III borrowed many of these elements from the second church, arranging them in a new style and sequence.

The interior of St. Bartholomew's II had an even less Romanesque, or Lombard, appearance than the exterior (fig. 7). Columnar piers with Gothicizing capitals supported a nave elevation with triforium and large stained-glass windows; the ceiling was rib vaulted. Indeed, the design had closer affinities with High Victorian Gothic than with Italian Romanesque architecture.

The appointment of David Hummel Greer as pastor in 1888 dramatically changed the course of St. Bartholomew's parish. As leader of a fashionable congregation, whose members included some of the richest men in New York, he preached the necessity of service to the less fortunate— not only in the parish community, but also in the city and the nation.

Finding in his flock a tendency to elitism, he fought it by placing a sign outside the church that read "Strangers welcome," and he took advertisements in the newspapers to announce church services. While his expansion

7 · St. Bartholomew's Church II, interior.

of parish membership was important, his achievements in community work were even more remarkable. By 1903, the parish was operating six Sunday schools in five languages (English, German, Swedish, Armenian, and Chinese), technical trade schools, guilds and clubs with a membership of about 3,000, kindergartens, an employment bureau, a loan association, a boarding house, and a medical clinic. These various services operated from a number of locations in New York; some of the most important were concentrated on East Forty-second Street. At 116 East Forty-second was the Rescue Mission for "down and outs" (later moved to the new Parish House), and further east, at numbers 205, 207, and 208, the Parish House served the lower middle class. The medical clinic, next to the Parish House, was staffed with fifty physicians and surgeons; in 1910, it served 15,646 new patients and 37,222 old ones.

Thus the community served by St. Bartholomew's Church during Greer's rectorship was far-reaching and far more numerous than the communicants of the church itself, who were estimated at 3,226 in 1910. In an obituary for Greer, who died in 1919, the *New York Times* wrote, "He built up at St. Bartholomew's a great educational, patriotic, labor, race-amalgamated and generally useful system of Christian charity and helpfulness."

Under Greer, the parish of St. Bartholomew's was committed to the role of an "institutional parish"—that is, an urban parish that provides social services as well as worship and instruction. This connection between religion and social work was, in some ways, almost as old as Christianity itself. Its roots may be traced at least as far back as the first century, particularly to the Pauline message to the rich:

> Tell them that they are to do good, and be rich in good works, to be generous and willing to share—this is the way they can save up a good capital sum for the future if they want to make sure of the only life that is real. (1 Timothy 6:18–19)

By the fourth century, Christian welfare centers were owned by the church and operated by laymen.[2] But the model for the kind of large-scale social philanthropy exercised at St. Bartholomew's had taken form in Renaissance England, arising from the conviction that Protestant laymen should fulfill a duty to urban society.[3]

From England, the idea of "Christian socialism"[4] spread to the United States, and in 1890 was expressed in a sermon by George Hodges, of Pittsburgh:

> Christianity is interested in everything which is meant to make earth more like heaven,—in the progress of education and its universal extension; in the improvement of machinery; in the discoveries of the men of science; in the researches of the scholars; in political reform and social betterment. . . . The Church . . . is concerned with what is commonly called religion . . . but just as much with politics.[5]

In the absence of city, state, and federal aid for the poor and immigrant population of late-nineteenth-century New York, Episcopal parishes such as Grace Church, St. George's, and St. Bartholomew's were leaders in providing social services. Assuredly, it was hoped that some of the poor might be converted, but this was not the direct aim of church social work. Christian socialism, fired by the effects of the Industrial Revolution, implied a reconsideration of the nature and aims of the church itself. This new ideal, inspired by a new conception of the relation between church and state, aimed at more than the conversion of souls.

For such Protestant liberals as Greer and Leighton Parks, his successor as rector and the patron of the present St. Bartholomew's Church, heaven, or eternal bliss in union with God, was to be attained not after death, but within the context of life on earth. The revelation of God "should be sought in history, which is the sphere of moral growth and development."[6] In the view of Protestant liberals, ethical action aimed at realizing the kingdom of God in the here and now, and thus a godly life was of necessity a socially oriented life of action.[7]

Accompanying this conviction of the immanence of God was, for American Episcopalians at least, a commitment to the realization in modern society of the ideals of American democracy. Thus in 1913, the General Convention of the Episcopal Church resolved that "the Church stands for the ideal of social justice," and it called on "every communicant, clerical and lay, so to act that the present prejudice and injustice may be supplanted by mutual understanding, sympathy and just dealings, and the ideal of a thorough-going democracy may be finally realized in our land."[8]

These views regarding the role and nature of the modern church characterized the rectorship of Leighton Parks (fig. 4), who succeeded Greer in 1904. Continuing Greer's liberal politics, Parks stressed the necessity of bringing "the tradition of Christian belief and practice into closer relation with the intellectual habit and social aspiration of our own time,"[9] seeking to find "within the Church's treasure 'things new as well as old.' "[10]

But if Parks believed that the church should be "relevant," he was no popularizer in the pejorative sense. His academic preparation was one of high scholarship: B.D. from General Theological Seminary, D.D. from St. John's College, and S.T.D. from Harvard University. He used his scholarship and great eloquence to confront what he perceived as a situation of religious crisis. The titles of his books suggest the nature of the problem: *Moral Leadership; The Crisis of the Churches; What Is Modernism?* The moral leadership that Parks had in mind was best exemplified for him (and not only for him) in the person of Phillips Brooks, the great preacher of Trinity Church, Boston, and, in the last year of his life, bishop of Massachusetts.

Parks, who had been rector of Emmanuel Church, Boston, was an intimate friend and a fervent admirer of Brooks. In his eulogy of that preacher, he defined one of the central causes of crisis in the modern church—its relation to the authority and tradition of the past:

How did he [Brooks] believe his Creed? Not as a piece of tradition; not as something that had once been a power in the past, but of no power now, but must be recited simply in order that men might receive the emoluments that came because of that recitation. Far from it. He said his Creed with that free spirit in which he did everything else, because those grand historic words did express his profound conviction in regard to the Gospel of our Savior, that God is our Creator-Father, that Jesus Christ is the manifestation of the living God, that the Spirit of God is in the heart of every man. [11]

Anticipating the declaration of the Liberal Evangelical Movement that "it is the mind of Christ, not the letter of Holy Scripture, which is authoritative," [12] Parks believed that although the core of Christianity was unchangeable, its forms were and should be mutable. Thus he rejected the idea of the inerrant Bible and the infallible church. For him, the *form* of Christian ministry was subject to evolution, and it therefore required continual redefinition. [13] This relativist position owed much to the impact of the scientific discoveries that had revolutionized nineteenth-century theology and were transforming contemporary society. His response to the new knowledge was positive and energetic: he cast traditional Christian belief in terms appropriate to a new age.

This did not entail a rejection of all historical forms, such as the Creed. Indeed, he felt that they retained their validity as vehicles for modern spirituality. But these statements of belief had to be freely chosen by each person for him- or herself. Parks's emphasis on people's freedom to choose their way of faith and on the psychological and ethical component of religion came, of course, from his participation in the liberal current of thought in Protestantism. In his eulogy of Brooks, Parks praised him on these grounds:

Nothing . . . could shake his faith in the people and in the purifying power of freedom, not because it freed man from restraint, but because it opened up to every man the possibility of the completion of his character by the exercise of all his faculties untrammeled by oppression, and called to their highest opportunity by the voice of God himself. [14]

Like other Liberal Episcopalians, Parks felt that patriotism, love of democracy, and the Episcopal ministry were closely intertwined. He thoroughly opposed the reforms of the Tractarians, who—against liberalism, the new science, and the church's involvement in social and political matters—called for renewed emphasis on spirituality and ritual. Stressing the importance of the sacraments, particularly Communion, they urged a return to the practices and piety of the medieval church. Arguing against this view, Parks wrote,

The weakness of Protestantism at this point, cannot be denied, but the cure is to be found not in an attempt to revive the splendors of the Medieval

Church nor the supposed purity of the mythical undivided Church of the first three centuries. It is to be cured by more Protestantism, more liberty, truer equality, more widespread fraternity. For in the last analysis, what are these notes of Protestantism and of Democracy? They are the notes of the religion of Jesus.[15]

For Parks, as for Greer, the figure of Jesus was the central focus of faith. The keynote of their belief was "Jesus Christ, the same yesterday, and today, and forever" (Hebrews 13:8). Less concerned with sin, atonement, and judgment, Parks's piety, like that of other Broad Churchmen, focused on Jesus Christ in his role of revealing God to men. For him, Jesus the man represented human nature at its purest and best, holding God within his mind and will. Further, God is "always being actualized, fulfilled and expressed in Man; and Man only comes to full consciousness—the fullness of his potentiality—in God."[16]

This, then, was the character of his immanentism: God is in man, and the proof of this is the Man, Jesus Christ. Parks's message was preeminently an ethical one: people must choose to fulfill their potential, thus bringing the kingdom of heaven to earth. The main task of Parks's ministry was to provide moral leadership from the pulpit, interpreting the body of Christian belief in a modern spirit.

But this theologian and preacher was forced by events to become a builder. In 1904, Parks's first year at St. Bartholomew's, the question of moving from the Madison Avenue church was proposed. Parks put it aside. By 1914, however, the situation had dramatically worsened, and action was necessary. The next eleven years of Parks's rectorship were occupied with the construction of the present St. Bartholomew's Church, and his last acts as rector were attempts to bring the project to completion. At Parks's retirement in 1925, the building was little more than a shell; its decoration took place under Robert Norwood, who was rector from 1925 to 1931, along lines that departed from the original intentions of both the patrons and the architect.

LEIGHTON PARKS

Although Parks does not seem to have had previous experience with building, he was sensitive to architecture and had clearly defined ideas about it. What he liked was the "gorgeous French Gothic"[17] of St. Thomas Church, completed by Goodhue in the same year he designed St. Bartholomew's. Parks's eventual rejection of Gothic, culminating in his panegyric of Romanesque architecture in 1923,[18] is an interesting example of the prevalence of spiritual and moral over aesthetic values.

Parks consoled his parishioners, who were unhappy about leaving St.

Bartholomew's II, with the promise that "what is best in this [church] we can take with us."[19] Indeed, the new St. Bartholomew's is tied to the old in many ways; it incorporates practically everything movable from the second church: reredos, altar rail, altar painting, marble pavement, stained glass, pews, choir stalls, pew cushions, columns, and memorial plaques. Most significantly, the most famous feature of St. Bartholomew's II—the portal by Stanford White—was the focal point for the design of the new church. This portal, executed in 1902 to 1903, had been erected as a memorial to Cornelius Vanderbilt by his wife and children after his death in 1899. Said by the critic Royal Cortissoz to be the most beautiful sculpture outside Florence,[20] it is a loose copy of the mid-twelfth-century portal of St. Gilles-du-Gard in southern France (fig. 20). The choice of a Romanesque model for the Vanderbilt portal may have been influenced by a desire to match the style of St. Bartholomew's II, said to be Lombard Romanesque,[21] and it certainly determined the selection of "Lombard Romanesque" as the style of the present building. The reuse of the portal also established the maximum possible width of the façade as 75 feet, the same as that of the Madison Avenue church.

At St. Bartholomew's III, then, the continuity of the parish was expressed through the continuity of at least parts of its physical setting. Although it is true that since the new church was furnished in wartime, money was not obtainable for completely new fixtures and that it would have been undiplomatic to discard an important and recent gift made to the church by such prominent parishioners as the Vanderbilts, the reuse of materials in the new church has a deeper significance. Parks believed in the importance of tradition and in the need to invest old forms with new meaning. These objects, representing the specific traditions and experience of the parish, were irreplaceable. Part of the cultural richness of the present church is attributable to the subtle dissonance produced by its stylistic variety.

Throughout the construction, Parks kept the congregation up to date on the work in progress and interpreted its significance. The project was consistently presented in moral terms, and the congregation was led through the successive phases of building as through a spiritual exercise.

In his first sermon on the subject, delivered on April 19, 1914 (Appendix of Texts), Parks presented the necessity of abandoning the old church as a test of the congregation's obedience to Divine Will, choosing as his text "at the commandment of the Lord they journeyed" (Numbers 9:23). But the challenge was also a positive one, for the congregation was asked to accept the move as an opportunity to create

the Ideal Church, where the rich and poor meet together; in which the beauty of holiness is prefigured by beauty of worship; where the concentrated energies of the congregation are enlisted for every good work; where the stranger is welcomed as a member of the family and the pure word of God is preached for the saving of souls.

The ideal to be realized was, of course, an extension of the concepts of Christian socialism and Liberal Protestantism. More particular to Parks, perhaps, was the idea that worship has three components. There are

> three elements in divine service, and every one of them ought to be ministered to. There is the emotional, which should be ministered to by beauty. There is the devotional, or spiritual, which should be ministered to by communion. And there is the intellectual or ethical, which should be ministered to by preaching.[22]

In his sermon, Parks connected the new building with the first component—the ministry of beauty. But if the building per se belonged to the first category, it also had to provide for the functional requirements of the other two. Parks's aim as patron was to build a church that would minister to these three needs.

Ministry of Beauty

The ministry of beauty actually had two parts: the architecture of the church, and the performance of music within it. The architecture, in turn, had two roles: the ministry to the congregation during service, and the ministry to the city and nation for the conversion of souls. This larger, evangelical, aim seems to have had great importance for Parks. In his sermon, he spoke only of the exterior appearance of the new building and how it would look to the passer-by. Its frontage on a broad avenue would permit "a better artistic effect than can easily be found today." His audience was urged to imagine the complex thus: "the land to the south and west covered with stately buildings and a church worthy of the present facade lifting itself into the sunlight." The parishioners were challenged to consider the needs of others before their own, for it is a "privilege to place at the beginning of a new avenue, a thing of beauty which will give joy and peace and comfort to those who pass by." For Parks, the work of conversion was a task for the urban, rather than the rural, church, and it was directed at not only the urban masses, but also out-of-towners who "come for weeks at a time not—as we sometimes think—for shopping and frivolity alone, but also because of the educational and artistic and medical advantages of the city." To the classic definition of the city as a marketplace and the locus of social exchange, Parks added the city as the center of culture and social service.

The architecture of the church, seen in this cultural and social role, belonged as much to the urban landscape of the city as it did to the parishioners. As an instrument for the ministry of beauty, it had to satisfy urban spectators' emotional needs by stimulating their imagination: "no small part of the influence of our church in this city is due to its appeal to the imagination."[23] As evidence of this, Parks led his congregation on an imaginary tour of New York that, like medieval guidebooks, traced urban geography between the fixed points of the city's great churches: Old Trinity, Grace Church, Old St. Paul's, St. Thomas. To this list was to be added, of course, St. Bartholomew's.

Another aspect of the intended civic role of the new building had to do with urban development. Grand Central Terminal had been built astride Park Avenue between 1908 and 1913, and it was clear that this area would undergo significant improvement in the coming years. The new church claimed a place as one of the first structures to define a new center of urban development. Because Parks saw little, if any, separation between the interests of church and state, he urged his parishioners to make "a great gift of beauty to the city." For, he said, he and his parishioners owed a great deal to New York, and that debt should be acknowledged: "would it not be fine to give the city an object of beauty that would be a joy forever?"[24]

The aim of this gift of beauty to the city was, again, moral and evangelical. If liberty, fraternity, and equality were the guiding values of both the Episcopal church and American democracy, then the building, embodying these values, should testify to and tangibly express the soul of America. The architect was asked to design a structure that would be the equivalent in stone of Greer's statement, "I preach to the United States."[25] The style of the new church had to provide moral leadership to American architecture, as Parks provided moral leadership from the pulpit.

This view was clearly stated in Parks's sermon of February 27, 1916 (Appendix of Texts). That the Americans were "the most idealistic people the world has ever seen" was evident, Parks said, from modern American architecture. But this idealism was in need of guidance from the church:

> Some of you can remember the Hudson River Railroad Station on 28th or 29th Streets, some of you can remember the New Haven Railroad on 32nd Street, some of you can remember the sheds of the Pennsylvania Railroad in Jersey City. Well, they were serviceable, you could buy your ticket and find your train and start on your journey. But now we must have great palaces built over the gates of the splendid city that is about to come. Why even our stores rival in their towers the cathedrals of old! We have private houses like Italian palaces, we are no longer content with the useful, we are insisting that in banks, insurance companies, stores, railroads, libraries, private houses there be some expression of the beauty which underlies our somewhat sordid life. . . . If the Church . . . falls below the artistic demand of the community it will fail to do the work that it desires to do.

For Parks, the style of the church was replete with moral significance and purpose, and thus it was successful. It opened "a new era in American church architecture."[26] How and why this was so was spelled out in his sermon of May 6, 1923 (Appendix of Texts), the Sunday following the church's consecration. Parks began by establishing the historical place of the new church's architecture within the evolution of Protestant spirituality. His discussion started with the Reformation. The Renaissance was not considered because although

> the Renaissance is often spoken of as the root of the Reformation . . . there could be no more fatal mistake. While that great movement undoubtedly liberated the human mind, it was so essentially immoral that it would have led to the destruction of society. The Reformation saved the world from the decadence of the Renaissance.[27]

And although in the Renaissance, "the revelation of classic beauty awoke the latent artistic spirit in Italy and France . . . beauty became so sensual that the Renaissance produced an orgy of immorality no less deadly because refined and subtle."[28]

The first architecture that successfully embodied Protestant spiritual values was that of Christopher Wren. This architecture was suitable to a faith that believed that "every word in the sacred Scriptures had been uttered by God," and "it was solemn, sober, ethical, character-moulding." But it did not adequately express the nature of man's relationship with God, as this came to be understood in later times. So the architecture of Wren gave way, under pressure from the Oxford Movement in the nineteenth century, to an architecture that "turned back to the mediaeval thought which was expressed by that sublime architecture which we know as 'Gothic.'" In aesthetic terms, said Parks, the Gothic is the highest and final form of church architecture. But the idea of God and of man that it expresses is alien to the modern mind, "in direct opposition to the thought of the Reformation," and incompatible with scientific knowledge. Its idea of man and God derives from St. Augustine's views on original sin and the depravity of man; it focuses on the judgment made on man by a "Transcendent God who could be brought to the altar only by the magic influence of a priest"; and it fosters an attitude of fear. Because of the unsuitability of the religious ideas embodied in the Gothic style, it could not be chosen for the new church of St. Bartholomew's.

Instead, Parks went on, an earlier style, the Romanesque, had been chosen. It can be recognized by five stylistic characteristics, each of which has moral significance: the round arch; the apsidal chancel; the dome; clearglass, instead of stained-glass, windows; the bell tower, or campanile.

In Parks's view, the Romanesque round arch, inherited from Roman architecture, signifies human brotherhood and acceptance of this life, as contrasted with the desire to escape this life and strive upward toward heaven, symbolized by the Gothic pointed arch. Thus it was appropriate for a parish dedicated to community service and the realization of a moral ideal in every person's life.

The apsidal chancel recalls the equality between bishop and clergy in the early church, when the bishop's throne did not exist and the whole clergy sat on benches ringing the semicircular wall of the apse. The placement of the altar in the sanctuary enabled minister and congregation to gather around it like a family. Parks's remarks at this point were aimed at distinguishing the Episcopalian priesthood, which conforms to early Christian practice, from the Catholic priesthood, which Catholic congregations regarded as "a special order with magical powers." Further, they were addressed to a movement within the Episcopal church that wanted to drop the word *Protestant* from the title of the *Book of Common Prayer*. Parks opposed this on the grounds that an essential characteristic of the Episcopal faith, deriving from the Reformation, is that each priest, instead of the bishop alone, is invested with the responsibility to maintain sound doctrine. Hence, he thought, while the name "Episcopal church" states that the bishops, rather than the pope, are at the head of the ecclesiastical administration, "Protestant Episcopal" adds that all the clergy, not just the bishops, may formulate church doctrine. Since Parks's whole ministry of preaching was predicated on his right and duty, as an ordained priest, to search out the applications of church doctrine to modern life and to interpret in the light of his own understanding the ways in which that doctrine had evolved, he predictably favored an apsidal arrangement that stated the equality between bishop and clergy.

The dome, which was brought to Western architecture from the East, traces its origins back to the tents used for Hebrew worship, according to Parks. It was developed in the Byzantine Empire, at Constantinople, and appeared first in Italy at San Marco. Since Romanesque "arose out of the Byzantine," it is also characterized by the use of the dome. The dome signifies "not the transcendence but the immanence of God, God dwelling amongst His people." Its meaning calls attention to the Incarnation and is in accord both with the values of the early church and with modern thought. In contrast, the idea of the transcendence of God was linked to the medieval emphasis on atonement and sin, the central concepts of modern Catholicism and Gothic, or neo-Gothic, architecture. Moreover, the most majestic buildings in the world—Parks lists Hagia Sophia in Istanbul, St. Peter's in Rome, Les Invalides in Paris, and the Capitol in Washington—have domes. Indeed, the dome "typifies a majesty that overshadows and unifies and sanctifies human life." For Parks, the definition of the dome was identical to the definition of the Godhead, and Goodhue's original extraordinary design for this part of the church needs to be evaluated in this light.

In regard to the windows, it might at first seem, said the rector, that Romanesque was inferior to Gothic because of the absence of stained glass. But the builders of Romanesque churches preferred "the clear light of heaven" to illuminate their churches, finding in it a metaphor for the promise of redemption. This clear light was to have fallen on the glorious color of mosaics, pictures, and blue and gold tiles. "It is the illumination by the light of Christ which brings out the hidden glories of the soul which the Romanesque sought to symbolise."

The campanile, the last feature of Romanesque style, is typical of Lombardy and was an architectural innovation of the Romanesque period:

> It showed that while the Romanesque builders were profoundly influenced by the past and wished to perpetuate that sense of the brotherhood of mankind which the Roman Empire had failed to spiritualize, and that Divine Presence which the Greek Church witnessed to, and the Light which is the life of men, they did not wish to prevent progress in religious thought.

Although St. Bartholomew's had no campanile, Parks felt that this point about the appropriateness of Romanesque to the modern Episcopal church had to be made. If the church's positive attitude toward progress in religious thought was not expressed by the inclusion of a campanile at St. Bartholomew's, it was nonetheless evident from the sermons preached there and from the fact that the whole church was designed for preaching.

As a whole, these comments on the spiritual significance of Romanesque equate that style with the spiritual character of the early church and the modern Episcopal church. Romanesque is defined in contradistinction to Gothic, here equated with Catholicism and medievalism in its pejorative senses: superstition, magic, lack of respect for the individual, and pessimism.

In his closing remarks on the subject, Parks summed up. The Gothic cathedral, with its long aisles and noble columns, was perfectly suited to the sort of worship that the medieval mind desired: the people were separated from the priest; there was no need for them to hear; there was no need for them to see; the "sacring" bell would remind them when to abase and cross themselves. In a Romanesque church, on the contrary, the congregation gathered beneath the dome "to see and hear and participate in the service."

The style of the new church embodied the main tenets of Parks's ministry. It was traditional, and yet modern. It was in accord with the intellectual, spiritual, and scientific culture of contemporary America; it embodied these values and promoted a religious experience that drew from them. Although Parks preferred the "gorgeous French Gothic" from an aesthetic point of view, Romanesque was the style of democracy—in which all participate in brotherhood beneath the unifying dome, are equally illuminated by the clear light of grace, and are free to seek perfection in their earthly lives. As the style that embodied the guiding principles of American life, Romanesque was the correct style for modern architecture, and the Episcopal church had a duty to make this known: "the congregation had an opportunity to build a church which would not only be a glory to the city, but also reveal to the people that a Romanesque, or Byzantine architecture, was well adapted to this cosmopolitan city."[29]

The ministry of beauty was exercised not only through architecture, but also through music. In 1892, Greer had established a surpliced lay choir in the chancel of St. Bartholomew's II, and Parks saw to it that the choir had brilliant direction. In 1905, in his second year as rector, he invited Leopold Stokowski to come from London as choirmaster and organist. When Stokowski left in 1908, he was replaced by Arthur S. Hyde, who had studied with Charles-Marie Widor in Paris and had been organist at Parks's parish church in Boston. The size of the budget allotted to music increased steadily during Parks's rectorship. In line with Parks's views, the choice of music to be performed achieved a balance between modern and traditional composers. Indeed, the organists of St. Bartholomew's have often been distinguished composers in their own right.[30]

The importance of the ministry of music created special problems in the design of the church. Since the professional choir of seventy voices would be placed between the congregation and the altar, a deep and wide chancel was needed. Care had to be taken that the choir would be hidden from sight in high choir stalls, thus not intruding its presence on the service. But high choir stalls might obscure the congregation's view of the altar. To avoid this, the choir stalls were placed in a chancel that is 44 feet wide, permitting a clear view between them into the apse beyond. Further, the chancel was raised some 4 feet above the pavement of the nave. In this way, the choir is effectively hidden within its pews, while the altar gains additional visibility.

While not to be seen, the choir was certainly intended to be heard, and thus an acoustically favorable environment had to be created. An acoustics expert from Harvard was retained as consultant throughout the project. At St. Bartholomew's, many features of plan and style were determined by acoustic, rather than aesthetic, exigencies: the sheathing of the wall surfaces with brown acoustic tile; the use of barrel rather than rib vaults or domes; the extensive, uninterrupted wall surfaces; and the absence of interior spatial divisions.

Ministry of Communion

The second aspect of ministry, for Parks, was the devotional, or spiritual, which focused on divine service at the altar. The rector had less to say about this component of worship than about the other aspects of ministry. In part, this was because the requirements of divine service were traditional and well defined, thus needing little explication or defense. However, it is also true that Parks, as a "modernist," was less concerned with the transcendant spirituality of the Eucharist than with other aspects of the Incarnation. For him, salvation through the word of God, and the perception of his immanence, took precedence over the mystical sharing of the body of Christ. Although less a subject of discussion, Communion at the altar remained a fundamental part of worship, imposing its own practical demands on the design of the church. The altar had to be both visible and easily accessible. The wide, raised chancel contributed to the satisfaction of the first of these needs, as did the arrangement of the pews in the nave.[31] In the old church, the altar had had poor access: "the communicants are often wearied by waiting and sometimes jostled by those trying to return to their seats."[32] The broad entrance to the apse in the new church permitted the installation of a long communion railing, and the wide chancel favors an orderly flow of movement toward the apse. Return corridors opening off the east end of the chancel and exiting into the nave side aisles complete this efficient pattern of movement.

Ministry of Preaching

For Parks, the most important part of ministry was the intellectual, or ethical, which was the province of preaching. The primary importance of this function for the new building is clear from Parks's first sermon in the new church, delivered on October 20, 1918 (Appendix of Texts):

> the two essential things that the Vestry had in mind, in the construction of this building, I hope are entirely successful. We believe that the acoustic conditions of the church are favorable to an intelligent participation in the services of the church and that the seating of the congregation is such that each worshipper has an unobstructed view of the lectern and pulpit.

The pulpit had to be visible to all. The means for satisfying this requirement had been found at Phillips Brooks's preaching church in Boston, consecrated in 1877 (fig. 29). H. H. Richardson had laid out Trinity Church with a wide crossing and transepts, bringing the maximum number of people down to the end of the nave, near the pulpit. Galleries in the transept arms provide additional seating. The pulpit itself was brought forward, outside the chancel enclosure and into the nave. Side aisles in the nave were suppressed, so that all nave seating has unobstructed views of the pulpit. This arrangement, adopted at St. Bartholomew's, had far-reaching consequences not only for the church's plan, but also for its elevation.

Parks's views on Christian ministry had profound effects on the form and function of the new church. His numerous and varied requirements touched all aspects of the project: location, style, size, layout, and materials. Further, he endowed the project with moral significance for his parishioners, enlisting their participation as in a spiritual exercise.

His ideas about the church and parish are illustrated in the iconographic program of sculpture and inscriptions, in which his literary erudition found ample scope for expression and his perception of the church could be expressed in a concrete and systematic fashion. Although this program will be discussed in greater detail, some of Parks's choices are worth noting here. The four larger than life-size figures on the west façade—St. Paul, St. Francis of Assisi, Martin Luther, and Phillips Brooks—represent great preachers and reformers (pl. III). They testify to the unbroken tradition of Christian faith within a changing ecclesiastical organization and to the primary dedication of St. Bartholomew's to preaching. The twelve portraits ornamenting the narthex capitals are also representative of the concerns and commitments of St. Bartholomew's (pl. XII). St. Athanasius, the champion of the doctrine of Incarnation, is there, as are two great early preachers who taught that God's presence is revealed in human activity: St. Paul and St. Clement of Alexandria. The historical tradition of the Protestant Episcopal church is represented by Pope Gregory the Great, whose missionaries converted the Anglo-Saxons to Christianity; John Wycliffe, English forerunner of the Protestant reformers; Thomas Cranmer, the first bishop of the reformed Church of England; Martin Luther, the great reformer; John Wesley, the founder of the Methodist faith; and William White, who drafted the constitution of the Protestant Episcopal church in the United States. The commitment of St. Bartholomew's to social work is affirmed most dramatically by the inclusion of portraits of Florence Nightingale and Louis Pasteur, as well as of William Augustus Muhlenberg, the Episcopal clergyman who founded St. Luke's Hospital, and George Williams, the founder of the Young Men's Christian Association. The central role of preaching at St. Bartholomew's is again suggested by the portrait of John Chrysostom, a preacher especially admired by Parks, as well as by many of the other great preachers already mentioned.

THE VESTRY

If the rector was concerned with defining the practical needs and spiritual significance of the new church, the vestry was entrusted with its realization. At St. Bartholomew's, all the work of construction was financed by donations and offerings to the church and was administered by the vestry as a whole and through its committees. Whenever building was contemplated, a Building Committee of three to six men was constituted. The committee solicited and disbursed funds, hired architects and construction contractors, and made decisions about the forms and function of what was to be built. Although the clergy were often represented on the Building Committee and the rector might be a member of it, this was not always the case. Usually, however, the rector had an important role in the choice of the committee members, and one must suppose that a good deal of informal consultation with him took place.

Some idea of the importance of these committees for the parish may be gained by reviewing the construction projects that they oversaw in the late nineteenth and early twentieth centuries. St. Bartholomew's II was constructed in 1872 at a cost of $228,584 on land bought for $150,000.[33] Additions made in 1892, including a new organ, a mosaic floor for the chancel, a sculpture of the Last Supper for the altar, and an altar rail of colored marbles and mosaic, cost $103,000. The Parish House, built in the 1890s, cost $335,143.16 on land donated by Cornelius Vanderbilt, a member of the vestry. Improvements to the church in 1892 cost another $103,000, and expansion of its facilities in 1909 came to $90,000. The expansion of the medical clinic cost $200,000 in 1900, and its rearrangement as a hospital in 1919 cost $300,000. This does not, of course, take into account smaller projects, such as the various missions and the boarding house, whose individual costs were much lower. From this sampling, it emerges that the vestry was responsible for about $1.5 million of construction between 1870 and 1920, not including the cost of the present Park Avenue church. With that added, the expenditure reaches over $3 million. Considering that in 1910, the annual income of the church was $279,000, pressure to find funds and to contain costs was a constant problem. As we trace the construction of the present church, we will see the members of the vestry again and again acting as hard bargainers with the architect and contractor. Although one is tempted to criticize their willingness to sacrifice architectural excellence in order to cut costs, their actions should be evaluated within the larger picture of the total costs being sustained by the parish, of which the new church was only a part. It is clear from the many commitments and financial burdens on the parish during this period that the vestry must have been extremely able administrators.

Almost all the members of the vestry were men distinguished by success in the business world and by their wealth. They belonged, in short, to that class of patron Lewis Mumford so scathingly described,

> whose vulgarity sought to mask itself in the hand-me-downs of culture, revarnished and framed, at fabulous prices by equally adroit financial manipulators, like Joseph Duveen. These men were no longer creators but gaping and goggle-eyed connoisseurs: no longer builders but buyers: and their values, being based on the counters of finance, were as derivative as they were abstract. They pictured themselves as the Caesars and the Borgias and Napoleons of their era: and instead of taking chances in buying original works of art or financing contemporary buildings, they wanted only gilt-edged esthetic securities whose value was well-established on the market-place.[34]

Although Mumford regarded the new urban patrons as powerful forces of reactionary behavior in the early twentieth century, the evidence regarding the members of St. Bartholomew's vestry during this period suggests a different conclusion. They chose to serve a parish dedicated to community service and social welfare, and their conduct implemented the ethical recommendations of T. W. Higginson, in his article "A Word to the Rich": "the day has come for him to show other men that his life and his work are henceforth for them and not for his own gratification. He must prove that he has labored for the common good, and that he knows the rightful, wise use of profits."[35] While this contention may seem overly flattering to the patrons of St. Bartholomew's, the biographies of these individuals provide firm support for it (Appendix of Members of the Vestry).

Of the twenty-two men who served on the vestry between 1914 and 1930, during the construction of the new church, two-thirds were deeply involved in some kind of lay charity work or otherwise active as defenders of the poor. While almost all were in high-level business positions or were lawyers, many of them devoted their free time to cultural enterprises. Their records are distinguished by service to the church, to society, and to the country.

Not all of these men played active roles in directing the project, nor were all involved with it from its inception in 1914 to its completion in 1930. Three of the most distinguished vestrymen, Elgin Gould, John Gray, and William Sloane, died in 1915, before the final designs for the church were approved. But they helped to choose the architect and were involved in the genesis of the project. Gould, the first chairman of the Building Committee, was probably chosen for that position because of his experience with the construction industry. An article in the *New York Times* of January 17, 1916, described him as the main figure behind the move from the old church and suggested that his death had delayed the preparation of plans for the new one.

Of the men who oversaw the creation of the building, one of the most important was James Lane, chairman of the Building Committee from 1915 to 1918. He had been a member of the committee from its creation in 1914. As chairman, he handled all correspondence with Goodhue; their relationship does not seem to have been a warm one. Part of Lane's coolness was probably due to his opposition to the organization of the project along too specialized or professional lines, insisting that much of the decision-making power remain with the vestry, rather than being given to the architect. For him, the architect should be the instrument of the vestry's will. Lane stepped down as chairman only after he became warden of the church in 1919, and he continued to serve the committee ex officio until his death in 1927. His loyalty is further attested by his donation of $100,000 to the project at a crucial moment in the construction.

Robert Brewster replaced Lane as chairman in 1919, and became head of the Art Committee in 1929. Thus it was he who oversaw the completion of the building. The nature of his participation, however, does not emerge from the extant documents.

Alvin Krech's activity is more easily traced. He was involved in the initial search for the architect, and it was on his recommendation as chairman of the Art Committee that the vestry chose Goodhue. He did not serve on the Building Committee officially, although he frequently attended its meetings, but was probably a member of the Art Committee, of which he again became chairman in 1927, the last year of his life. His activity had a rather independent character; in 1918, he decided to place additional pews in the church in a way contrary to Goodhue's design, and in the 1920s, he privately undertook a research project on church decoration that led to the adoption of a mosaic program for the church. His influence, then, while less evident than Lane's, was at least as important in terms of determining the form of the church.

The other members of the original Building Committee were William Field (appointed in 1914), William Greer (1915), Henry Morris (1915), and William Appleton (1914). Greer, treasurer of the Parish House, probably served as treasurer of the committee. Appleton came from an old parish family; his father had served as vestryman for twenty-three years, and Appleton had been on the vestry since 1899. Hence his membership in the committee represented the continuation of parish interests in the new building. Morris had served on the vestry even longer, since 1877, and had been a warden since 1899. Like Appleton, Morris had serious cultural interests as well as a deep loyalty to the parish. As a mechanical engineer, Field was probably chosen for the committee because of his professional knowledge and experience.

The make-up of the Building Committee represented a balanced cross section of interests. Chairman Lane was a financial man responsible for the business organization of the project. He was aided in this by the treasurer, Greer. Field informed the committee about architectural procedures and problems from an engineering point of view, while Morris and Appleton contributed their experience as vestrymen familiar with earlier projects and as men of culture. We know much less about the composition of the Art Committee, although it is clear that its guiding forces were Krech and Parks.

THE HARKNESSES AND VANDERBILTS

Two families were important as patrons of the church, even though they were not represented on the vestry: the Harknesses and the Vanderbilts.

Charles William Harkness, a lawyer and railroad magnate, was a generous contributor to the project. In 1916, the year of his death, he donated $100,000 to the construction (one of four such gifts made that year), and he and his wife established an endowment fund of $500,000 for the future needs of the parish. Another fund, of $50,000, was given for the decoration of the chapel. Harkness seems to have taken no active role in the decision making about the form of the church or in the administration of the project. His donations seem to demonstrate his loyalty to the parish rather than any particular interest in architecture.

The role of the Vanderbilt family in the construction of the new church is very difficult to assess. William Vanderbilt and Cornelius Vanderbilt had served as vestrymen and wardens in the nineteenth century, and the family had made a number of substantial gifts to the parish, including the land for the Parish House on Madison Avenue.

Alice Gwynne Vanderbilt, Cornelius's widow, had donated the Stanford White portal in memory of her husband. The flattering references to the portal in Parks's sermons and Goodhue's pamplet "The Proposed New St. Bartholomew's Church" (Appendix of Texts) and the decision to design the new church around this feature suggest the continuing importance of the Vanderbilts in the parish. Yet, although the family had considerable experience in building, both in Newport and in New York, none of its members served as adviser or principal donor to the new church. Two family members viewed Goodhue's model of the new church on January 17, 1916, and declared themselves pleased with the effect of the portal in his design, yet the family's only recorded donation to the project, of $20,000 in 1916, was by no means the most generous received in that year.[36] When one considers that the initial cost (before enlargement) of the Vanderbilt mansion on Fifty-seventh Street and Fifth Avenue was over $3 million, the $1.5 million spent by the parish on the new church represented a relatively modest sum.

The absence of Vanderbilt participation in the new project seems inexplicable. It is true, however, that the family was indirectly represented on the Building Committee. William Field, one of the first appointees to the committee, was married to Lila Vanderbilt Sloane, daughter of the vestryman John Gray and Emily T. Vanderbilt (daughter of William Vanderbilt). Gray, who died in 1915, served during only the initial stages of the project, and his contribution is not clear. Field was a very active member of the Building and Art committees, well qualified by his own interests and profession to have been chosen. Whether the fact that his wife was a Vanderbilt also had an influence on his selection is difficult to determine.

In 1923, the year of consecration of the new church, Alice Gwynne Vanderbilt seems to have had a falling out with Parks and, in any case, became a parishioner of St. Thomas. Her daughter, Gertrude Vanderbilt Whitney, remained in the parish, but resided much of the time on Long Island. There is no evidence that Whitney, who took so great an interest in contemporary art, was consulted in the project of decorating the church with byzantinizing mosaics. It is not likely that she would have approved of this choice.

It is interesting that until 1923, the new church was described as Romanesque, as was the Vanderbilt portal, and that almost immediately after Alice Vanderbilt left the parish, it was referred to as Byzantine. Possibly, the original decision to build in the Romanesque style was taken, in part, to please the Vanderbilts; the architect's presentation booklet strongly suggests this. With Vanderbilt's departure, it became possible to choose more freely among the various stylistic options available for decoration and to adopt the Byzantine. That this choice was totally foreign to the taste and interests of one of the remaining Vanderbilt parishioners suggests a decline in their importance in the parish. But when it was decided in the 1940s to fill the rose window with stained glass, the glass was donated by Emily Vanderbilt White. Widow of William Sloane, a vestryman at the time of his death in 1915, White also donated the mosaic decoration of the narthex in the late 1920s. Thus the Vanderbilt connection with St. Bartholomew's was not severed in 1923.

As patrons, then, the Vanderbilts were at once all-important to, and relatively absent from, the project. Although the Vanderbilt portal determined the style of the new church, the construction of St. Bartholomew's III seems to have elicited little Vanderbilt interest.

8 · Bertram Grosvenor Goodhue.

2 · THE ARCHITECT

I N 1914, when Bertram Grosvenor Goodhue was commissioned to design St. Bartholomew's, he was known primarily as a partner in the
firm of Cram, Goodhue, and Ferguson.[1] This firm, especially respected
for its skill in designing meticulously accurate neo-Gothic buildings, was
completing St. Thomas Church in New York (fig. 9), the last work that
Goodhue excuted in partnership; St. Bartholomew's is perhaps the first
designed independently. If St. Thomas marks the culmination of Goodhue's early career, St. Bartholomew's illustrates his first steps toward a
late, personal style and is a transitional building in his *œuvre*. As such, it
displays some continuity with Goodhue's earlier thought and practice, and
it shows the architect experimenting with the new design principles that
would be fully mastered in his late works. Although St. Bartholomew's
marks a change in Goodhue's development, his entire career may be seen
as a unified and coherent process through which he sought an appropriate
formal language with which to embody his architectural vision. Because
of the peculiar position of St. Bartholomew's in Goodhue's work, some
aspects of both his earlier and his later career need to be examined, beginning with the formative influences on his thinking about architecture and
the nature of his creative process.

THE FORMATION OF THE ARCHITECT

When Goodhue, born on April 28, 1869, was fifteen years old, he became
an apprentice in the office of Renwick, Aspinwall, and Russell, and remained with the firm for seven and a half years. At this time, James Renwick's firm, which had completed St. Bartholomew's II in 1872, was finishing St. Patrick's Cathedral in New York. Thus Goodhue's earliest
practical experience with architecture, and his only formal architectural
training, plunged him into neo-Gothic style: "All I know of architecture
(little enough, my professional opponents say) I got in this period and by
dint of office work and by reading and drawing at night."[2]

If during the day, Goodhue learned how to construct neo-Gothic churches,
at night he studied the theoretical underpinnings of this style. The staples

9 · Cram, Goodhue, and Ferguson. St. Thomas Church, New York (1914).

of his book education were the works of Augustus Pugin and Eugène Viollet-le-Duc: "in those days the gospels . . . were Pugin's various books, and as a sort of thoroughly credible Apocrypha, the works of Viollet-le-Duc."[3] But even in this early period, Goodhue's interests ranged far beyond the boundaries of neo-Gothic; he read "everything I could get my hands on."[4]

A list of books that Goodhue recommended as being useful to an architect's training includes works on Egyptian, Classical, Byzantine, Gothic, Renaissance, and Spanish Colonial architecture.[5] Although Goodhue compiled this list late in his life, one of his earliest projects—the competition

entry for the Cathedral Church of St. John the Divine in New York—
reveals his acquaintance with a variety of historical styles. In this design,
Byzantine, Romanesque, Gothic, and Renaissance motifs are—not very
skillfully—combined (fig. 10).[6]

Goodhue seems to have been an avid student of all styles except the
Classical, for which he felt a kind of allergic reaction triggered by his
dislike for the professional training given in architectural schools:

> Unfortunately, or at least unfortunately from my point of view, modern
> architecture as largely practiced and as necessarily taught in the schools is a
> matter of copying more or less closely the buildings of classical antiquity.
> . . . This is the sort of thing I don't like and can't see any excuse for on
> the part of an architect of genuine artistic ability, one that is born for the
> job and for no other. And this is why I prefer the freer styles—those less
> hampered by rules.[7]

This theme of the born architect was a favorite of Goodhue's. By it, he
seems to have meant, in part, someone who had not studied in an architectural school, who shunned the Ecole des Beaux Arts, and who in general refused to design within a set of norms or rules. He thought that

the reason architectural schools teach formal Classic architecture is because,
thanks to Vitruvius, Vignola, and other lesser men, there is a sort of code,
a set of rules, governing the use of these classic forms, and no such code is

10 · Goodhue. Competition design
for the Cathedral Church of St. John
the Divine, New York (1888).

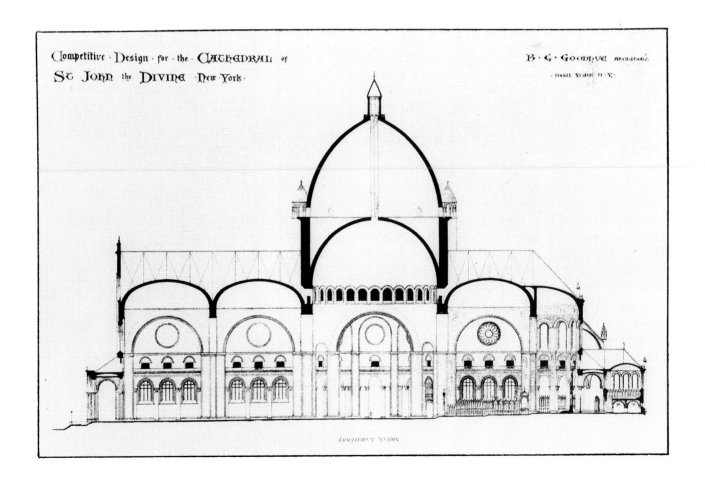

the case of any other style; in fact there can't be, and thanks to this difficulty the styles other than the Classic ones can't be taught—and there you
are.[8]

Goodhue's idea of the born architect, then, was based on his conviction
that it is not possible to teach anyone how to design, but only how to
copy buildings and memorize rules. The only possible product of such
instruction would be Neoclassic architecture, which was hack work. For
example, expressing his opposition to the President's Art Commission,
established in 1909, Goodhue explained that "official art has always been
a very terrible thing, and none of the great art epochs in the world have
owed their impetus to anything other than an instinct in the public." He
went on to equate "art by statute" with Neoclassic work, since both follow rules, and concluded that "me and my partners ain't classicists."[9]

While Goodhue's attitude to Neoclassic, or classicizing, architecture is
clearly and consistently stated, his views about the value of other historical
styles are less easily grasped. It is particularly difficult to assess Goodhue's
opinions during the twenty-two years of his association with Ralph Adams
Cram (1891–1913), who, as an ardent neo-Gothicist, made sure that most
of the buildings designed by the firm were in that style. Goodhue avoided
confronting the problem of the past, apparently content with the professional success that his skill in neo-Gothic design brought. As a result, he
earned a reputation for having purely aesthetic concerns.[10] Since he never
felt a profound theoretical or moral commitment to the Gothic, this esti-
mation was partly true. But his main concern with architecture was not
aesthetic, but spiritual:

> Contrary to what I suppose is the generally accepted view, I hold no brief
> for Gothic as opposed to any other style. Gothic seems to be the generally
> accepted spirit in which churches should be built; also I find its forms at-
> tractive, and therefore a good deal of Gothic work must be laid at my door;
> but I assure you I dream of something very much bigger and finer and
> more suited to our present-day civilization than any Gothic church could
> possibly be.[11]

Goodhue's indifference to Gothic reflected his belief that the past was
dead. This conviction distinguished him from many, perhaps most, of his
contemporaries. His partner Cram, for instance, did not believe that the
past had really died; enthusiasm and hard work could revive it: "The rav-
elled end of the golden cord that snapped four centuries ago is being sought
again that it may be knit once more with the flying end now in our hands,
and religious and aesthetic continuity restored."[12] For Cram, as for John
Ruskin, the golden age was, of course, not classical antiquity, but the
High Middle Ages, whose ideals had been subverted by the Renaissance
in fifteenth-century Italy. These ideals, obscured but not destroyed, could
be returned to their rightful position of leadership and would result in an

architectural expression almost identical to that originally developed for them—the Gothic. For Cram, since the continuing validity of an ideal predicated the continuing appropriateness of the forms that express it, the relation of the present to the past was one of continuity in the form of renewal.

To this, Goodhue replied that "nothing that apes the past is genuine Art. The whole of modern civilization is based on other ideals."[13] This condemnation applied to his own work as well. For example, he told a friend that praise of St. Thomas Church was unjustified, "for, although I did the best that in me lay, it was always with the rather mournful conviction that to rival the past in this fashion could never result in anything but comparative failure."[14] During his partnership with Cram, Goodhue tried to maintain a position of compromise, advocating the creation of "modern Gothic," since "Medieval Gothic is now impossible and must remain Medieval, and the Gothic we do today, if it is to be vital, and beautiful, and true, and good, and therefore Art, must be of our own times."[15] But he felt no real conviction that such a style as "modern Gothic" really existed.

What was really at issue, uneasily suppressed beneath Goodhue's statements, was a profoundly important matter that had little to do with the formal aesthetic value of Gothic or any other style. If art is indeed a manifestation of the social, intellectual, moral, and spiritual character of a given period (as Goodhue's mentor Charles Eliot Norton, and Norton's friend Ruskin, believed) and if it arises "from an instinct in the public" (as Goodhue claimed), then the revival of any historical style is a betrayal of art. But Goodhue's adherence to this view was only partial because, he said, in a "false and soulless age" art should not express its historical period. Instead, "we should strive to comprehend and enjoy only the greatest epochs."[16] Goodhue believed that his own age was not an admirable one; indeed, "every modern church is a failure compared with what was done in less materially advanced but infinitely more spiritual and instinctively artistic periods."[17] Because modern culture lacked a vital spiritual life, its art merely repeated the received truths of the past and was incapable of stating its own truth. This was the dilemma of many modern architects: Should the architect express the values of his own culture, whatever they may be? Or should he seek to give form to an ideal, regardless of its importance for the present?

Goodhue's solution to this problem is complex. Its clearest expression is in "The Villa Fosca," a "Voyage Imaginaire" that recounts a conversation between Signor Orgogliese, the owner of an Italian villa, and Goodhue, his guest. Troubled by his host's failure to explain what the aim of art should be, Goodhue strolls out into the garden. But while nature lulls and calms him, it does not hold the answer to this problem either. The answer, instead, is provided by art. A sailor is overheard singing "Di Provenza il mare, il suol," Germont's aria in Verdi's *La Traviata*. The aria, says Goodhue, is "well-remembered yet unworn." That is, it belongs to a living tradition, spontaneously preserved by the people, rather than being either artificially revived (Gothic), or kept alive by rules and precedent (Classical). Valid artistic traditions cannot be chosen; they must be recognized as vital, self-supporting aspects of culture.

But what is the content of this art? Verdi's aria provides the clue; in it, a father urges his prodigal son to remember the joy and peace of his native land, far away and apparently forgotten. Goodhue concludes that this aria sums up "all that Italy has been, is, or may yet be, all the pathos and glamour of a forever vanished past." His meaning is that the greatness of Italian art lies in its unending yearning for an ideal that once existed, or is thought to have existed, and that can be evoked in the present through art. For Goodhue, this yearning constituted the living core of artistic tradition. Although the past is dead (the ideal is unattainable), it becomes perfectly real and present through the expression of its idea in art. Thus the aim of art is illusion. But, of course, the realization of the ideal is more general and more formal. That Goodhue intended this meaning to be gleaned from "The Villa Fosca" is suggested by his comment on its publication: "bad as it is, you can see that I had a certain idea, almost an ideal, in the back of my head."[18]

It remains to determine the kind of ideal that Goodhue sought to represent. He approached this ideal through imagination, intuition, and aesthetic response rather than through intellect. His capacity for intense—indeed, all-consuming—involvement in imaginative mental activity impressed those who knew him.[19] Cram remarked that "amateur theatricals, costume parties of every sort, anything, in fact, that took on an aspect of beauty recovered out of the past, appealed to him in the strongest possible fashion."[20] This might suggest that Goodhue was, after all, concerned solely with beauty. But although he was extremely reticent about his deeply held beliefs, almost always expressing them in flippant style, scattered remarks show him to have been a deeply spiritual man.

He usually spoke of himself as "irreligious"[21] or even "anti-religious,"[22] although he had been a theosophist in his youth.[23] Yet in a rare moment of self-disclosure, he admitted that he was a religious person who had always enjoyed the designing and building of churches more than anything else "because of the idea or ideal behind such."[24] That these are almost the same words used to describe "The Villa Fosca" is no coincidence. For Goodhue, the core of art was the aspiration toward divinity (understood as ideal perfection) and the urge to embody both the yearning for and the vision of divinity in concrete form.

Goodhue's religious sentiment, or spirituality, had little to do with organized religion. He felt that Christianity tended to be "a direct hindrance rather than help in furthering the utopia toward which we all are looking so longingly."[25] Nor did it have much to do with the fundamental Creeds of the church: "the God of the Protestant Episcopal Church in America [is] a person whom I wholly refuse to recognize as the right one."[26] For

Goodhue, all great religions possessed truth, and their meaningful core was ethical.[27]

We have seen that Goodhue thought that the aim of art is not to reflect its age, but to embody an ideal. This ideal is not inherent to organized religion, although it stands behind all religions. It seems to have no dogmatic or literary content, and very little intellectual content. In fact, it is a spiritual ideal that Goodhue never—and could never have—explained in words: "humanity hasn't the words, and shouldn't have the words, with which to formulate such a thing."[28] Art was the vehicle that Goodhue used to express the ideal that he perceived and longed to realize. There is a hint, for one of his churches, of some of the qualities of that ideal. Writing of the recently completed St. Bartholomew's, he said that it does not look like a Christian church, but like something from the Arabian Nights or the last act of *Parsifal*.[29] Despite the lightness of his tone, Goodhue's analogy between architecture and other forms of art is again revealing. The church was to appear distant in time and place and to excite the imagination by its strange effect.

The reference to Wagner's opera is even more enlightening. *Parsifal* is an exploration of the mystery of the penetration of the divine into the human (what Leighton Parks would have called immanence). It focuses on the relationship between human actions (ethical behavior) and grace. In the last act, the healing Grail reveals itself to sight: the ideal is attained. For Goodhue, this experience of the divine, of the "awful and unknowable power that stands behind everything,"[30] was not verbal, but visual and aural; its setting was not life, but art. The ecstasy of the spirit, operating through the medium of beauty, was Goodhue's ideal in church architecture, as in his life as an architect.

THE ST. BARTHOLOMEW'S PROJECT

When the Art Committee of St. Bartholomew's approached Goodhue in early 1914, he was at a turning point in his professional career. The dissolution of his partnership with Cram had become effective in January 1914, and Goodhue was completing the last of their joint projects—St. Thomas Church.[31] Goodhue's skills as a designer had grown steadily during the years of partnership, and St. Thomas is testimony to his ability to control effects of light, color, and texture. Now he was ready to practice on his own. That the New York Chapter of the American Institute of Architects had awarded him its Medal of Honor in 1913 was both an encouragement and a practical aid, since Goodhue needed commissions.

Important for gaining a place within the New York architectural Establishment, and decisive for obtaining the St. Bartholomew's commission, was Goodhue's membership in the Century Association. When he was nominated for membership in 1910, some of the most distinguished New

York architects and art critics had written on his behalf: Cass Gilbert, John M. Carrere (of Carrere and Hastings), Frederick Law Olmsted, Jr., Montgomery Schuyler, and W. Rutherford Mead (of McKim, Mead, and White).[32] Goodhue's friendship with the influential critic Royal Cortissoz sealed his acceptance by the New York Establishment.[33]

At the Century Association, Goodhue could have met six members of St. Bartholomew's vestry: William Butterworth, William Appleton, William Field, Alvin Krech, Robert Brewster, and Elgin Gould. Two of the three original members of the Building Committee were Centurians, and Krech was the chairman of the Art Committee and the man who drafted the recommendation that Goodhue be hired.[34]

Although Krech was, in this and in many other ways, a figure of crucial importance for the new church, he could hardly have acted alone. Indeed, Goodhue's first recorded contact with the church, on April 29, 1914, involved another member of the Art Committee: Arthur C. Jackson. Jackson had apparently hinted that if Goodhue would make him a partner, the St. Bartholomew's job was his. Goodhue tried to ignore the implications of the offer and urged Jackson to convince the committee that he worked not only in Gothic, but also in "the Romanesque of Italy and Southern France."[35] Thus while Goodhue had come to the attention of the Art Committee through his recent neo-Gothic works in New York and, particularly, through Parks's admiration for St. Thomas, it was clear before the commission was even awarded that the style of the new church would be, like the Vanderbilt portal, Romanesque.

Goodhue must have known about the intended style of the church through conversations with Krech or perhaps with his friend Charles Mathews. Mathews, himself an architect, was a parishioner of St. Bartholomew's and served as an informal consultant during the construction and decoration of the church.[36] His loyal partisanship of Goodhue is evident from their letters and from his attempts to reconcile the differences of opinion between Goodhue and Parks.[37] Goodhue acknowledged this loyalty, and perhaps expressed his thanks for having received the St. Bartholomew's commission, by recommending Mathews for membership in the Century Association in 1915.[38]

The Art Committee also consulted with Wallace Sabine, an expert on acoustics who was a professor of physics at Harvard and yet another member of the Century Association (he had recommended Goodhue for membership in 1910).[39] Sabine, who had assured Goodhue of his desire to continue working with him after the end of his association with Cram in 1914, had excellent reasons to recommend Goodhue for the St. Bartholomew's job. Goodhue had introduced Sabine to Rafael Guastavino, a manufacturer of clay tiles, and they were developing an acoustic form of this tile, Akoustolith, for Goodhue's use.[40] To patrons concerned with the acoustic properties of their church, Sabine could hardly have recommended anyone better suited than his friend and associate Bertram Goodhue.

Goodhue won the commission, then, with the help of his acquaintances at the Century Association and his friends within the parish of St. Bartholomew's, as well as through his demonstrated architectural skill.

During the summer of 1914, when Goodhue was making his first sketches for the new church, his office was busy indeed. Some projects, St. Thomas and the Chapel of the Intercession (at One Hundred Fifty-fifth Street and Broadway), still required attention, and two new jobs had been accepted: the First Congregational Church in Montclair, New Jersey, and St. Vincent Ferrer (at Sixty-sixth Street and Lexington Avenue). Goodhue was able to boast that he had twenty-two draftsmen working for him, which was "far and away more than any other architect in this part of the world, so they tell me. McKim, Mead, and White have only ten, Carrere and Hastings only two or three and Warren and Wetmore only two."[41] The success of his office need not suggest that Goodhue was esteemed as a great creative artist. It more probably reflects his ability to deal with patrons and fulfill their needs, his reliability in terms of quality of workmanship and adherence to time schedules, and his fair prices.

The small church in Montclair was completed rapidly (dedicated in 1916) and at little cost: $300,000. It served as an experiment with the acoustic tile that later had extensive application at St. Bartholomew's. St. Vincent Ferrer (fig. 11), consecrated in 1923, proceeded concurrently with St. Bartholomew's. Although it is a good-sized church, it cost only one-half the approximately $1.2 million spent to construct St. Bartholomew's. Indeed, of all of Goodhue's ecclesiastical works, only St. Thomas, at $1.1 million, comes near to St. Bartholomew's in cost.[42] Thus of the three new commissions taken on in 1914, St. Bartholomew's was both the biggest and the most important. This explains why Goodhue put his best draftsman, Clarence Stein, in charge of the project.[43]

Despite this importance, Goodhue consistently disparaged St. Bartholomew's in comparison with St. Vincent Ferrer. Even in their earliest stages of design, he claimed that "the Roman one is the best I have done, but I am by no means so confident of the quality of the second."[44] When construction of both began, their relative merits had not changed in his mind; while St. Bartholomew's was "going to be good," St. Vincent Ferrer was "going to be a corker."[45] And at their completion, Goodhue declared that St. Vincent Ferrer "acoustically is just as good as St. Bartholomew's and architecturally much—No: I'd better not say it."[46]

While the neo-Gothic St. Vincent Ferrer represents a distillation of all that Goodhue had done—for example, at St. Thomas and at the Chapel of the Intercession—St. Bartholomew's is an experimental building. Its experimental nature was acknowledged by the patrons at an early stage; in the *Year Book* of 1915, Parks reported that the vestry

have invited Mr. Bertram Goodhue to draw plans which, should they prove satisfactory, will in due time be presented to the congregation for sugges-

11 · Goodhue. St. Vincent Ferrer,
New York (1914–23).

tion. We have a number of beautiful Gothic churches in this country but
few of any other style. But the doors and facade of this Church do not
permit us to avail ourselves of the experience of most Church architects
who have designed almost nothing but Gothic churches and we do not
expect soon a design which will be such as we want.[47]

Although Goodhue had persuaded the vestry of his ability to design a
Romanesque church, he was poorly prepared to execute the commission.

Acquiring a mastery of this historical style was only one of his problems. Another was his desire, having broken with Cram, to explore his own capabilities as an architect and to develop a vocabulary that would express his personal vision of form. Whereas the architectural ideas of the neo-Gothic St. Vincent Ferrer were skillfully and completely realized, the novelty of St. Bartholomew's made it, of necessity, a flawed work. Thus Goodhue's judgment of the former as the more successful building is, from a professional point of view, justified. But it is the less important building in terms of Goodhue's development as an architect, for St. Bartholomew's was the practice ground for Goodhue's best buildings, those of his late style.[48]

Goodhue's own difficulties in devising a new sort of ecclesiastical architecture were exacerbated by the patrons of the church. Although they seem to have been agreed in renouncing Gothic style, they were unprepared for the sorts of novelties that the architect asked them to consider. Set after set of drawings was rejected, and, reluctant to approve even the brick and stone masonry intended for the church, the vestry demanded that Goodhue erect a sample wall in his studio.[49]

Goodhue's letters written between 1914 and 1918 often contrast the sunny relations he enjoyed with the patrons of St. Vincent Ferrer with the storms and lightning bolts over St. Bartholomew's. One example will serve for all:

> I am anti-religious and strongly anti-Catholic; but I must say that I like their methods [at St. Vincent Ferrer] a great deal better than those of one other church I could name, but won't. They pay their bills and keep out of the newspapers, and so long as I give them their practical requirements for the money they can afford they are content to trust that I know more about architecture than they do.[50]

In a more public vein, Goodhue's scathing description of the process of modern church building was almost certainly aimed at St. Bartholomew's, although the church is not mentioned by name:

> When a parish wishes to build a new church, it invariably goes about the matter in the wrong way; for the beginnings of the movement are withheld from the architect as being no concern of his. When the site, which may, it is likely, be very poor instead of very good, is chosen, the hard-headed businessmen, of which the vestry is usually made up, determine the amount the parish will "invest" in the new building, keeping clearly in mind too, what has already been paid for the site. The Rector then states what, in his opinion, is the seating capacity needed. Usually far in advance of what can ever be expected, this is promptly cut down by the afore-said hard-headed businessmen to a much more reasonable figure, though still—take an architect's word for it—too large, invariably bigger than can be worthily provided with the funds in hand. The architect is then informed of the state of affairs, and told to begin work on tentative sketches. If a conscientious as

well as intelligent practitioner, he there and then points out the impossibility of giving his clients a "Gothic" church or anything that shall bear more than the most superficial resemblance to a "Gothic" church for twenty-five cents per cubic foot, even though Mr. Smith the senior warden did recently build an apartment house for 33⅓ cents.[51]

Except for the comments about the site, which Goodhue approved of for St. Bartholomew's, and the style, the description is supported by the documents that relate to the St. Bartholomew's project. The attempt to match the amount of money that the vestry was willing to spend with the enormous size and ambitious design of the church that it demanded was an ongoing nightmare for Goodhue.[52] Further, the members of the vestry had no intention of leaving important decisions to the architect, and they intervened in the project in many ways.[53]

At first, Goodhue seems to have thought that the vestry could be humored. But his original pretense of accepting the proposed budget came back to haunt him. Although he had never believed that the church could be built for $500,000, the vestry held up to him his initial agreement to this figure and (from their point of view rightly) accused him of dishonesty.[54]

As it became clear to Goodhue that the vestrymen would not take a step until they were completely satisfied with his designs, he grew resentful; his imprudent comments becoming known to them, he was fired (to be rehired two weeks later).[55] Goodhue could ill afford to lose his most lucrative commission, but his subsequent willingness to sacrifice much of what he had planned for St. Bartholomew's, in order to contain its cost, concealed a growing bitterness toward his employers. This unhappy relationship may have been another factor influencing Goodhue's negative assessment of the finished church.

Despite personal friction, evident in the unkind comments about Parks that pepper Goodhue's correspondence, the rector and the architect had remarkably similar views about church building, and their collaboration was a fruitful, if not a happy, one. Parks, as we have seen, believed that the past was of significance for the present, but that the old forms had to be invested with new meaning. Goodhue felt that "architecture should represent a decent reverence for the historic past of the art"[56] and that the task of the ecclesiastical architect, in particular, was "to suggest the old, and so carry on the great ethnic tradition to which the American Church, no less than the American people is heir."[57] At St. Bartholomew's, the traditional element was represented by the use of a historical style and by the reuse of as much as possible of the material from St. Bartholomew's II.

Just as Parks opposed the idea of reviving medieval forms of piety, insisting instead on the affirmation of a modern conception of God and man, so Goodhue tried to reconcile tradition and progress at St. Bartholomew's. Progress, in architectural terms, was a question of new constructional materials and a new theory of design principles.

In particular, the "steel frame, or reinforced concrete, construction" was extremely difficult to reconcile with the historical styles.[58] Goodhue, who had read Pugin and Viollet-le-Duc, felt that construction had to be honest; that is, it would not do for the visible support system of a building to differ in character from the actual structure. But how could a steel frame be honestly accommodated to a historical style? Or, to put the problem more generally, when the methods and materials of construction are no longer traditional, how could traditional forms be retained?

St. Bartholomew's is built with modern materials; its basic structure combines timbrel tile vaults (both for a platform beneath the church and as its ceiling) with reinforced-concrete piers. The transept galleries are supported on steel girders, and the whole interior is faced with an acoustic material that had just become available. Having chosen these materials, Goodhue faced an aesthetic, ethical decision. To explore the aesthetic potential of these new materials fully would have meant believing that progress excluded tradition. Instead, Goodhue reconciled progress and tradition, choosing architectural models and precedents in which revetted piers and vaults constitute the vocabulary of structure. The pier form of San Marco was an ideal model for St. Bartholomew's, since its planar, blocky character minimizes the visual suggestion that a weight-support dynamic is at work (fig. 41).[59] Further, the pier form at St. Bartholomew's, while almost identical in design to that of San Marco, is just as much the logical consequence of its steel core. Quite literally, the steel core was coated with concrete and faced with acoustic tile without significant alteration in shape.

As Parks believed that modern faith must express a new relationship between God and man, so Goodhue felt that new functional needs were the controlling concern of the designer: "now all great art arises in response to some great need—some great practical need."[60] The need of paramount importance for St. Bartholomew's was that the congregation be able to hear and see the preacher. His belief that functional demand determines form led Goodhue to view the historical past typologically rather than stylistically. From this point of view, churches that provide maximum space near the pulpit constituted a coherent group from which he might borrow ideas. This meant that centralized churches, or at least churches in which the crossing is the central design feature, made up this typological category. In this respect, San Marco, Sant'Andrea in Mantua, and Ely Cathedral belong to the same group, and all are major sources for St. Bartholomew's, despite their different styles. As Parks said, the forms are mutable, but the content is constant.

Parks believed that Christian belief should not be codified, but that each individual had to interpret his faith according to conscience and inspiration, guided by tradition. By the same token, Goodhue rejected all styles that followed rules, preferring the "freer" styles. And, finally, just as Parks felt that a modern church should provide moral leadership for the United States, contributing to the realization of an ideal, spiritualized democracy, so Goodhue longed for that utopia in which spiritual values would prevail.

ST. BARTHOLOMEW'S AND GOODHUE'S LATE STYLE

Goodhue was troubled by the dilemma of the modern architect, caught between the conflicting values of tradition and progress. And he was aware of the need either to invent or to revive a style that would express the modern age. His stand on these matters is hinted at in some of his writings:

> It is probable that we shall never again have a distinctive style, but what I hope and believe we shall some day possess is something akin to a style— so flexible that it can be made to meet every practical and constructive need, so beautiful and complete as to harmonize the heretofore discordant notes of Art and Science and to challenge comparison with the wonders of past ages yet malleable enough to be molded at the designer's will.[61]

What he hoped for was not the adoption of a unified formal vocabulary, not an official style, but a common way of approaching architecture, employing modern materials, and serving modern needs. The imaginative element should be harmonized with the rational, and the new architecture should be monumental in its ambition and vision.

In terms of a personal stylistic idiom, Goodhue moved from a fascination with ornament toward a desire for an almost abstract architecture of enclosed volumes.[62] By the last years of his life, he was able to express his formal (but not his spiritual) ideal: "architectural expression reaches its height in finely proportioned solids and surfaces, devoid of all detail excepting that of noble sculpture," and "architecture is preeminently an art of relative proportions."[63] Thus Goodhue's late style is planar and geometric, and calculated juxtapositions of shapes, scale, and spatial ambience constitute its aesthetic center.[64]

It was at St. Bartholomew's that Goodhue took his first steps toward a design governed by this ideal. A comparison of St. Thomas and St. Bartholomew's reveals that the difference between these churches is precisely that the latter rejects a vocabulary of line and light in favor of that of the well-proportioned plane. The vast, curved surfaces of the vaults at St. Bartholomew's, activated only by the gold mortar beds, contrast, in their simplicity and obvious utility, with the interlacing ribs and arches of the vaulting at St. Thomas. Whereas at St. Thomas, sculpture substitutes for structure (see the reredos), at St. Bartholomew's, the structure is revealed and sculpture enlivens it.

At St. Bartholomew's, then, Goodhue designed for the first time in terms of large, simple geometric units. Their surfaces are flat or curved and plainly utilitarian; ornament is embedded in the structure rather than being independent of it or a substitute for it. In these ways, St. Bartholomew's is a work of the late style. But it is also a transitional building in Goodhue's work, first because it displays continuity with some of his earlier designs and attitudes, and second because it is a vehicle of expression for an ideal of architectural form that inspires all of his work, but is fully realized only in Goodhue's last buildings.

It would be surprising indeed if Goodhue had completely abandoned the forms with which he had worked for twenty years in the few months between the completion of St. Thomas and the design of St. Bartholomew's. In fact, he did not. Many features of St. Bartholomew's have precedent in his earlier work: some aspects of the plan, the rose window, the tracery windows in the nave and west façade, the colonnettes on the nave piers, the figural carving of the wooden organ screen.

But while Goodhue continued, at St. Bartholomew's, to give much attention to small-scale, intricately wrought ornament, these passages have a new purpose. Rather than constituting the main value of the whole design, the ornamental areas serve as contrast to the monumental volumes of the spaces and to the extensive wall planes. Thus the very small and delicate heightens and enlivens an abstract composition of mass and space that is the new conceptual core of St. Bartholomew's. Such abstract compositions characterize Goodhue's latest works as well: the Nebraska State Capitol, in Lincoln (fig. 12), and the National Academy of Sciences, in Washington, D.C. (fig. 13). In both buildings, architectural sculpture is

12 · Goodhue. Nebraska State Capitol, Lincoln (1920–32).

13 · Goodhue.
National Academy of
Sciences, Washington,
D.C. (1919–24).

used for powerful effect, but sparingly, and it is inseparable from the wall structure; that is, it does not obscure the planar character of its support. At St. Bartholomew's, the ornament of the north and south transept façades points the way to this late style.

Goodhue's early buildings are activated by colored light entering the interior through stained-glass windows. At St. Bartholomew's, the color becomes structural, literally embedded in the walls. There is a new exploration of pattern and color as qualities inherent to the materials of the building. A particularly clear example of this is the marble inlay pattern on the west buttress of the south transept (pl. VII). In an architectural detail some 3 feet high, eighteen types of marble and stone are used: Westfield Green, Tinos Green no. 3, Numidian Breche Sanguine, Levanto, Sienna Yellow, Alps Green, Campan Vert, Nebo Golden, Red Numidian, Windsor Green, White, Red Sandstone, Vesta Yellow, Red Verona, Dark Tennessee, Eastern Green, Emerald Green, limestone.[65] The National Academy of Sciences and the Nebraska State Capitol continue and extend this exploitation of colored materials, particularly in the use of tile mosaic, also intended for the interior of St. Bartholomew's.

Whereas in his earlier ecclesiastical work, Goodhue tended to draw from one historical style, usually Gothic, the historical references of St. Bartholomew's are diverse. Gothic is certainly one. But other sources—Byzantine and Romanesque, in particular—are also evident. Although Goodhue had previously drawn motifs from these styles, the borrowings are increasingly mingled according to a personal vision of form that tends to obscure their origins. This tendency is further developed in the late works.[66] For example, the rotunda of the National Academy of Sciences is a variant of Brunelleschi's Pazzi Chapel or some other central-plan building with barrel-vaulted arms and a dome on pendentives, to which Roman (or Palladian) thermal windows and Byzantine mosaics have been added.

Perhaps the clearest definition of the place of St. Bartholomew's within Goodhue's development may be drawn from its central tower (fig. 15). Goodhue had used such high, multiple-staged crossing towers in his earlier work, and they appear in the fantasy sketches of the "Voyages Imaginaires." But those towers rise as a vertical extension of the lower parts, in visual continuity with them. At St. Bartholomew's, however, the upper and lower portions of the building are in formal contrast. This design concept, of contrast between tall vertical and low horizontal masses, was crucial for the famous exterior massing of the Nebraska State Capitol.[67] The great span of the interior dome projected for St. Bartholomew's, over 40 feet, and its height, more than 150 feet above pavement level, would be almost exactly reproduced at Nebraska.

The tower of St. Bartholomew's, which was not built, was to have been the culminating feature of its design. Its roots are to be found not only in Goodhue's earlier practice, but also in an early experience that I believe haunted the architect throughout his career. For it was as a novice that Goodhue, himself a competitor for the design of the Cathedral Church of St. John the Divine, saw Halsey Wood's "astounding" entry, *Jerusalem the Golden* (fig. 32).

For Cram, this design anticipated "the significant trend towards vital design that ultimately was initiated by that equally great genius Louis Sullivan, carried forward by . . . Frank Lloyd Wright, and brought to its climax in Goodhue's Nebraska State Capitol."[68] Wood died soon after the design competition, leaving little significant contribution to architecture. Goodhue began his career at the point where Wood left off, as a visionary architect using a neo-Gothic style. But he pursued the implications of his and Wood's vision beyond the Gothic, to a new conception of monumental form. Sharing with Sullivan an interest in exquisitely designed ornament inspired by, rather than copied from, diverse historical sources, and with Wright an appreciation for the beauty of pure, juxtaposed volumes, Goodhue moved toward increasingly greater abstraction and purity in his designs. However, his personal style was at once more sensual and more transcendentally spiritual than theirs.[69] It was, in its essence, closer to the ecstatic vision of Halsey Wood.

St. Bartholomews Church. Park Av & 50 to 51st Sts.
Made Aug. 16. 1917
Bertram G. Goodhue Architect N.Y.C.
Marc Eidlitz & Son Builders N.Y.C.

14 · St. Bartholomew's Church under
construction (1917).

3 · THE BUILDING HISTORY

T HE STORY OF the present St. Bartholomew's Church began in 1914, when the rector and vestry realized that St. Bartholomew's II would have to be abandoned. Its foundations had settled so badly that the floor sagged and the entire roof had to be replaced; the stability of the structure was endangered and could not be restored by repair. A new church would have to be built, either on the Madison Avenue site or on a new one. The vestry did not consider very seriously the possibility of rebuilding on the same site. The surrounding neighborhood, no longer predominantly residential, was becoming filled by tall commercial structures that, complained Leighton Parks, created a canyon on Madison Avenue down which strong winds blew, causing uncomfortable drafts in the church. Further, the church had become so hemmed in by large buildings that it was no longer possible to step far enough away from the bronze doors of its façade to appreciate them. These complaints constitute a first list of desiderata for the new St. Bartholomew's: solid construction on firm foundations, location in a residential neighborhood, and a clear view of the Vanderbilt portal.

In a sermon preached on April 19, 1914 (Appendix of Texts), Parks laid these considerations before the congregation, basing his remarks on the text "at the commandment of the Lord they rested in the tents, and at the commandment of the Lord they journeyed" (Numbers 9:23). The vestry, he informed his parishioners, had voted to relocate, and he urged acceptance of this decision as an opportunity to realize

> the Ideal Church, where the rich and poor meet together; in which the beauty of holiness is prefigured by beauty of worship; where the concentrated energies of the congregation are enlisted for every good work; where the stranger is welcomed as a member of the family and the pure word of God is preached for the saving of souls.

From the first, then, Parks conceived the role of the new church as embracing a congregation larger and more varied than its regular parishioners at that time. It was to be dedicated to community, service, and conversion. Its essential mission was evangelical. At least some of the strangers welcomed by Parks were the poor and needy served by the various welfare and health centers operated by the parish. Whereas their religious needs had previously been met outside the parish church, now they would be integrated into its congregation. It seems unlikely that the rector's determination to erase the barriers between helpers and helped was received with unqualified enthusiasm by all the parishioners. Other strangers whom Parks hoped to attract were the commuters whose point of entry to and exit from the city was Grand Central Terminal, completed in 1913, and tourists staying in midtown hotels.

In selecting the new location, however, the most important consideration was its convenience for the present parishioners. The vestry had, accordingly, analyzed the distribution of their current addresses and taken note of the boundaries of other midtown parishes. A suitable lot, in terms of this information, was found on Park Avenue between Fiftieth and Fifty-first streets. The lot was roughly square: 200 feet on Park Avenue, 225 feet down Fiftieth Street, and 250 feet down Fifty-first. This slight irregularity was to be of great importance for the design of the church. The site had numerous practical and aesthetic advantages. Restrictions placed by the owners on the land to the south of the lot guaranteed that all future buildings there would not exceed a height of seven stories; hence light and air for the new church were ensured. Further, the frontage on broad Park Avenue permitted the portal "a better artistic effect than can easily be found today." The rock bed beneath the lot would make the laying of sound foundations easy. Finally, the site was convenient not only to the homes of the parishioners, but also to those of the poor who used the parish welfare center on Forty-second Street and to Grand Central Terminal.

The only defect of the site was its ugliness. Parks described it as "an unattractive brewery backed by mean houses and flanked by the obtrusive power-house." The brewery belonged to the Schaefer Brewing Company, which was to vacate the premises on May 1, 1915. Thus the first, or planning, stage of the project would, of necessity, last one year—from April 1914 to May 1915.

Having decided on the site, the next step was to find an architect. The search was conducted by the Art Committee, led by Alvin Krech, one of the most prominent members of the vestry. But since Parks sometimes acted as spokesman for the committee, he probably had considerable influence on its decisions. There is no record of the candidates who were considered or of the formal process of selection. It seems likely that since the Stanford White portal was the nucleus around which the new church was to be designed, the firm of McKim, Mead, and White was a favored competitor. But White had since died, and McKim had retired; evidently, the office was unable to convince the committee of its ability to satisfy the very particular requirements of the new project.

These requirements were, beyond those already noted, functional, financial, and aesthetic. The rector wanted a building that could seat 1,500 people—400 more than in St. Bartholomew's II. The vestry, however, wished to finance the building in such a way that it would cost the parish nothing. The intent was to pay for the new land and building with the proceeds of the sale of the Madison Avenue property and of half of the new lot. The vestry hoped to receive $1.4 million for the Madison Avenue site (it was sold for $1,525,000 in 1919)—the price of the Park Avenue lot. The sale of the northern half of the new property would bring $500,000 (it was estimated in 1915 as being worth $575,000), which would cover the cost of the new church. When one considers that St. Thomas, finished in 1914 and occupying almost the same size lot in midtown Manhattan, cost $1.1 million to build, it becomes clear that the vestry was willing to spend very little on the new church. And yet it was a structure much like St. Thomas that the rector had in mind. Parks admired this building, considering it to be one of the most notable Episcopal churches in New York, and he preferred its Gothic style to all other architectural styles.

THE COMMISSION

Goodhue probably came to the attention of St. Bartholomew's through his recent works in New York for Episcopal congregations (St. Thomas and the Chapel of the Intercession) and through his contacts at the Century Association, where, in particular, Krech's acquaintance may have been valuable for obtaining the commission. Within ten days of Parks's announcement of the proposed move, Goodhue had seen the building site and was preparing sketches. Goodhue wanted the commission badly, as is evident from his letters of April 29 and May 15, 1914,[1] and he was willing to design in a style consonant with the Stanford White portal in order to get it. Although he gave only aesthetic reasons for the choice of Romanesque style, Goodhue was too skilled a professional not to have weighed the economic and diplomatic aspects of the design. The small sum allotted for the new church put any complex, and therefore costly, structure beyond reach. The stone masonry of Gothic and its structural system of piers, ribs, buttresses, and tracery were expensive. Italian Romanesque, however, would be simple and inexpensive, since local brick and tile could be used as primary building materials. The impression of splendor could be effected through the use of finish materials and added ornament. Goodhue understood that the Stanford White portal would be retained for the new church not only because it was only a decade old, but also because the Vanderbilts were among the most important of St. Bartholomew's parishioners. A design that made the neo-Romanesque portal the criterion of stylistic choice was likely to win favor with the Art Committee. Goodhue guessed right; on June 4, the Art Committee declared itself impressed not only by the architect's ability, but also by his "peculiar qualifications for the work" and recommended that he be hired.[2]

On the surface, all seemed rosy in June 1914, with the new lot acquired and the architect chosen, but the foundations had been laid for a decade of conflict. Although the Gothic style was out of the question for aesthetic, functional, symbolic, and financial reasons, the vestry members had no clear idea of or liking for the Romanesque that Goodhue promised them. It would require two years of design preparation before an acceptable non-Gothic solution was found. Goodhue, too, was groping in the dark; he referred to the style of the new church as "Byzantine, Romanesque or whatever you call it."[3]

Further, the vestry was not sure whether to use the whole lot or only half of it. Goodhue knew that the southern half of the lot alone was too small to allow the desired seating capacity, but that $500,000 was too little a sum to construct a church that would occupy the whole lot. Indeed, such a small budget made it unlikely that a building of much artistic merit could be built on even half the lot. These problems would plague the building project for its duration, and dramatic clashes, abrupt changes of plan, and growing mistrust on both sides characterize the years of construction.

Between July 10, 1914, when Goodhue signed the contract, and December of that year, the architect made sketches and discussed them with Parks and the Art Committee. Within a month of signing the contract, Goodhue had conceived of a design for the church and had talked about it with Parks. The plan of new St. Bartholomew's would be inspired by San Marco (fig. 39); its elevation, by the recently completed Westminister Cathedral in London, itself derived in part from San Marco (fig. 34). The exterior masonry was to be of random courses of brick and stone. Although San Marco and Westminister Cathedral might be considered Byzantine, or at least byzantinizing, structures, Goodhue suggested that Parks visit the major Lombard, Emilian, and Apulian Romanesque monuments during his vacation in Italy, in order to form some idea of the style to be used at St. Bartholomew's. Goodhue may have known the northern Italian examples from photographs; he certainly had never seen them in person, for he mentioned in a letter written in 1922 that he had never been north of Rome.[4] These byzantinizing and northern Italian Romanesque buildings are the primary sources for the present St. Bartholomew's Church, and despite numerous adjustments to this first scheme, the building as executed carried out Goodhue's initial solution for it, at least in general lines.

Goodhue's treatment of these sources is discussed in depth in Chapter 4, but it is useful to examine some of the practical considerations that shaped his choice of Romanesque/Byzantine, rather than Gothic, style. The economic, aesthetic, symbolic, and diplomatic reasons have already been mentioned. To understand why, specifically, the plan of San Marco was adopted, we must look at the functional requirements of the new building. Three functional requirements, in particular, were stipulated by Parks: that the entire congregation be able to see the pulpit, hear the sermon, and hear the music. (That the people be able to see the divine service at the altar was a traditional requirement, not particular to St. Bartholomew's, and therefore not a subject that required discussion.) The means of satisfying these requirements were the arrangement of the pews and the acoustic properties of the building.

Goodhue's own statements confirm that the starting point of the design was the seating arrangement: "a church building should be built to fit around the proper location of the pews. St. Bartholomew's was built to fit around the pews as arranged by us and approved by the Building Committee."[5] The seating at St. Bartholomew's, with no pews in the side aisles and as many as possible in the transepts and crossing, derives from late-nineteenth-century preaching churches and, in particular, from the evangelical current in the Episcopal faith. This disposition, in turn, had a decisive effect on the layout of the church as a whole and on its elevation. Building plans that focus on the crossing—with broad transepts, nave, and choir—are not common to all architectural styles. The Gothic, for instance, presents few examples of this type. Renaissance models exist, and they had some influence on the design of St. Bartholomew's. But the best-known prototypes are Byzantine, and within this category San Marco enjoyed a status rivaled only by Hagia Sophia, which has no transepts. Not only was the plan of San Marco ideal for the seating arrangements of St. Bartholomew's, but its elevation provides long expanses of flat surfaces well suited to the acoustic requirements of the building.

Goodhue needed the help of an acoustics expert in designing a church in which both the music and the sermon would be audible, and references to Wallace Sabine, an acoustics expert from Harvard University, are in the documents of these first months. At St. Bartholomew's, the acoustic needs conflicted with each other. An acoustic setting ideal for the single voice of the preacher would be too reverberative for the music, while the proper level of reverberation for the music would render the preacher inaudible. In the end, a compromise was decided on: the building is not quite reverberative enough for the preacher (who now uses a microphone), while it is slightly too reverberative for the music. In order to obtain this very precise acoustic balance, the nature and extension of the mural surface had to be carefully calculated. Once again, the richly articulated stone surfaces of Gothic, or even of French Romanesque, architecture were inappropriate to these needs. Even the domical coverings of San Marco (fig. 41) had to be rejected in favor of the flat, curved surfaces of barrel vaults. Barrel vaults, derived from Byzantine and Romanesque models, had recently been experimented with successfully at Westminster Cathedral (fig. 34).

The upper parts of St. Bartholomew's—the gallery level and vaults—were to be covered by Akoustolith. Akoustolith, Guastavino tile with acoustic properties, was designed by Wallace Sabine and Rafael Guastavino in order to solve "the long vexed question as to how to guarantee in advance that the preacher and music will be satisfactorily heard in an as yet unbuilt church."[6] Goodhue described it as "a material of great beauty, both in colour and texture, slightly rough, and of a soft and rather warm coffee colour, whose greatest value lies not in its beauty but in its acoustic value."[7] Although a similar tile, Rumford tile, had been used at St. Thomas, the more refined Akoustolith was first tried out at Goodhue's First Congregational Church in Montclair, New Jersey, and then applied to St. Bartholomew's.[8]

Akoustolith, which can be used as a finish material, is the final layer of a timbrel tile vault. Such vaults, composed of mortar and thin tiles, had become very popular in the United States since they were introduced by McKim, Mead, and White in 1892 (at the Boston Public Library). Quick to erect and amazingly strong once in place, timbrel tile vaults are non-combustible and therefore serve as a fire-proofing device. At St. Bartholomew's, not only are the high vaults constructed of timbrel tile, but the entire pavement of the church rests on a system of such vaults.[9]

Goodhue's letters of October and November 1914 reveal a certain resistance to his ideas on the part of the vestry: "they hate what I have done in the way of design but they find it impossible to give the least hint of what they want,"[10] and "it seems impossible to suit them, try as I may."[11] Nonetheless, by December 14, Parks considered the plans far enough along to appoint a Building Committee.

Three points, in particular, were still up in the air. First, the vestry was skeptical about the stone and brick exterior masonry. Goodhue had assured Parks that he would avoid an effect of zebra striping, but his plan to graduate the masonry from a mostly stone lower wall to a mostly brick upper wall apparently raised visions of rainbows in the minds of his patrons. On December 14, he was requested to build a sample wall, illustrating the intended effect, in his studio. Second, the nature of the covering over the crossing had not yet been decided. Although Goodhue favored a multiple-staged "ciborio," he feared that its great height might interfere with the acoustic properties of the church. He consulted Sabine about whether it would be better to use a hemispheric dome. Sabine responded on December 18 that if the ciborio were lined with absorbent material, it would be even better acoustically than a dome. Third, the question of whether to use the whole lot was still open, and the architect was therefore obliged to continue making two sets of drawings.

On January 6, 1915, several sets of drawings (now lost) were presented to the vestry for approval. They were found to be unsatisfactory, as was the sample wall that Goodhue had constructed in his studio. However, the vestrymen agreed to adopt one of the proposed schemes if it could be modified to meet their criticisms: that the Fiftieth Street façade of the church was too secular, the ciborio was unacceptable, and the narthex was too plain. From the discussion, it is clear that the vestry had decided to build the church on the southern side of the lot and to sell the northern half. However, in order to retain the aesthetic advantage of using the whole

Park Avenue frontage, the first 32 feet of the northern portion was to be left without buildings.

By January 22, Goodhue had prepared a new set of drawings. In a meeting with the vestry, "the question of the desirability of building the particular kind of church shown in the drawings or any other kind was thoroughly discussed," and unanimous approval was given to some of the drawings.[12] On the architect's assurance that this design could be built for $500,000, he was instructed to prepare working drawings. Since ten days later, Goodhue told a friend that St. Bartholomew's would cost $600,000 to $700,000, his assurance to the vestry was an empty promise, intended to humor his patrons for the moment.

On March 1, Parks established a new Building Committee of five members, replacing the committee set up in the previous year. William Appleton was not reappointed to the new committee; Elgin Gould was made its chairman. This committee administered the financial and practical aspects of the project, while the Art Committee, led by Krech and Parks, remained responsible for the aesthetic decisions. Since the vestry did not intend to approve the working drawings until the model was finished and various other matters were resolved, permission was given to the Schaefer Brewing Company to extend its occupancy of the site until May 1, 1916.

Between March and June, the Art Committee rejected three more sets of brick samples. Goodhue continued to solicit various firms for samples of a hard brick of salmon color, not too even in its shape. By June, the vestry had decided to have a scale model of the exterior of the church made, which would show "all stone and brick courses carefully lined off and colored."[13] Apparently, the vestry was still unconvinced that random masonry in salmon-colored brick and stone was what it wanted.

Despite the difficulty regarding materials, Goodhue was preparing working drawings and had asked the vestry to hire the engineers who would lay the foundations and design the heating and ventilating system. As the architect worked in greater detail, he realized that the church "may cost almost anything—certainly $800,000 or $900,000,"[14] a realization he did not share with his patrons.

During the summer, the vestry prepared to sell the northern part of the lot, which on July 14 had been estimated to be worth $575,000. The Racquet and Tennis Club made an offer for this land, and by October 22 the parish was ready to grant a sixty-day option to buy. But before this arrangement could be concluded, the vestry was again considering using the northern half of the lot for the church. The irregularity of the lot, 25 feet deeper on the northern than on the southern side, had not seemed important until the Building Committee decided, on June 15, to eliminate the 150 seats that Goodhue had planned for the west gallery in order to place the organ there. These seats could not be accommodated elsewhere in the church except by reducing the width of the main aisle to 6 feet, which the architect thought would be too narrow for processions. Thus the only way to obtain the number of seats that Parks wanted was to lengthen the church, which could be done only by placing it on the northern, instead of the southern, side of the lot. Goodhue favored this solution, although "the Church will get practically no sun, the chapel no sun at all," and the cost of the building would have to be increased by $100,000.[15]

According to this new scheme, the design of the building was to remain unchanged except for the addition of a third nave bay. Thus Goodhue's comment that placement on the northern side of the lot would "very greatly enhance the beauty of the building" must be understood as referring primarily to the interior disposition of the seating and only secondarily to the augmented scale of the church.[16] This exchange reveals that in Goodhue's original proposal, the building was to have been almost centralized in layout; that is, the nave would have been only slightly longer than the transepts and east end. It was transformed into a longitudinal basilica only in response to the need for increased seating capacity.

By early January 1916, the model (ordered on June 10, 1915) had been seen and approved by the vestry, and invitations were sent to the parishioners to view it in Goodhue's studio. A pamphlet describing the new church, prepared by the architect for the occasion, was distributed to the congregation on Sunday, January 16 (Appendix of Texts). Thus equipped, the parishioners proceeded to view the large model of the church, at one-twenty-fourth full size. Unfortunately, this model, so large that two people could enter it at once, has been lost, but an article in the *New York Times* of January 18, 1916, and the presentation booklet describe it: the Vanderbilt portal dominated the lower portion of the west façade, its horizontal extension balanced by the verticality of the upper portion of the façade, into which a great window was set. The volumes of the nave and transepts were pure geometric solids whose surfaces were pierced with windows and columnar galleries. The whole was dominated by a fenestrated, multiple-staged tower over the crossing. The reporter from the *Times* who viewed the model on January 17 thought (or was told) that the style of the building was Romanesque, and it seemed to him to make a strongly Italian effect because the exterior was of colored brick and stone.

Apparently, the parishioners learned for the first time at the presentation of the model that the vestry did not intend to use the whole Park Avenue frontage. Instead of the Italian garden and Italian villa that they had expected to see flanking the church, the model showed an apartment building occupying 75 feet of frontage. There is no evidence about whether the church occupied the northern or the southern side of the lot. Goodhue refused to estimate the cost of the church, but denied rumors that it would cost $3 million and that the parish was trying to rival St. Thomas Church in expenditure.

While the parishioners were viewing the model, discussion about where to place the building and whether to sell part of the lot gained momentum. Parks urged the vestry to use the whole plot, as it "should without doubt

I · West façade.

II · West façade, portal zone
(Stanford White, 1902).

III · West façade, window.

IV · View from the south.

V · South transept, rose window.

VI · South transept, St. Bartholomew.

VII · South transept, ornamental detail.

VIII · Dome (Bertram Grosvenor
Goodhue Associates, 1930).

IX · South flank, dwarf gallery.

X · Narthex.

XI · Narthex, Genesis cupola
(Hildredth Meiere, 1930).

XII · Narthex, capital depicting
John Wycliffe (ca. 1917).

XIII · View toward the east, showing
the nave and apse.

XIV · Chancel and apse.

XV · Crossing, interior
of the dome.

XVI · Nave barrel vault, detail.

XVII · Nave elevation, view from the northeast.

XVIII · View toward the west,
showing the organ loft.

XIX · West gallery, detail.

XX · Apse, Transfiguration
(Hildredth Meiere, 1929).

XXI · Apse, revetment and liturgical furniture.

XXII · Chancel pavement (ca. 1918).

XXIII · North transept, *The Light of the World* (Francis Lathrop, 1893).

XXIV · South transept, rose window.

XXV · Lectern
(Lee Lawrie, 1923).

XXVI · Communion
rail
(Lee Lawrie, 1920s).

XXVII · Pulpit (Lee Lawrie, 1925).

XXVIII · Chapel.

add greatly to the beauty of the church and be a glory to the city."[17] Goodhue informed the vestry that it would cost $650,000 to construct the church on the northern part of the lot, and $1 million if the whole lot was used. The additional $350,000 would cover the cost of the cloister, garden, rectory, and parish building, which would adjoin the church if the whole lot was used. These estimates did not include all the originally planned ornamentation, but only "sufficient decoration to make the church presentable." These prices were not accurate, since Goodhue knew that to construct and fully finish even the shorter church alone might cost $900,000. Nonetheless, the vestry was appalled at the estimates and doubted that so much money could be raised. Not only was the church to cost twice as much as had been originally budgeted, but the source of money to pay for it (the sale of part of the lot) was to be lost. From an economic point of view, the use of the whole lot was folly.

By February, with the model approved and construction due to begin in six months, it became an urgent necessity to make a decision. On February 14, the Building Committee presented three possible solutions (A, B, and C) to these questions. Scheme A placed the church on the southern side of the lot, as originally planned, and released the northern portion for sale. Scheme B showed the church on the northern side and, using the whole lot, left nothing for sale. Scheme C used the whole frontage on Park Avenue, but not the whole depth of the lot, leaving small plots for sale behind or to the side of the church on both Fiftieth and Fifty-first streets. It is not stipulated for scheme C where the church was to be placed, but its length must have been at maximum 225, not 250, feet.

At this point, the vestry made an amazing decision, declaring that scheme B was superior to the others "in point of excellence of design, architectural beauty and serviceability" and resolving to finance this scheme or to abandon all plans made until then and begin anew.[18] What were the advantages of scheme B? First, it provided more seats than scheme A or C. While scheme A allowed a maximum of 1,300 seats, only 200 more than in St. Bartholomew's II,[19] scheme B accommodated 1,275 people in pews and 1,500 if folding chairs were placed in the aisles. Thus it gave the rector precisely the number of places that he had asked for.

Scheme B proposed an architectural complex of at least four separate structures. Whereas in scheme A, the Sunday school and offices would have been located in the basement of the church, now they would occupy the southeastern quarter of the lot. Presumably, scheme A did not provide for a rectory or a cloister. A watercolor of the project shows that the sloping grade of the site was to be utilized so that most of these structures would be partially hidden from view (fig. 15). The passer-by on Park Avenue would see the huge church rising next to a pretty garden with a charming house in it. The aesthetic effect aimed for was contrast: the monumental was contrasted with the minute; the imposing, with the picturesque; art, with nature. Thus the subsidiary buildings were designed on a small scale in order to emphasize the nobility, severity, and grandeur of the church. Although at least part of this complex was erected, the subsidiary buildings were torn down within a few years to make room for the present Community House. Further, urban development in the surrounding neighborhood has reversed the effect that Goodhue envisioned; while the relationship of St. Bartholomew's to its environment remains a positive one, the church has become a jewel in a monumental setting (fig. 1).

Scheme B must have been architecturally richer or more complex than scheme A, since there was a $20,000 difference in Goodhue's fee for executing them ($79,695, as compared with $59,650) and since he now claimed that St. Bartholomew's would "be regarded as a monument among the churches of America, something that will take its place beside Old Trinity, Grace, the Brick Church, the new Cathedral and the Chapel of the Intercession as a permanent, not a temporary landmark in New York."[20] Scheme B, then, represented something different in both quality and kind from what had earlier been approved. It projected an architectural complex rather than a church building alone, and it would bring prestige to the parish, rivaling the most notable examples of Episcopal church building in New York.

Cost estimates from several contractors were appended to the three

15 · Goodhue. Presentation drawing for St. Bartholomew's Church (1916).

schemes. According to the Eidlitz Company (the firm that eventually built the church), $428,000 would have to be raised to build scheme A, $1,071,275 for scheme C, and $1,226,325 for scheme B. The ever-prudent vestry was not optimistic about the possibility that such a large sum could be raised, but giving in to Parks's determination to have the largest church on the whole site and its own recognition of the superiority of scheme B, a compromise was reached: the rector, who loathed fund raising, was requested to seek the necessary money from the congregation.

This he did, bringing the matter to his parishioners in a sermon preached on February 27, 1916 (Appendix of Texts). After reviewing the history of the project and pointing out the inadequacies of seating capacity and church facilities in scheme A, he urged the acceptance of scheme B:

> if after having seen the larger and more beautiful and efficient thing, we content ourselves with something that is less desirable, we may save money but we may lose something for which the Parish exists. For first of all I fear that an inconspicuous Church, and a Church having no appeal to the imagination and a Church that does not stand out in this great city will fail to draw into its doors the great multitude of people from all parts of this country who year by year settle in this city.

For Parks, the new building was a crucial instrument in his evangelical ministry. Scheme B should be built not for the pleasure or pride of the parishioners, but for the saving of souls. While his appeal challenged the self-respect of the parish, its deeper message urged a tangible commitment to the spreading of the faith beyond parish boundaries. Thus St. Bartholomew's, which is the realization (if an imperfect one) of scheme B, was built as something more than a parish church. Its architecture was expected to carry a spiritual message to all who see it, and it was designed on the model of a cathedral, rather than on that of a parish church.

The vestry was willing to follow the rector's lead in committing the parish to this costly project, but it did not intend to abandon sound business procedure in carrying it out. No work would begin until most of the full sum—$1 million—was in hand. In April, subscription forms were sent to the parishioners, who were urged to make gifts of $100,000 or more. If the financial goal was not reached by December, the whole project was to be abandoned. The vestry did not intend to incur debts or to begin construction without the certainty of completion. Thus the parishioners were challenged to act swiftly and generously, or not at all.

At this moment, with the parish on the verge of committing itself to an architectural project far more grandiose than originally foreseen, the whole enterprise exploded. Perhaps in reaction to the architect's urgings or in a momentary failure of nerve, Parks turned against Goodhue. Parks now challenged the most recent cost estimate of $684,700 for the construction of the church building, claiming that Goodhue had promised to keep the cost at $500,000. As we have seen, Goodhue never believed that the church could be built for that sum, and in the light of his own earlier private estimates, $684,700 was very reasonable. But his past attempts to humor the patron were interpreted as willful dishonesty.

In a letter of April 14, Goodhue defended himself against Parks's charges, reminding him that "when this sum [$500,000] first was put forward, I smiled and said that you never could build such a building for such a sum; but that we might call it that for the time being."[21] On April 18, Parks asked Goodhue to resign. As attempts at mediation failed, more causes of discontent surfaced. Apparently, Parks had gotten wind of some of Goodhue's criticisms of him and felt that his confidence had been betrayed. Again, Parks suspected Goodhue of trying to manipulate the parish into accepting his design by refusing to consider alternatives, withholding information, and, in short, giving his patrons the run-around.

Faced with this open confrontation, Goodhue backed down. All humility and contrition, he begged pardon and, in a show of good will, suggested ways in which the cost might be trimmed. By May 1, peace had formally been reestablished. Who had really been at fault? The incomplete evidence suggests that while Goodhue had indeed been high-handed and condescending in his attitude, he had been fundamentally honest about the building's cost. After all, if in 1915, Goodhue had thought that the first design might cost $600,000 to $700,000 and if his estimate a year later was within these bounds, there is no reason to believe that he was artifically inflating the projected cost. Further, approximately this estimate had been accepted as reasonable by the vestry in 1916. Why was it being questioned now, when the subscription forms had already been sent out? It seems likely that the rupture was provoked more by the parish's fear of the financial commitment and its outrage at Goodhue's gossip, than by his dishonesty. Although peace was made, trust was irrevocably broken. From this moment on, the vestry sought to curb Goodhue's power and control his decisions. James Lane, appointed chairman of the Building Committee after Gould's death, grumbled that he did not see why it was necessary to leave decisions in the hands of "architects or of experts from outside,"[22] and the committee sought a building firm that would act as a watchdog over Goodhue.

Goodhue tried to avoid further misunderstandings, informing Parks of every step he made. Thus new drawings were approved on June 7. This attitude explains his refusal to accept the contract prepared by the building contractor for the church. The contract was inadequate, he said, because it would lead to "an endless series of difficulties that might and certainly should have been avoided."[23]

Goodhue's caution was unrewarded. While on July 3, he wrote that "our last troubles are over with regard to St. Bartholomew's,"[24] on July 6, the vestry resolved to leave certain portions of the church unfinished. Although money for the project had begun to come in (in June, a bank account for it was opened), the $1 million was not yet in hand and construction was scheduled to begin in September. Thus the vestry decided to finish the church, but to postpone the completion of the chapel.

The actual situation was much more serious than the vestry had imagined. When the bids for the construction contract were opened on September 5, they were 20 percent higher than anticipated in April. The vestry dug in its heels: either the architect found a way to reduce the cost, or the project would be abandoned. Goodhue responded that the cost could be lowered only by eliminating parts of the design and using cheaper materials for the rest. His appended list of proposed reductions was gloomy indeed. To be eliminated were all decorative marble columns, bronze grilles, all sculpture, wall veneers, and window tracery. Nor would this alone suffice. The height of the church would have to be lowered by 2.5 feet, and its length shortened by one bay (returning to the original proposal).

The vestry turned to Eidlitz for advice, distrusting the truth of Goodhue's assertions. Goodhue protested that the vestry did not have full confidence in him and objected to its selection of Eidlitz as building contractor. Lane confirmed this in his reply. Indeed, he wrote on September 15, since Goodhue had first claimed that prices had risen by 30 percent and now maintained that they had risen by only 15 percent, there was no reason to believe that even this second figure was reliable. Lane concluded that Goodhue would have to work with Eidlitz whether he liked him or not, their mutual mistrust guaranteeing that the church would obtain the best services at the lowest price. This exchange seems to have silenced Goodhue, whom we next encounter in a more cooperative frame of mind.

During October, the vestry examined six proposals for reducing the cost of the church. At this point, faced with the prospect of the mutilation of his design, Goodhue prepared new drawings, meekly assuring the vestry that "in case the cost of the new design proves too high or in case it does not meet with the approval of the Building Committee, I will make no charge to cover the cost to me of these new drawings."[25]

A sheet of cost estimates submitted at the November 10 meeting of the vestry gives a fairly clear picture of the financial situation at that time. The rise in cost since the February estimate was $260,505, bringing the total to $1,544,550. The reductions to the project proposed in October had eliminated this extra cost, mostly by lowering the cost of the church building (cut by $234,950, to a total of $920,000) and the architect's fee (cut by $10,000, to $80,000). Following the November 10 meeting, further cuts were decided. Eidlitz submitted a scheme for reductions that would decrease the cost of the church by another $120,000, to $800,000. This scheme, examined on November 15 and approved on November 23, called for a gilded coffered ceiling instead of a crossing tower, lowering the height of the church by almost 4 feet, omitting the cloister, the chapel sacristy, the marble veneers, and the bronze grilles, and replacing the blue slate floor with tiles and cut stone with cast stone in the interior.

These proposals had a drastic effect on the appearance of the building.

From the first, Goodhue had aimed to achieve his main effect through the tower and the use of beautiful finish materials. Now they were eliminated, and only a poor skeletal structure remained. Even the vestry members felt that they had gone too far. On December 20, they voted to add $10,000 to the budget so that the height of the church would not have to be lowered and the chapel could keep its sacristy. The other changes, more important to the design, were irrevocably confirmed.

On January 7, 1917, Parks informed the congregation of these recent events (Appendix of Texts). He began on a positive note, rejoicing that $1 million had been received by the December deadline. But, he admitted, during the time that had elapsed while raising the money, prices had risen. In effect, he told the parishioners that it was no longer possible to complete the church for which they had pledged their funds, but he cast this news in as positive a fashion as he could, referring only to "simplification of detail" and assuring them that the changes would improve the design, "inasmuch as there is always danger of over-ornamentation in Romanesque." The crossing tower and cloister, he said, would be built later. The congregation was invited to inspect a drawing that shows how the finished church would look (fig. 16). This drawing, which is still in the possession of the church, depicts the building from the exterior, with the truncated crossing tower as the only visibly changed element. A view of the interior, denuded of ornament, would have been more distressing.

Preparations for construction had begun in earnest. Contracts were signed for the timbrel tile vaulting, structural steel, rubble masonry, modeling and carving, cutting and setting of cast and cut stone and of marble, brick, and roofing tile.[26]

After discussions, on February 15 and March 7, about whether to lay acoustic material in the foundations, excavation began on the site. Almost immediately, it was discovered that unforeseen difficulties in laying the foundations would add $4,000 or $5,000 to the cost of the church. In fact, the extra cost for the foundations was $11,901.

While this work was going on, the Art Committee and Parks worked out the iconographic program for the church and made recommendations to the architect in regard to the subjects of the interior and exterior sculptural ornamentation. The program was approved on May 14 (Appendix of Iconography).

On April 26, in a last-minute reversal before construction began, it was decided to substitute natural for cast stone on the interior. Although the building had been designed with natural stone in mind, two of the vestrymen had pressed Goodhue on September 21 and 22, 1916, to substitute cast stone in order to reduce costs. But, said Goodhue, the "cut stone people of New York" had reduced their original estimate in order to undersell the cast-stone company,[27] and thus "thanks to a combination of wicked labour union methods and trade rivalries directed against Wheeler's concrete stone, only the other day we managed to change all of the

16 · Modified proposal for St. Bartholomew's Church (1916).

interior from this material into real yellow Ohio stone."[28] Contracts for Tammany Buff stone, Bluestone, and marble were signed on March 30 and April 11. Thus Goodhue was able to rescue a portion of his original scheme, and he declared with satisfaction that "St. Bartholomew's, P.E. and Italian Romanesque . . . is going to be good I think, even though the style is so strange to us here."[29]

With both the form and the content of St. Bartholomew's planned and approved, the moment to begin construction had come. On May 1, 1917, the cornerstone of the new church was laid by David Hummel Greer, the bishop of New York and former rector of St. Bartholomew's. The inscription on the stone reads:

TO THE GLORY OF GOD THIS FOUNDATION STONE WAS LAID ON THE FIRST DAY OF MAY IN THE YEAR OF OUR LORD MDCCCCXVII AND OF THE REFORMATION THE FOUR HUNDREDTH, BY THE RIGHT REVEREND DAVID HUMMEL GREER D.D., L.L.D., BISHOP OF NEW YORK AND SOMETIME RECTOR OF THIS PARISH.

Within the stone were laid a Bible, the *Book of Common Prayer,* a hymnal, the Journal of the General Convention of 1916, the *Year Book of St. Bartholomew's Parish* for 1917, a vellum sheet with the history of the parish, Parks's sermon of April 19, 1914 (Appendix of Texts), Greer's and Parks's sermons of February 27, 1916 (Appendix of Texts), the Order of Service for the laying of the cornerstone, copies of the *New York Times, Tribune, Herald,* and *Sun* of May 1, 1917, American currency (a $20 gold piece, a $10 gold piece, a $2.50 gold piece, a fifty-cent piece, a quarter, a dime, and a penny), photographs of the working drawings, photographs of the old church, a list of those responsible for the design and construction of the new church, a medal struck for the occasion, a photograph of the Park Avenue plot, and a list of the contributors to the project.

The medal, designed by Goodhue and executed by Piccirilli Brothers, is an important piece of evidence for the architect's original intentions for the completed church (fig. 17). In particular, the representation of the church on the medal, together with the presentation drawing for scheme B, depict Goodhue's design for the crossing tower (fig. 15). That Goodhue included the tower on the medal, although it had been decided not to build it in the foreseeable future, suggests how crucial it was, in his mind, to the exterior profile of the building and to its intended effect of grandeur. The tower would pull all the volumes of the building together and would be the architectural focus of the whole design. That on the medal it is shown rising above adjacent skyscrapers implies that Goodhue conceived of the tower as the ecclesiastical equivalent of the new secular architecture. The tendency of contemporary commercial architecture to multiple-staged verticality could be followed in religious buildings only through the upward thrust of the crossing tower. The tower of St. Bartholomew's, despite the historical references of its specific form, would have designated the new church as a modern building and placed it within the avant-garde of stylistic developments.[30]

The medal also suggests that the other major distinguishing feature of the church was to be the Vanderbilt portal, which is represented prominently on the model of the church held by St. Bartholomew and on a larger scale, to his right. The section of a barrel vault visible immediately to his left may be Goodhue's testimony to the importance of Guastavino tile for modern construction. On the reverse of the coin, coats of arms symbolize the loyalties and membership of the new church: the parish of St. Bartholomew's, the diocese of New York, the city of New York, and the United States of America. Thus the interdependence of church and state asserted in Parks's sermons is reiterated by the medal's imagery.[31]

17 · Goodhue. Medal struck to commemorate the laying of the cornerstone (1917).

CONSTRUCTION

The erection of the church took place between May and July 1917, when the roof was put on (fig. 14). As Goodhue had intended, the skeleton of the building was quick, easy, and thus cheap to construct. The church would not be ready for use, however, for another fifteen months, since its finish and ornament were to claim most of the time and money spent. By September 10, the parish had spent $1,272,818.43 on the project, of which about $280,000 was for the church, and it was anticipated that another $1 million would be needed to complete the project. In January 1918, with money tight again, it was decided not to complete the garden that was to be adjacent to the church and to omit the ornamental tiles that were to have been set into the Akoustolith. Since these reductions would save only about $20,000, the vestry asked Goodhue whether he could reuse the pews from the old church, saving the cost of new ones.

At this point, in early 1918, work was far advanced. Payments to the sculptor Lee Lawrie and to the Piccirilli Brothers sculptural firm had been made in November 1917, suggesting that the ornamentation of the church structure was under way. The transfer of the Vanderbilt portal to its new location was scheduled for March 1. Indeed, the whole parish was beginning to prepare for the move, which was scheduled to take place within ninety days after March 1.

To mark the occasion of this announcement, Parks delivered a sermon in which he summarized the history and traditions of the parish (Appendix of Texts). The building of the new church was presented as the culmination of almost 100 years of devotion to the ideals of worship and community service. But, admitted Parks, his promises regarding the completion of the building could not be kept. The First World War had intervened; costs of material and labor had jumped; and, in short, a deficit of about $100,000 was projected. This deficit, however, was on the cost of the land, not of construction. In regard to the latter, he said, the vestry had held firm against the architect's attempts to make expensive additions to the original plans, and the cost of the building had remained within the budgeted amount. But the documents do not support Parks's version of the financial situation and its causes.

By the spring of 1918, work was in its final phase. Eidlitz was given permission to enter St. Bartholomew's II on May 1 in order to remove the materials and furnishings that would be reused in the new building, and the Art Committee consulted with Goodhue about where to place them. During the summer, some stained glass was transferred from the old church, and some new glass was made by G. Owen Bonawit. The G. Brown Company took out the marble paving in St. Bartholomew's II and used it for part of the paving of the new chancel. The chancel rail of the old church was cut down for reuse; the old choir stalls were adapted to the new chancel; the painting over the altar was installed in the north transept (pl. XXIII); and the reredos was placed in the baptistery.

Finally, on October 20, the first service was held in the new church. In his welcoming address, Parks connected the celebration with the triumph of virtue over vice that was about to end the war (Appendix of Texts). This was why, he said, the service had begun with the singing of the national anthem and the saluting of the American flag in the chancel. "And now we hope that this work, planned in the days of peace, carried on amid the tumult of war, dedicated in the dawn of victory, will be an instrument of God's glory by preparing the way of the Lord in the new world which has been revealed."

In regard to the work completed, Parks praised the architect, the contractor, and the wardens and vestry of the church, particularly James Lane, chairman of the Building Committee. He rejoiced that the building had been erected in only eighteen months and that the contractor and vestry had succeeded in containing its cost. The two essential aims of the new church had been fully realized by its acoustic properties (hearing the sermon and the music) and its seating arrangement (seeing the preacher). As to its appearance, however, Parks once again expressed regret. Not only had the original scheme been truncated by the deletion of many features, but even the work planned was still unfinished. The marble revetment in the chancel had not yet been installed; the acoustic tiles for the interior were not yet in place; and the exterior on the north side was incomplete. Nonetheless, Parks felt that it was already clear "that Mr. Goodhue has struck a new note and designed a building which marks a new era in American church architecture."

The response of the congregation to Parks's appeal for funds to finish the building was, once again, loyal. Throughout the autumn, private donations were received, and by April 1919, estimates for the completion of Goodhue's crossing tower were being considered. In the meantime, the Parish House had been occupied, on December 21, 1918, and the landscaping of the garden was going ahead. In June, the possibility of erecting the cloister was discussed, and estimates for a lectern and pulpit were solicited. But while some of this work was made possible by donations, funds remained limited. The tower and the cloister were not built, and it was decided that the parish could not afford $2,520 for windows (stained glass?) in the nave. On December 8, the treasurer reported that $47,667.38 was left in the building fund, and on March 14, 1920, the vestry asked the rector to try to raise a badly needed $136,000 from the congregation. More than $98,000 had been collected by January 1921.

There is no documented building activity between late 1919 and the end of 1921. By March 1922, Goodhue was urging the Building Committee to take action, particularly in regard to the completion of the interior and the substitution of the temporary covering over the crossing. "The church," wrote Goodhue, "as it is, is in some ways a good deal of a barn and, with the exception of the Chapel, doesn't redound at all to my credit."[32] The vestry continued, however, to pursue its by-now-traditional policy: until the indebtedness of the church was removed, no further work would be undertaken. It was not until April 1923 that the $155,000 needed to pay the debt was raised. Finally, the date for the consecration of the church was set. It took place on May 1, and on May 6, the rector explained the style and the significance of the building to his parishioners (Appendix of

Texts). His sermon on the preferability and superiority of Romanesque architecture led him to an analysis of some features of this style, such as the campanile, that were neither present in St. Bartholomew's nor ever planned for it. Nonetheless, the sermon is of invaluable help in understanding not so much what the building is, as what it was thought and intended to be by its patrons and architect.

In 1924, the leading actors in the drama of construction left the stage. Goodhue died on April 23, and seven months later, Parks resigned from his post. These men had represented the artistic and intellectual core of the enterprise. Without their inspiration and guidance, the project would never be carried to completion as originally planned. Instead, new leaders would change its character, using different aesthetic and practical criteria in finishing the church and its adjacent buildings.

In his last months as rector, Parks pushed hard for two goals: the completion of the church as planned in scheme B, and the establishment of an endowment fund to protect it in the future. He reminded the congregation that its moral obligation had to be fulfilled: the completion of a church with a tower, garden, and cloister. Moreover, some of the largest donations had been made with the understanding that this would be the final appearance of the whole; thus it had to be carried out.

In regard to the endowment, Mr. and Mrs. Charles William Harkness had given $500,000 to the church "so that when the day . . . came, when the city churches could no longer count upon a congregation of people of large means and must either be abandoned or minister to a community unable to support them, this church would be a house of prayer for all people."[33] In order to increase the endowment, two sources of revenue were suggested: the rental of pews and the purchase of memorial tablets. The deeds of all privately owned pews were reclaimed by the vestry, and on April 11, 1923, it was decided that new rentals would be issued at $1,000 each. The right to place memorial tablets on the walls of the church would be offered to all parishioners at a cost of $5,000 a tablet. Other, simpler memorials could be obtained for $1,000. Parks had alerted his congregation to the necessity of securing the future of the church, and with this prophetic warning, he stepped down from the pulpit that he had occupied for twenty years.

Under Parks's successor, Robert Norwood, construction and embellishment of the church complex was taken up with renewed enthusiasm. By January 1926, within one year of his appointment on May 3, 1925, Norwood had the vestry considering sketches for a new Parish House. By April, the budget of $575,000 had been approved, and an architectural firm—Bertram Grosvenor Goodhue Associates—was chosen. (Goodhue Associates, a firm directed by F. L. S. Mayers, Hardie Phillip, and O. H. Murray, renegotiated contracts for works unfinished at Goodhue's death.) The contractor, Cauldwell-Wingate Company, was appointed in June, and work on the demolition of the structures on the southeastern quarter of the lot was begun. The Community House was dedicated on November 29, 1927.

This project was the positive consequence of the closing of the Parish House on Forty-second Street. The character of that neighborhood had changed; the poor had moved elsewhere; and the Parish House ministry was no longer necessary. A new group of people needed the help of the church: young professionals and college graduates making their careers in the city. Norwood envisaged a center that would be "a home for people of mental and aesthetic perception where they may express their social impulse in an environment of kindred selves. The club rooms take care for that. For their physical selves there is the gymnasium and swimming pool in which wholesome exercise is provided."[34] Thus the southern half of the lot was needed for functions not foreseen in Goodhue's time. A more intensive use of the land was required, and the separate, low structures in a garden setting were demolished, to be replaced by a five-story edifice.

While Goodhue's plan (fig. 15) embodied the principle of contrast between the church and its setting, the 1926 project produced a relation of continuity between the two. Under the circumstances, Goodhue Associates probably made the most sensible decision possible: to use the same exterior materials for the Community House as had been used for the church and to design the simplest of volumes in the hope that at least a neutral relationship of coexistence might be obtained.

Norwood was also eager to complete the decoration of the church interior. The pulpit and lectern, carved by Lee Lawrie, had been given as private memorials to the church, as had the bronze doors of the chapel, but the overall decoration of the interior had not progressed. In January 1927, Goodhue's designs for this decoration were reexamined, and in February, Goodhue Associates (specifically, Mayers and Murray) was asked to provide new sketches.

The fragments that survive of Goodhue's original drawings for the apse decoration suggest that the present revetment of the sanctuary, in which large fields of colored marble are separated by vertical stripes of geometric ornament, follows his scheme (fig. 18).[35] The chancel rail, altar, apsidal bench, and chairs, while not directly designed by Goodhue, bear the unmistakable imprint of Lawrie, Goodhue's most trusted collaborator. Since Lawrie had always had a good deal of freedom in working out Goodhue's sculptural ornamentation, one may suppose that—except for the influence of Lawrie's own stylistic development in the intervening years—the design of these parts reflects Goodhue's intentions. The design and furnishings of the lower parts of the sanctuary represent a continuation and further development of Goodhue's scheme. The revetment, whose application in 1929 was made possible by the Easter offering of $123,637, was dedicated to the memory of Bishop Greer as "a sacrament of the mystical union between God and all who worship in St. Bartholomew's."

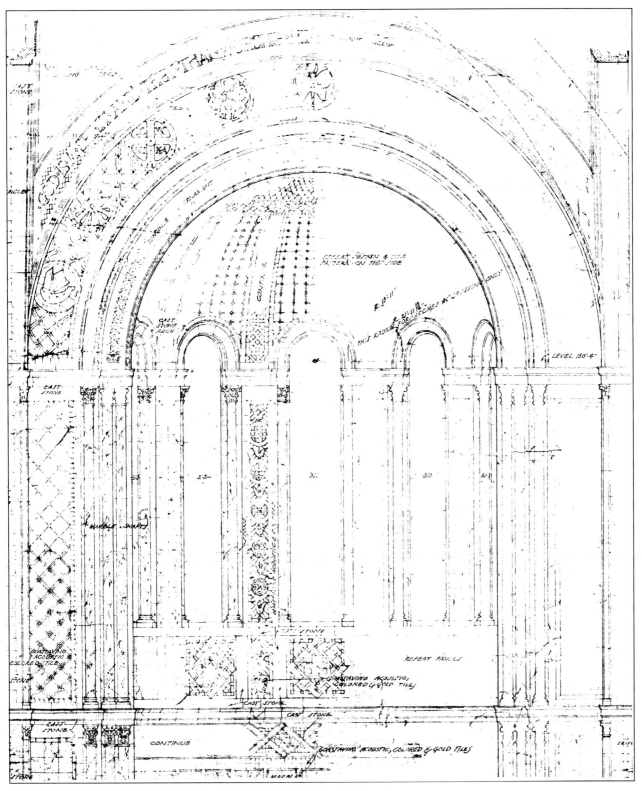

18 · Goodhue. Design for apse
decoration, St. Bartholomew's
Church (1916).

While the sanctuary was being completed, the Art Committee, chaired by Krech, was examining the larger question of the embellishment of the walls of the church. In a report of 1928, the committee stated that "the two main features which are lacking to make St. Bartholomew's Church in the City of New York a unique example of twentieth century expression of Byzantine architecture in America, the realization of which was interrupted by the Great War, are the dome and the interior embellishment."[36] It will be recalled that at its consecration only five years earlier, the church had been described—and at length—as Romanesque. So, too, is it described in Goodhue's presentation booklet of 1916, which Krech, who had served on the vestry since 1912, was perfectly familiar with. Why, then, was it suddenly described as Byzantine?[37]

Krech had personally undertaken the task of researching the style of decoration that would be most appropriate to the church. In his report to the vestry on behalf of the Art Committee, he explained the choice:

> the conclusion of the Committee to adopt the Byzantine style of mosaic wall decoration was naturally inevitable; its use covering a period of nearly a thousand years preceded the revival of the art of painting in Italy just as the Byzantine influence gave way to the Gothic in church architecture. Its main characteristics are dignity of design, combined with colorful and jewel-like brilliancy.[38]

Krech's search for a pre-Gothic, pre-Renaissance, but post-Classical style of decoration led him, predictably enough, to Byzantine mosaics. Moreover, Goodhue's design, with marble revetment on the lower walls and gold tile in the vaults, owed a debt to Byzantine example. If Goodhue had blurred the boundary between Romanesque and Byzantine architecture, following the example of his model, San Marco, Krech erased it altogether. For him, Byzantine was the medieval style that had preceded Gothic in western Europe, and it must therefore be the style of St. Bartholomew's.

This new commitment to Byzantine decoration for the interior led to a negation of some of Goodhue's ideas for the church. Goodhue had designed the church without figural decoration, except for the architectural sculpture. All the ornamentation planned for the upper parts of the building was to have been abstract, and iconographic content in those areas was to have been conveyed only through inscriptions. Now it was decided to cover the vaults with a narrative mosaic scheme. That the Art Committee was unable to devise a coherent iconographic program for the whole church is hardly surprising; only Goodhue could have done it, and he had not wished to. As a start, it was decided to place a depiction of the Transfiguration in the apse, and then to see about the rest (pl. xx). Preliminary designs were prepared by Goodhue Associates, working with the mosaicist Hildredth Meiere, in October 1927; a model of the apse mosaic was exhibited in May 1928. The work of installation began in October, continued through the winter and following summer, and was completed in October 1929.

On January 10, 1929, the Art Committee had reviewed the cost of the work on the church still to be done. The construction of the dome was the most expensive item listed, estimated at $350,000. The rest—the decoration of the narthex, covering the four crossing arches with mosaics, and covering the rest of the exposed stone with mosaics—came to about $200,000. Evidently, the idea of sheathing all the vaults in mosaics had been abandoned, probably for acoustic reasons (it would have covered the Guastavino tile). Now, instead, the aim seems to have been to create mosaic borders around the surface planes.

Between January and October, the vestry was busy raising these funds, and by December, there was enough money in hand to proceed with the mosaic decoration of the four crossing arches and with the construction of the dome, for which working drawings had been prepared. The records are silent about why Goodhue's tower design was rejected, but its cost probably was prohibitive. By December, the donation promised in 1927 by Emily Vanderbilt White for a celestial organ, to be placed in the dome, had been received; the same donor paid for the completion of the narthex in 1930. The walls and windows of the narthex had just received their marble ornamentation, and sketches for the Creation cycle of mosaics for the domes of the narthex were ready. Final gifts—a green marble altar, a marble credence table, and chancel chairs—given in 1930 brought the church to completion.

On December 9, 1930, a ceremony of dedication for the decoration was held, and Norwood could record with pride in the *Year Book* that

> what were formerly brick surfaces have now given way to marble facings, mosaics and great stone arches. Stately bronze doors adorn the entrances to the baptistery and chapel, a number of stained glass windows appear in the transepts, a beautiful altar and altar rail have been installed and a celestial organ is the means of adding further beauty to our music. Last but not least there has been erected a dome which is outwardly appropriate to its surroundings and inwardly a work of art.[39]

Norwood had accomplished much, and the church he left at his death in 1932 has remained much as we see it today; the most notable additions are the stained-glass windows of the gallery and west windows. The vestry, too, had served admirably; the entire debt for construction had been liquidated by December 20, 1932.

19 · San Marco, Venice (begun 1063).

4 · THE HISTORICAL SOURCES

IT WAS MY INTENTION, in considering the historical sources for St. Bartholomew's, to treat the church as a revival of Italian Romanesque style and, through visual comparisons of such models with St. Bartholomew's, to assess both its historical accuracy and its originality. Such an approach was suggested by the numerous statements made about historical style by Bertram Goodhue and Leighton Parks, by the need to dispel the confusion caused by recent definitions of the church's style, and by the many borrowings from the past evident in the building itself.

The task seemed straightforward, even simple; even before Goodhue was hired, it had been decided to build in the Romanesque style. Since the new building was to conform to the Vanderbilt portal, the question of its architectural style determined itself. Moreover, it is clear from Parks's sermon celebrating the consecration of St. Bartholomew's in 1923, "The Spiritual Significance of the Romanesque," that he believed that a neo-Romanesque church had been erected.

Goodhue's description of the church even named the specific sources for the design: the narthex was to imitate that of St. Gilles-du-Gard (fig. 20), the model for the Vanderbilt portal (pl. II); the rose window in the south transept would be "reminiscent of such Italian examples as St. Francis at Assisi" (fig. 21; pl. v); the "ciborium," or crossing tower, was to be based on that of Santa Maria delle Grazie in Milan and the Certosa di Pavia (figs. 15, 22, 23); the chapel ceiling derived from that of San Miniato al Monte in Florence (fig. 24; pl. XXVIII); and, finally, the exterior masonry of brick and stone would "give a somewhat similar effect of richness to that which one finds in the Romanesque churches of Milan and Bologna."[1]

But the characterization of St. Bartholomew's as Italian seemed to be too simple—indeed, inadequate—to account for its appearance. It assumed, for example, that Goodhue had been able to identify buildings in the Romanesque style. Of the five buildings he named as sources, two are Romanesque, one is Gothic, and two are Renaissance; thus this assumption seemed unwarranted. Further, it assumed that he had been concerned with reproducing the medieval styles of his models. His letters cast doubt on this. In a letter to Parks in which he urged the rector to visit the major examples of Lombard, Emilian, and Apulian Romanesque architecture during his vacation in Italy, Goodhue declared that "the structural princi-

20 · St. Gilles-du-Gard,
Provence (ca. 1170).

21 · San Francesco,
Assisi (ca. 1250).

22 · Bramante. Santa Maria delle Grazie, Milan (1492).

23 · Certosa di Pavia, Pavia (1429–73).

ple underlying the design [of St. Bartholomew's] is the same as that of Westminster Cathedral," a neo-Byzantine church designed by John Francis Bentley that had been completed in 1903.[2] Finally, it seemed naïve to assume that Goodhue had been telling the truth. Although he recommended that Parks look at northern Italian Romanesque monuments, Goodhue had seen them only in photographs and knew them only slightly. The historical sources listed in his presentation booklet are equally misleading: three are not the real sources for the features mentioned, and many other actual sources for the design are omitted. Indeed, some of the architect's private statements suggest his own confusion about the historical style of the building: "for the moment I have set pinnacles, flying buttresses and pointed arches to one side in favor of the style—Byzantine, Romanesque or whatever you call it—of the new St. Bartholomew's."[3] This ambiguity about whether the style of St. Bartholomew's is Byzantine or Romanesque was in the architect's mind at the inception of the project, and helps to account for recent critics' definition of the style as Byzantine, even though the patrons regarded it as Romanesque.[4] Finally, some evidence suggests that the whole question of historical style was secondary to Goodhue:

> You speak of a Gothicless life as something you hate to contemplate. Here we are taking up such a life from preference. God knows St. Bartholomew's is anything but Gothic—indeed when completed, if ever, and with its roc's egg hanging from its central dome, it will look more like Arabian Nights or the last act of Parsifal than any Christian Church.[5]

The discussion of the historical sources for St. Bartholomew's, then, became a series a questions about Goodhue's culture and about his intentions and aims for the building. The process of answering these questions led to realizations of a general nature that in effect undermined the validity of the original object of research—that is, the definition of St. Bartholomew's in terms of its historical style.

The designing of St. Bartholomew's was a complex process in which a number of demands had to be met, the most important of which were functional, not stylistic. First of all were the acoustic requirements of the building. The second consideration was that the congregation be able to see the altar and the pulpit. This is, specifically, a question of seating arrangement. The third matter was available funds, which necessarily influenced the style, materials, and constructional system of the church as much as did the functional requirements. The liturgy to be performed in the church was another factor to be weighed. There was, in addition, the question of decorum, or appropriateness of style. Since different styles connote different philosophical, social, and institutional associations, Goodhue had to choose a style that would be consonant with the nature of the project. Finally, the matter of aesthetics—form, pure and simple— had to be pondered.

24 · San Miniato al Monte, Florence (ca. 1100).

These demands were often in conflict. Although an auditorium or a theater may be the best hall acoustically, its form is unsuited to the Episcopalian ritual, and it is deficient in religious associations. A traditional ecclesiastical structure—Gothic, for instance—may be satisfactory in terms of liturgy, but is unsuited to a focus on preaching. The form of St. Bartholomew's was determined by functional considerations, illustrating Goodhue's belief that all art arises in response to a need. The process of design, then, was a process of problem solving in which the architect was challenged to propose architectural forms that not only would accommodate, but also would tangibly express an array of functional and spiritual needs.

Thus it seems extremely unlikely that Goodhue intended to reproduce Italian medieval models with much fidelity. Few, if any, such churches possess the acoustic properties or the visibility adequate for modern needs. The idea of Goodhue as a romantic, immersed in his nostalgia for a real or an imagined past, must give way to the less glamorous image of the professional architect wrestling with conflicting requirements and a limited budget.[6] This realization has an important consequence for the definition of St. Bartholomew's. The modern tendency, so widespread as to be practically universal, to define in terms of stylistic categories has to be questioned, for it seems doubtful that the definition of St. Bartholomew's as "modified Byzantine eclectic" (to give but one recent example) can, by its very nature, explain much that is significant about the building.[7] Such descriptions are not useful for a number of reasons, not least of which is the general public's inability to envision the stylistic referent. Even more important may be the assumption of such definitions that the history of architecture is the history of stylistic categories. That formalist criticism should dominate the art that is most intimately linked to function is to be regretted. Such an approach not only falsifies the entire basis of architecture in convenience and necessity, but also obscures the nature of the design process.

If St. Bartholomew's is "modified Byzantine eclectic," then its style is illogical and inconsistent. Such a building cannot display unity or wholeness, and thus it must be of poor quality. But since Goodhue did not regard the history of architecture as the history of style, but as the history of functional and structural types, the definition really misses the point. St. Bartholomew's is a coherent, carefully thought-out building. Its style is modern because, despite the historical references of its formal vocabulary, the functions that determined its form and the structure by which that form is realized are modern. To define the church by its relation to historical styles, as has been done (both accurately and inaccurately), is to overlook the actual historical context of the building in the early twentieth century. St. Bartholomew's is not a flawed attempt to revive "Byzantine grandeurs," but a successful realization of complex functional, aesthetic, and spiritual requirements. That these needs were satisfied with the aid of historical precedent is true, but the church must be recognized as something more than an exercise in archaeological reconstruction. Thus while the epithet "modified Byzantine eclectic" may be a fairly accurate description of the style of St. Bartholomew's (although "byzantinizing Romanesque eclectic" would be more precise), it does not adequately define the architectural monument.

A SPACE FOR SEEING AND HEARING

Goodhue's first and most important concern in designing St. Bartholomew's was to provide the best spatial arrangement and distribution of masses for a church in which the whole congregation could see and hear the preacher, and as many worshippers as possible could see the altar.[8] His solution, in which four barrel-vaulted arms center on an immense domed crossing, was the fruit of recent experiments in building cathedrals in England and the United States.

Although the American Episcopal church had no cathedrals until the mid-nineteenth century, a veritable "cathedral movement" was under way by 1870. These buildings were designed to meet many of the same functional and aesthetic requirements as St. Bartholomew's. Indeed, the intimate connection between St. Bartholomew's and contemporary cathedrals has not yet been appreciated. The central concern of the projects for the Cathedral Church of St. John the Divine in New York, Westminster Cathedral in London, and Liverpool Cathedral was the creation of a space for seeing and hearing. The question of what style could most effectively satisfy this need was thoroughly discussed, and often hotly debated, by both architects and critics, whose views amplify and confirm our understanding of this issue at St. Bartholomew's.

In addition to their similar solutions to the central problems of acoustics and seating, St. Bartholomew's and the cathedrals are analogous in respects that have passed unnoticed. One is size: Alexander James Beresford Hope estimated that "cathedral size" is "not less than 200 or 250 feet in length, and of other dimensions in proportion"[9]—exactly the size of St. Bartholomew's. Such a building, which seats roughly 1,500 people, cannot follow the stylistic conventions of a parish church that averages a cozy 90 feet in length, and the connections of St. Bartholomew's with parish-church designs are very limited.

Size is not the only consideration that suggests the cathedral model. The location of St. Bartholomew's on a broad avenue, forming a visual pendant to the monumental Grand Central Terminal and surrounded by buildings that averaged twelve stories in height, also elicited design on a grand scale, if the building was to hold its own in the urban environment (fig. 25). Moreover, Parks wanted the church to make a visual impact on the city and even on the country. Thus the seating capacity, physical relationship with the neighborhood, and symbolic intent of St. Bartholomew's are associated with cathedrals, not parish churches.

Cathedral Church of St. John the Divine, New York

The project for the Episcopal cathedral of New York was the closest to Goodhue in time and space, and he knew it well both as a competitor for the commission in 1888 (fig. 10) and, after 1911, when Ralph Adams Cram took over its construction.

The problem of style was particularly dramatic. The original design for the interior, by George Louis Heins and C. Grant La Farge, was Romanesque/Byzantine and very closely related to Goodhue's design for St. Bartholomew's. But after taking over the commission, Cram transformed this scheme into Gothic. The issues latent in this controversial change of plan were pinpointed by the critic Montgomery Schuyler in 1911. He agreed that the sentiment of "Anglicanism" appropriate for an Episcopal cathedral did suggest the use of fourteenth-century Gothic style, but argued that modern functional requirements demanded that a different stylistic choice be made. The new conditions were "the need to a cathedral of a great 'auditorium,' a preaching-space in which can be assembled as large a congregation as can be brought within the range of a human voice." Modern structural materials also posed new conditions—for example, "the modern tile arch, which to clothe in the forms of the groined vault of the old Gothic minsters were to indulge in a fiction or a masquerade."[10]

Schuyler's points, that timbrel tile vaulting and the modern emphasis on preaching precluded the use of Gothic—with its long, narrow, groin-vaulted nave—were of crucial importance for the definition of Goodhue's design concept at St. Bartholomew's. Goodhue's acceptance of them is proved by his own belief that Romanesque was much better suited to preaching and congregational worship than was Gothic. It is important to realize that this debate about historical styles did not focus on aesthetic criteria, or even on historical justifications, but was about function, constructional systems, and materials. To some extent, this attitude toward historical styles had

25 · St. Bartholomew's Church in the 1920s, view from the southwest.

its roots in the nineteenth-century Ecclesiological Movement. For example, an article written by F. M. Simpson in 1901 argued that the essence of architectural style is not formal vocabulary, but constructional method. All architecture can be understood as belonging to one of two groups: (1) in which the supports are large and few (Roman, Byzantine, Romanesque, and Renaissance architecture), and (2) in which the supports are small and numerous (Greek and Gothic architecture). The first group, which produces "a large open un-encumbered floor space," is better for modern use, since "there must not be too many piers or columns to obstruct the view of the service and render some portions of the building inferior to others for seeing and hearing."[11] The modern requirement that all members of the congregation be able to see and hear the service rendered Gothic old-fashioned and inadequate.

But did this mean that the requirements of Episcopalian congregations were the same as those of Catholic congregations? R. F. Bach thought that it did. In an article written in 1916, he summarized the history of American church planning.[12] Two historically and liturgically different traditions could be discerned among the various Christian faiths. The first, that of the ritual or liturgical faiths, include the Catholic, Anglican, and American Episcopalian creeds. Their focus of worship is at the altar. Space is needed for processions before, during, and after the service, and a numerous clergy has to be provided with places separate from the congregation. As an example of a good, traditional plan of the ritual type, Bach's article illustrated St. Paul's Cathedral in Detroit, designed by Cram, Goodhue, and Ferguson. It is Gothic in style and has a large narthex, where processions can form; narrow side aisles flanking a wide nave, whose center aisle accommodates processions; shallow transepts; a broad and deep chancel for the choir; and a simple apse. The plan, devised in such a way that all seats have an unobstructed view of the altar, has many features in common with St. Bartholomew's. The second tradition, that of nonritual or denominational faiths, is composed of other Protestant groups—Methodist, Lutheran, Baptist, and so on. Their liturgy centers on the pulpit, and their churches do not require pathways for processions and a large chancel area for clergy and choir. The ideal form for their churches is the auditorium. Approaching church design from a functional point of view, Bach saw its forms as determined by the nature of the liturgy to be performed and, in particular, by the relative importance of altar and pulpit.

For Cram, to whom the sacramental aspect of divine service was most important, the Gothic was a viable style for modern use. The long nave favors splendid processions; the deep chancel houses the choir; and the elaborate altar treatment makes the Eucharist the visual focus of the interior. Thus he felt justified in transforming St. John the Divine into a Gothic cathedral.[13]

But for other groups, particularly Low Church Episcopalians and liberals, the focus of divine service was the sermon, which could not be

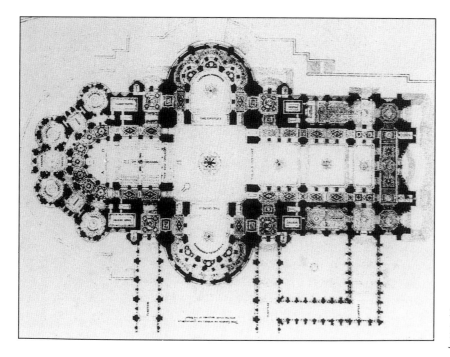

26 · Heins and La Farge. Competition
plan for the Cathedral Church of St.
John the Divine (1888).

heard well in a Gothic structure. Further, since the mid-nineteenth century, some Anglicans had wished to set themselves apart from Catholics,
preferring architectural styles that were "untainted" by later medieval Catholicism. That Parks was an active believer in the tenets of the Ecclesiological Movement is proved by his sermon in which he claimed that the
ideological and liturgical differences between the faiths could be defined in
terms of architecture.[14] Goodhue, too, believed that this was so. In an
article written in 1917, he complained that insufficient attention was paid
to architectural, liturgical, and ideological differences in church design.[15]

At St. John the Divine, then, the problem of Romanesque or Gothic
style was, most profoundly, a problem of function and dramatized a conflict about the nature of the Episcopal liturgy. In the end, the question was
which current of faith should have its beliefs expressed in stone.

Most of the designs entered in the competition of 1888 were neo-Gothic,
but some drew their inspiration from Byzantine and Renaissance architecture. The latter, of course, favored using constructional systems designed
to facilitate hearing and seeing the service. Almost all the entries, regardless of style, featured an extremely large—sometimes disproportionate—
crossing area. This was recognized by Schuyler, in his article criticizing
Cram's changes: "every one of the four selected designs indeed made a
point of enlarging the crossing and increasing its capacity to the utmost."[16] And La Farge, describing his winning design (fig. 26), wrote that
"it will be seen, then, that through the central idea of a great crossing we
strike, as it were, the keynote of the present design."[17]

Why was this? In a preaching church, the best seats are near the pulpit. Thus the large open space of the crossing, combined with broad but shallow transepts, constitute an auditorium space along the transverse axis of the church. Moreover, the crossing, at the east end of the nave, offers the best view of the altar along the longitudinal axis of the church. Therefore, in a church designed to satisfy the potentially conflicting aims of seeing the altar and of seeing and hearing the preacher, the crossing is the ideal seating area and is enlarged as much as possible. (Of course, in a small parish church, this problem need not arise, since the altar and pulpit are visible from all points.)

The modern Episcopal faith, then, is both ritual and nonritual (to use Bach's categories) in function. Longitudinal extension and articulation are needed for the movement of the clergy during the service and for the focus on the celebration at the altar. But an auditorium space on the transverse axis, in front of the pulpit, is of equal importance. Since these two functions are entirely satisfied only in the crossing, this area became the center of the whole design. Indeed, the crossing of both St. John the Divine and St. Bartholomew's was the first part built, and the four arms of the church were appended to it (fig. 14).

The huge crossing of St. John the Divine generated problems in elevation. On the interior, the covering had to be fairly low, for acoustic reasons; but on the exterior, as the focus of all the massing, the crossing

27 · Heins and La Farge. Competition design for St. John the Divine, exterior.

element had to balance the combined volumes of nave, transepts, and east end. These conflicting needs could best be harmonized by using a double-shell structure: an exterior tower and interior dome (figs. 27, 28). So it is described and approved in an editorial in the *Architectural Record:*

> The dome which is the central feature of the new cathedral internally, is covered and masked by the tower, which is the central feature exteriorly. The space covered by the dome and its immediate appendages, including the transepts and choir, is practically the cathedral, the nave being but an impressive approach. The whole space occupied by the transepts is available as a vast auditorium, and the one great difference between a modern and medieval cathedral is thus recognized and provided for.[18]

28 · Heins and La Farge. Competition design for St. John the Divine, interior.

29 · Richardson. Trinity Church, Boston (1872–77).

The pioneer in this design solution for Episcopal churches was Trinity Church, Boston, consecrated in 1877 (fig. 29). H. H. Richardson, the architect, was inspired by the crossing towers of Auvergnate Romanesque architecture, in which "the tower became, as it were, the church, and the composition took the outline of a pyramid, the apse, nave, and chapels forming only the base to the obelisk of the tower."[19] Richardson had suggested that the formal roots of this feature were in Byzantine architecture. La Farge, employing a functional model, acknowledged that the Byzantines had been the first to realize that change in function should be accompanied by change in plan, developing the dome for this purpose. But while Hagia Sophia was the first building to emphasize the center of the church in this way, he said, the motif had not long remained the exclusive possession of the Eastern Empire. The first Western use of the enlarged crossing for congregational needs was at Ely Cathedral (after 1322), making it "the only Gothic example of a church of cathedral type."[20] La Farge

30 · St. Bartholomew's Church,
interior.

was referring to the famous Ely octagon (fig. 55), which inspired his design for the exterior tower of St. John the Divine, as well as those by other competitors for the commission.

These considerations are of fundamental importance for the design of St. Bartholomew's, whose enlarged crossing was to be surmounted by a variant of the Ely octagon. Moreover, the closest source for the nave elevation of St. Bartholomew's is the choir bay of St. John the Divine, although its cool—even glacial—monumentality is far from the tone of Goodhue's church (figs. 28, 30). Heins and La Farge's design was essentially a reworking of the elevation of San Marco (fig. 41). In the choir bay of St. John the Divine, major and minor piers alternate, as at St. Bartholomew's. The gallery is pierced by tall arched openings, through which are visible the three lancet windows of the exterior wall. Heins and La Farge intended to place a mosaic in the apse, unlike Goodhue's decorative scheme for St. Bartholomew's, but the rest of the decoration—colored tiles in the vaults, marble sheathing on the lower parts of the walls, large inscriptions in the crossing—corresponds to the program planned for St. Bartholomew's.

Heins and La Farge's design for St. John the Divine was seminal for Goodhue. It defined the functional requirements of a large-scale, modern Episcopal church and showed the types of plan, structural system, and elevation that could satisfy those requirements. It demonstrated a new method for making use of historical styles and clarified the advantages that each style could offer the modern architect. Finally, it gave powerful endorsement to a new architectural ideal, in which the dominating crossing tower was the very symbol of the modern church.

None of the entries embodied this new symbolism as dramatically as Halsey Wood's competition entry, *Jerusalem the Golden* (figs. 31, 32). This extraordinary pastiche, in which a Late Gothic elevation rises from a plan based on that of San Marco, was called "astounding" by Cram. It is a kind of ecclesiastical skyscraper in which the crossing tower overwhelms and subsumes all the other parts of the building.

The design illustrates St. John's vision: "and I heard a great voice out of heaven, saying, Behold, the tabernacle of God is with men, and he will dwell with them and they shall be his people" (Revelation 21:3). Wood proposed to create a giant icon, a vehicle of connection between the contingent and the transcendent. Conveying the beauty and infinite splendor of heaven in a stone analogy, it was, above all, a statement of God's immanence and thus a representation of Liberal Protestant theology.

Wood's scheme was hardly buildable, and thus its formal links with St. Bartholomew's are tenuous. But if its influence was less tangible than that of Heins and La Farge's design, it was also more essential. Parks concluded his sermon celebrating the consecration of St. Bartholomew's with precisely those words from Revelation, summarizing the intended significance of the new building; they are also inscribed on the medal that com-

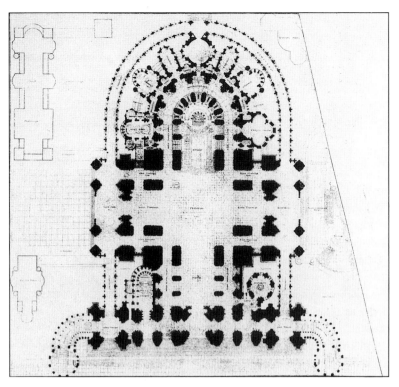

31 · Wood. Competition plan for the Cathedral Church of St. John the Divine (1888).

32 · Wood. Competition design for St. John the Divine, exterior.

memorates the foundation of the church. According to Parks, this meaning inhered, above all, in the dome, signifying "not the transcendence but the immanence of God."[21] Goodhue expressed this intention for St. Bartholomew's in different terms; he said that it would be like the last act of *Parsifal*—that is, the part of the opera in which God manifests himself to man. Wood's *Jerusalem the Golden* is, in the spiritual sense, the immediate inspiration for St. Bartholomew's Church.

The competition for the commission for St. John the Divine shows that the use of the dome, in conjunction with a non-Gothic plan, was firmly linked to a commitment to preaching. The greatest preachers of all time, said Parks, have preached in domed churches, not in Gothic ones. This connection, as we have seen, was also made by Goodhue.

Further, the dominating tower was identified with modernity; it was the single feature that distinguished the modern from the medieval cathedral. Goodhue consistently referred to the "ciborium," or tower, as the most important feature of his whole design.[22] Like most contemporary skyscrapers, it drew on historical sources for its specific forms. Its importance to the design of the church and its size, not its style, proclaimed St. Bartholomew's as a modern building and placed it in the forefront of developments in ecclesiastical architecture.

The structure of St. Bartholomew's was defined earlier in terms of two systems, its supports and its spatial arrangement, both of which are responses to functional requirements of the modern church, the need to see and, particularly, to hear. Goodhue's solutions at St. Bartholomew's followed the best available precedent, Heins and La Farge's design for the Cathedral Church of St. John the Divine. Thus St. Bartholomew's must be placed in the mainstream of modern cathedral design. But this does not adequately explain what the building is. The project of St. John the Divine was only one of many experiences that Goodhue absorbed and that influenced his own design. That St. Bartholomew's reflects the issues and stylistic modes of contemporary New York architecture is only to be expected. But its range of reference is far broader than the island of Manhattan, and thus our inquiry must be expanded.

Westminster Cathedral, London

In the summer of 1914, while making "exhibition drawings" of St. Bartholomew's, Goodhue wrote to Parks that "while the structural principal underlying the design [of St. Bartholomew's] is the same as that of Westminster cathedral, the sentiment of the whole is quite different, and the zebra effect so noticeable at Westminster entirely done away with."[23] Thus Westminster Cathedral in London, completed in 1903, must be considered one of the direct influences on Goodhue's design (fig. 33).

The Westminster project had many similarities with that of St. John the Divine. At both, the problem of historical style was considered in regard

33 · Bentley.
Westminster Cathedral,
London (1895–1903).

to the construction of an urban cathedral. Although Westminster is Roman Catholic, not Episcopal, and therefore its builders were less concerned with the provision of a preaching space, it was felt that the congregation should see and hear the liturgy.[24] To this end, it was decided not to build in the Gothic style, but in the Byzantine. Further, Byzantine was cheaper to construct than Gothic. John Francis Bentley, who had been known as a "Gothic man," was hired as architect. In 1895, he and his patron, Cardinal Vaughn, visited Italy in search of inspiration. Using W. R. Lethaby's recently published monograph on Hagia Sophia as a guide to style, they decided that San Marco and the monuments at Torcello and Ravenna could be adapted for the new cathedral.

In his letter to Parks, Goodhue wrote that the plan of St. Bartholomew's was derived from that of San Marco, which is true. But the basilica was known to the architect only from photographs. Thus Westminster Cathedral, which Goodhue visited in 1913, served as an intermediary between Goodhue and his Venetian model, permitting him to confirm and control his understanding of San Marco's spatial effect, illumination, and elevation. As we have seen, he studied Heins and La Farge's design for St. John the Divine with similar interest, but too little of it had been built by 1914 to provide much sense of how a neo-Byzantine interior would work. Further, Westminster had been approved by Lethaby,[25] whose ideas on architecture Goodhue admired, lending it additional authority in the architect's mind.

Lethaby had said that the most impressive aspect of the new cathedral was its interior space, which gave a sense of "reality, reason, power, serenity, and peace" (fig. 34). This effect was carefully studied by Goodhue

34 · Westminster Cathedral, interior.

for use in St. Bartholomew's, whose main vehicle of aesthetic expression is the enclosed space rather than the enclosing wall—the first of Goodhue's buildings to have this quality.

Further, Lethaby had provided historical justification for Goodhue's borrowing, since he had claimed that Westminster synthesized models in southwestern France and in Lombardy with the architecture of Constantinople. The distinction between Romanesque and Byzantine was blurred by Lethaby, as it had been by Heins and La Farge and as it would be by Goodhue at St. Bartholomew's.

Goodhue claimed to have borrowed Westminster's structural system. By this he meant a construction of brick and stone masonry, a system of large piers and entirely vaulted interior, and the use of internal buttressing (pl. XVI). La Farge, who had used a similar system for St. John the Divine (fig. 28), had explained that internal buttressing was a Romanesque feature that he had copied from Albi Cathedral in southern France (fig. 35).[26] With internal buttressing for the nave vault, the clerestory wall is practically eliminated and the gallery level is opened up between the pier buttresses. This permits light to enter through the windows in the exterior wall; filtering through the gallery at the periphery of the main space, the light reaches the nave. The nave is thus suffused with an even, soft light, and the spectator's eye is not distracted by spots of brightness from a visual focus on the main altar. Such indirect lighting (obtained, of course, with clear or tinted, but not stained, glass) heightens the sense of mystery in the interior and accentuates the sculptural quality of the exterior wall. The revival of internal buttressing was linked to the use of electric light, which, in tandem with natural light, can be utilized for special effects within the church.

Goodhue copied the placement and function of the windows of Westminster Cathedral, but he changed their form. The double lancet windows of Westminster leave the central axis of each bay without vertical accent. Goodhue corrected this:

> it's true that in my first sketches for the new St. Bartholomew's I had something of the same kind, but in the final result we changed it to a triple window, with arched openings, the whole enclosed by a tympanum, filled with a form of flat tracery quite reminiscent of Westminster [fig. 2].[27]

Goodhue declared himself satisfied with the proportions of the interior of St. Bartholomew's, which are "in somewhat the same fashion as Westminster."[28] The internal buttressing system provides a two-stage, rather than three-stage, elevation (because of the elimination of the clerestory wall), which permitted Goodhue to solve a problem that had bothered him since 1913, when he complained that even in the best Gothic churches, the triforium cuts the vertical height of the elevation in half.[29] A lower aisle arch and a taller clerestory, such as he was able to effect at St. Bartholomew's, give a "more impressive effect" and was more economical.

35 · Albi Cathedral
(thirteenth century).

Much of the sense of grandeur and monumentality at St. Bartholomew's
is due to the enormously high gallery arches and the windows they enclose.

Finally, Westminster Cathedral showed Goodhue how modern constructional materials could be used effectively. Although he assured Parks
that he would avoid the zebra-striped effect of Westminster's exterior, he
used its alternation of brick and stone courses as the point of departure for

his design for the irregular exterior masonry (figs. 2, 3). In Goodhue's version, the light-colored, hard-textured limestone of the lower part evolves into the darker, softer brick of the upper part of the wall. This effect was inspired by the interior of Westminister, where the lower wall is sheathed in shimmering marble, which contrasts with the austere brick surface of the vaults. Although this was something of an accident at Westminster, since Bentley had intended to cover the vaults with mosaic, Goodhue liked the result and designed the interior of St. Bartholomew's in a similar fashion, only adding gold and colored tiles and gold mortar beds in order to enliven the somber vaults (pl. XVII). This arrangement of color and tonalities has no precedent in Byzantine or Romanesque architecture and is one of the specifically modern features of St. Bartholomew's.

Liverpool Cathedral

The announcement of the Building Committee of Liverpool Cathedral in 1901 that "the style shall be Gothic" provoked an exceptionally heated and articulate controversy.[30] Having weathered a storm of criticism, the committee proceeded to reject all the competition entries on the grounds that they did not provide sufficient space for the congregation in front of the pulpit. This was, of course, to have been foreseen; by now, every professional knew that non-Gothic styles were superior in this respect. The problem at Liverpool, then, was to obtain the functional advantages of a Byzantine or Romanesque plan using a Gothic vocabulary.

The winning design, by Giles Gilbert Scott, proposed a most unusual solution, in which a centralized plan focuses on a mammoth square surmounted by a tower (fig. 36). Although the handling of the elevation is Gothic in idiom, its structure includes unorthodox elements, such as inter-

36 · Scott. Liverpool Cathedral, plan (begun 1904).

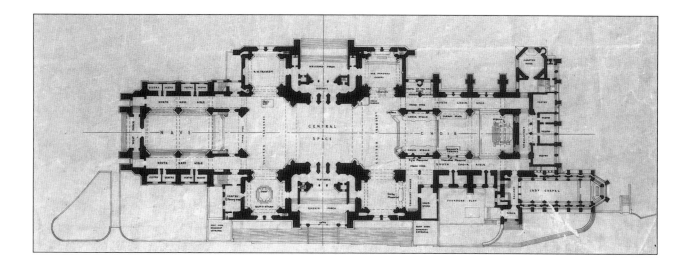

37 · Liverpool Cathedral, interior.

nal buttressing, which struck critics as "unusual in buildings of Gothic form."[31] Goodhue declared himself "quite mad over Scott's Liverpool Cathedral" and considered Scott "the greatest living ecclesiastical architect."[32]

Liverpool combines two features already familiar to Goodhue: the great central tower (as at St. John the Divine) and an uninterrupted perspective toward the altar (fig. 37). This clarity of focus on the altar in terms of massing and sight lines is very different from the loose, sequential spatial arrangements of Westminster Cathedral (fig. 34) and San Marco (fig. 41), but characteristic of St. Bartholomew's (fig. 30).

Above all, Liverpool demonstrates the shared concern of the architects with function in large-scale urban churches. All of them, whether Gothic, Byzantine, or Romanesque in vocabulary, tend toward centralized plans with few supports, internal buttressing, and a dramatic focus at the crossing. These buildings may be regarded as members of a unified functional group, offering very similar visual experiences to their congregatons: a clear visual focus on the altar; an absence of spatial interruptions, such as columns and piers; and an impression of grandeur and mystery provided by the even, indirect lighting, the immensity of the enclosed volumes, and the drama of the crossing tower. Seen together, they permit us to define a coherent, distinctively modern mode of religious experience. The question of their specific historical vocabulary not only is incidental to such a definition, but may obscure it.

St. Bartholomew's is a modern building that can be positioned historically as one of a group of structures responding to similar functional and experimental requirements. This group could be enlarged to include, for example, the Sacré-Cœur in Paris (Paul Abadie, 1874–1919), which is a particularly successful church of the same type. St. Bartholomew's was conceived as a building with two architectural foci corresponding to the two main events of the liturgy performed within it. Along the longitudinal axis, it focuses the congregation's attention on the altar and provides a path for processions in the nave. But the special importance accorded the sermon led to the design of an oversize crossing and the creation of an auditorium-like space along the transverse axis. This layout had far-reaching consequences for the elevation and for the style of the whole, since the side aisles are narrow, the supports are few and widely spaced, and the vaults are simple curves and covered with acoustic tile. It led Goodhue to plan in terms of large, uninterrupted volumes and thus to give greater attention to the spatial unity of the structure. Indeed, it changed Goodhue's personal style from one concerned with structure (parts and the relation among parts) to one concerned with mass (homogeneous matter enclosing space).

Contemporary New York Churches

When Goodhue designed St. Bartholomew's, he had been living in New York for more than a decade. As an architect whose professional reputation was to a large extent based on church design, he certainly was aware of recent, local developments in this sphere. Of the approximately twenty churches built in Manhattan between 1900 and 1920, six are (or have been described as) Romanesque, and four of these six have a central vault, as does the original design of St. Bartholomew's.

The pioneer of this type in New York was St. Agnes's Chapel (Episcopal), designed by William A. Potter in 1892. While it was thought to have been influenced by Trinity Church, Boston, it more probably is a miniature reflection of some of the competition entries for the Cathedral Church of St. John the Divine. According to the critic Montgomery Schuyler, "the peculiarity of the general design is the introduction of a central tower, or ciborium, which is not yet a tower but more properly a square dome, so to say, occupying the whole of the crossing and pierced with windows."[33] Thus the central feature of St. Bartholomew's had been tried out on a small scale in parish-church architecture in New York before it was eliminated from the design of the cathedral.

The execution of a plan with barrel-vaulted arms faced with Guastavino tile had also been tried out. Holy Trinity (Roman Catholic), built around 1900 by an unknown architect, must have been an important source for Goodhue. This very fine building, in the shape of a Greek cross, has galleries in the ends of three arms, as does St. Bartholomew's, and draws on much of the same historical material: Byzantine and Lombard Romanesque.

Another example of the same type, although smaller and more consistently Italian, is St. Paul's Chapel at Columbia University (Howells and Stokes, 1907). Particularly distinguishing this design are the inlaid patterns of the exterior masonry, further developed at St. Bartholomew's. Indeed, one is struck by the decided improvement in quality of the masonry at St. Bartholomew's in relation to earlier attempts at creating a Lombard Romanesque effect. The masonry patterns of Holy Trinity, Christ Church (Charles Haight, 1890), and the Judson Memorial Church (McKim, Mead, and White, 1892) are decidedly dreary by comparison.

There was a marked increase in the number of Romanesque- and Byzantine-style churches built in New York following the competition for St. John the Divine, particularly for Episcopal congregations, although Gothic remained the most popular style. The most interesting of the Romanesque churches had Guastavino tile applied to a system of vaults in a centralized layout. Their designs were probably influenced by the new importance accorded to preaching in the religious experience. While all are much smaller than St. Bartholomew's, they enabled Goodhue to assess the effects of spatial arrangement, material, and color that he intended to realize at St. Bartholomew's. Although the design of St. Bartholomew's was to some extent influenced by one current of New York architecture in the preceding two decades, the parish churches are but miniature reflections of the great urban cathedrals that were being built in the United States and England. St. Bartholomew's is more closely connected with this mainstream of architectural design than with its tributaries.

DECORUM: THE APPROPRIATENESS OF STYLE

While the relationship between historical styles and functional planning was an area of professional expertise, the philosophical or historical associations of styles concerned architects and patrons alike. Parks had firm opinions; he defended the Romanesque style as spiritually superior to the Gothic and as symbolic of democratic values. The question of decorum—that is, the appropriateness of style to subject—was defined by Parks's repugnance for Catholicism and conviction that the ideals of the American Episcopal church coincided with those of American democracy. The identification of Romanesque architecture with democratic values has its roots in nineteenth-century America, particularly in Robert Dale Owen's *Hints on Public Architecture* (1849), but also in the work of James Renwick and in the circle of H. H. Richardson.[34] There is, further, some evidence that Byzantine architecture, specifically San Marco, had earlier been regarded as opposing Catholicism.[35] There is no compelling reason to think that Goodhue shared Parks's interpretation of Romanesque or his religious, aesthetic, and social values.[36] It was, nonetheless, his task to embody them in an appropriate architectural style.

Goodhue's long partnership with Cram taught him to distinguish historical styles according to their institutional and philosophical connotations. The guidelines for such definitions were spelled out by Cram in *American Churches*.[37] Three architectural styles were suitable for modern ecclesiastical architecture: English Gothic, Lombard, and Colonial. Gothic, although sometimes chosen by Catholics, was best suited to Episcopalians. The Lombard style was recommended for Catholics, although it would also do for Presbyterians. Congregational churches should be in Colonial style.

The choice of style in each case was determined by the awareness of each faith's distinctive cultural tradition and the conviction that those separate traditions should be visibly expressed. As Cram put it, architecture should be "consistent with . . . that sense of historic and cultural continuity that I am persuaded is fundamental in all educational and ecclesiastical work." Thus, for example, the Episcopal faith had its roots in sixteenth-century England; its close ties with the Church of England, led by Canterbury Cathedral, dictated the use of Gothic style for its churches.

The last Episcopal church designed jointly by Goodhue and Cram, St. Thomas (fig. 9), is, of course, neo-Gothic. But at St. Bartholomew's, the necessities of incorporating the Romanesque portal designed by Stanford White and of honoring the views of Parks intruded on this ideal scheme. Like Cram, Parks preferred the aesthetic qualities of Gothic (and neo-Gothic) architecture. For him, too, diverse faiths (or, better, ways of conceiving the relationship between people and God) found expression in different architectural styles. But Parks's conception of the Episcopal faith was radically different from Cram's. While Cram thought that "Luther killed art,"[38]

Parks believed that Luther had been one of the great reformers, and had his image carved on the west façade of St. Bartholomew's. For the High Church Cram, the focus of the divine service was at the altar, while for the Low Church Parks, the Episcopal church should be first of all a preaching space. Thus Cram and Parks used the same criteria for the selection of styles; they differed in their definition of the Episcopal church. The requirements of the St. Bartholomew's commission forced Goodhue to abandon Cram's guidelines for style, which had determined his own designs. Yet other aspects of Cram's approach to architecture served Goodhue in his new commission.

Both Cram and Parks tended to consider tradition in historical and institutional terms. This attitude, recognizing the plurality of traditions within Western (specifically, modern Western) culture, suggests that architectural styles have relative, rather than absolute, value. Clearly, there can be no single "right" style, no ideal form, in architectural practice, but only right choices for specific situations. While such aesthetic relativity has often been denounced as the tyranny of mere taste, it expresses fundamental characteristics of American culture, not only in its denial of the validity of absolute values and its tendency to approach an issue in terms of problem solving, but also in its basis in pragmatism.

Although Cram and Goodhue were best known for their neo-Gothic work, they used other styles as the occasion demanded. For example, in designing Rice University in Houston, Texas (1910–12), the partners decided that since Houston had no architectural tradition of its own, something new, but southern in spirit, would have to be invented. Accordingly, they drew on motifs from the architectural traditions of "southern" countries and regions: France, Italy, Yugoslavia, Greece, the Byzantine Empire, Anatolia, Syria, Sicily, and Spain.[39] Thus eclecticism, or what Cram would have considered flexibility in cultural reference, was an important aspect of Goodhue's early professional experience, preparing him for the St. Bartholomew's commission.

Goodhue is silent on the philosophical merits of Romanesque and Byzantine architecture. But his choice at St. Bartholomew's must have influenced the always articulate Cram's design for the Park Avenue Methodist Church (1930). Explaining the style of this church, Cram said that "the Protestant congregation was averse to Medieval Catholicism both by inheritance and doctrine," and so, "let us go back to the first style that was evolved to express the Christian religion, long antedating the Gothic of the Catholic West. A Byzantine basis is what we should use."[40] Cram's logic, that a pre-Gothic but post-Classical Christian style would satisfy the Protestant desire to avoid association with medieval Catholicism, probably reflects Goodhue's own response to Parks's needs at St. Bartholomew's. Indeed, Cram's church, which joins a thoroughly Romanesque exterior to a vaguely byzantinizing interior, reveals his intimate knowledge of Goodhue's solution just ten blocks down Park Avenue.

That the scholar Cram would have mingled Romanesque and Byzantine might seem strange, for his eclecticism is difficult to explain as ignorance. Although he might well have known the difference between these two styles, he opposed the construction of buildings whose style was artifically pure. Cram did not believe that Gothic, his favorite style, was pure, since it revived elements of ancient Roman architecture. He understood the history of architecture as a continuous process, or ongoing tradition, in which motifs and styles are revitalized by their migration to new contexts. His ideal, from this point of view, was San Marco, which, "thanks be to God, is all sorts of things assembled and crystallized into a sort of apocalyptic unity in diversity."[41] Thus he advocated not only flexibility in terms of source material, but also multiplicity.

Heins and La Farge selected a Gothic crossing for St. John the Divine, although the plan and structural system of the cathedral are dependent on San Marco. Thus they, too, did not feel bound to maintain stylistic unity within their works. The eclecticism of St. John the Divine was the result of a conflict between the demands of function and the demands of decorum. It was widely believed that Gothic was the proper style for cathedral architecture; indeed, for many, the words *Gothic* and *cathedral* were synonyms.[42] But Gothic structure and spatial layout failed to meet modern needs. The first requirement being function, the plan and structural system of St. John the Divine were derived from Byzantine and Romanesque sources. But where possible, as in the elevation of the crossing, Gothic would be used. The resultant hybrid could, moreover, be justified on the grounds of both theory and precedent. Since architectural styles were thought to evolve from one another and, in particular, the Ely octagon was regarded as a descendant of the dome of Hagia Sophia, Gothic was legitimately related to Byzantine architecture, representing a later stage within the same evolutionary tradition. Further, the example of San Marco proved that Byzantine and Gothic vocabularies could successfully coexist within the same fabric.

For these architects, the problem of architectural unity, as distinct from architectural purity, was important. The complexity and multiplicity of modern needs could best be met by drawing on several traditions. Thus the functional requirements might be satisfied by a category of historical material different from that which responded to the decorum of the building. At St. Bartholomew's, decorum called for the use of Romanesque, which was, indeed, its official style. But because Romanesque could not have satisfied the acoustic, economic, aesthetic, and functional requirements of the commission, Goodhue drew on additional styles. Cram's praise of San Marco, moreover, makes it perfectly clear that he believed that the achievement of unity in diversity was the mark of architectural excellence. Unity alone might suggest a poverty of terms to define the specific character of a structure; diversity alone would imply that this character was inadequately defined. But unity in diversity was the essential quality of a "sane and logical type of Modernism."[43]

Historical styles, then, were to be plumbed for what they could contribute to present needs, rather than for their own sakes. Thus it is more correct to say that St. Bartholomew's refers to Romanesque architecture, than that it revives it. Parks's true concerns were American democracy and the modern Episcopal church, for whose values the forms of Romanesque architecture were metaphors. Since such an interest in the past is connotative, rather than historical, its categories correspond only approximately to the formal categories of architectural history. The category of post-Classical/pre-Gothic, for instance, is essentially a category of avoidance; it includes all architecture that is non-pagan, non-Catholic, and non-medieval (in the restricted sense of this term, as used by Cram and Goodhue). While its definition is clear and useful in negative terms, its positive reference is not at all precise; buildings in this category may be Byzantine, Romanesque, or a combination of the two.

ADDED ORNAMENT AND STRUCTURAL ORNAMENT

In an interview about Liverpool Cathedral, Scott divided the history of architecture into two building traditions: that in which ornament is structural, and that in which ornament is added:

> The Gothic style does not allow you to complete the fabric before adding detail, as the detail is part of the fabric; the ornament is part of the structure. It is not like Westminster Cathedral, where you can build a plain shell and cover it with marble and mosaics afterwards.[44]

Scott was explaining why, after almost fifty years of construction, Liverpool Cathedral was far from finished. Westminster Cathedral, in contrast, took only eight years to build; St. Bartholomew's, eighteen months. The added-ornament method is the cheaper and faster way of getting a building into use. It is also the more flexible, since the amount and quality of ornament can be adjusted as circumstances dictate. But as Scott pointed out, not all styles can be built in this mode. Essentially, styles using stone masonry with stone detail cannot. This includes, of course, Gothic; it also could include Greek, Roman, French Romanesque, Italian Renaissance, and Baroque. This leaves Byzantine, Italian Romanesque, and Italian Gothic styles as possibilities for added-ornament construction; they may be considered as a group.

Goodhue had been aware of this constructional group at least since 1910, when he and Cram designed Rice University. Since the budget was limited, they devised a method whereby "richness, variety, and a certain splendour were obtained through the use of unusually colored brick, marble columns, glazed tiles, and bronzes." In this way, they created a type of "magnificence that was possible at moderate cost about the year 1910."[45]

As we have seen, St. Bartholomew's was intended to impress by means of splended materials, rather than complex and costly structural properties. Such a solution has two prerequisites: that the ornament be added, rather than structural; and that tonal and textural, rather than tectonic, values determine its aesthetic quality.

Confirmation that these considerations guided Goodhue's choices at St. Bartholomew's is found in a letter he wrote in 1917, approving Lucian Smith's design for the First Methodist Episcopal Church in Asbury Park, New Jersey. Goodhue said that the architect was "absolutely right in his choice of architectural style, material, and system of construction," since the parish has "very considerable requirements" and only about $100,000 in hand. Goodhue himself had "come to precisely the same conclusion" in a "similar though larger church here in New York" for two reasons: "for an institutional church like yours requiring wide and unobstructed preaching space, Gothic seems to me very ill-suited indeed"; and "there can be no question but that it is a vastly more expensive style in which to build than the one Mr. Smith has chosen."[46] The church in Asbury Park is, like St. Bartholomew's, officially Lombard Romanesque, but looks rather more like Hagia Sophia.[47]

The decision to build St. Bartholomew's with local brick was a challenge to Goodhue, who had worked mainly within a stone-masonry tradition until 1914. Setting out to master a vast range of natural materials and craftsmanship techniques, he studied the Cosmati work of thirteenth-century Rome, Byzantine revetment, the stone intarsia of Emilian Romanesque, and the brick masonry of Lombard Romanesque architecture. In so doing, he was continuing the practice of High Victorian Gothic architects, such as William Butterfield and, above all, George Edmund Street.

Victorian Gothic architects exploited a variety of textures and colors for ornamental purposes, eschewing the monotone effects of stone-masonry architecture.[48] Indeed, although defined as Gothic Revival style, Victorian Gothic buildings, such as Butterfield's All Saints' Church, Margaret Street (1849–59), are really more eclectic in their sources, ready to adopt Romanesque or Byzantine wall treatments, patterns, and color schemes. The great, unsung genius of this new aesthetic was Street.[49]

Street worked in an eclectic style in which Italian Romanesque, Gothic, and Byzantine all had a part. Drawing on a knowledge of medieval architecture hardly equaled by his contemporaries, Street reveled in diversity, including myriad historical quotations in each edifice. While the richness of his effects may not be appreciated by some modern spectators, Goodhue seems to have been profoundly impressed by the performance. The aesthetic character of Street's work belongs to the same realm of taste as St. Bartholomew's, suggesting that the latter may have more in common with High Victorian Gothic than with Romanesque Revival architecture.[50]

Indeed, although Goodhue's dependence on the work of Richardson has often been cited, Richardson's muscular, assertive stone masonry belongs to an entirely different tradition from Goodhue's. Goodhue used stone to create colored surfaces, flat patterns, and illusions of texture and density, and to reflect light. This inattention to the tectonic quality of the wall mass recalls Ruskin, not Richardson. Ruskin's long eulogy of San Marco was not accompanied by a plan of the building, nor does it mention its spatial disposition. Instead, Ruskin saw the building as the sum of its colored surfaces, leading him to define its stylistic traits as the use of marble sheathing on brick walls and the dependence on color for effect.[51] This, of course, was Goodhue's formula for St. Bartholomew's.

For Ruskin, much of the beauty of Italian architecture resulted from the action of bright southern light on its surfaces. Evidently, Goodhue had this idea in mind when he wrote that he had used Italian medieval models for St. Bartholomew's because the bright skies of New York are similar to those of Italy.[52] Bright sunlight, said Ruskin, creates deep shadows and pronounced tonal contrasts that should be enhanced by making the dividing lines between the planes as sharp as possible.[53] The profiles of openings should be bold and simple; frames and tracery should be flush with the wall. Goodhue applied these principles to the exterior of St. Bartholomew's, where light and dark zones are dramatically juxtaposed and edges are sharp, even metallic. Further, the window tracery is flush with the wall, as Ruskin recommended. Thus not only is the added ornament intended for effects of pattern and color, but the design as a whole is conceived tonally.

Goodhue's decision to build in one of the added-ornament styles was undoubtedly motivated by economic, not stylistic, considerations, and it explains why a French Romanesque church was not joined to the existing French Romanesque portal. This choice involved much the same historical material as did the initial choice about the plan and essential layout. In both cases, Byzantine and Italian Romanesque buildings were the immediate models, with San Marco as the prototype. Logically, then, San Marco should be the primary source for St. Bartholomew's—and it is.

FORM: SAN MARCO AND OTHER HISTORICAL SOURCES

The requirements of function, decorum, and construction suggested that non-Gothic, specifically Italian byzantinizing or Romanesque, churches were best suited to serve as models for St. Bartholomew's. Within this group, San Marco was chosen as the point of departure for the new design, and the influence of this eleventh-century Venetian church is evident in the plan and elevation of St. Bartholomew's. The selection of this source may be connected with Goodhue's experience of St. John the Divine, for which several of the competition entries, including the winning Heins and La

Farge design, drew on San Marco. But it probably also reflects Goodhue's admiration for Lethaby, who wrote so sympathetically about San Marco, and, in the end, his absorption of Ruskin, who considered it to be one of the most beautiful examples of Western architecture.

Yet St. Bartholomew's is not a copy, in the modern sense, of that medieval church. San Marco may be regarded as a matrix onto which parts of other structures were grafted and from which parts of the original were deleted. The most important of these changes—the substitution of barrel vaults and a central tower for the five domes of San Marco—was necessitated by acoustic considerations (the need for an oversize crossing and acoustic-tile-faced surfaces). Yet in overall optical effect, the great unified volumes of St. Bartholomew's retain much of the spatial quality of its Venetian prototype.

Since neither the contents of Goodhue's library nor the extent of his photograph collection is known, many of the sources on which he drew cannot be positively identified. But examining the kind of structures he used as models will give some idea of the breadth of Goodhue's visual culture and the extraordinary level of synthesis that the design of St. Bartholomew's represents.

The Plan

In his presentation booklet, Goodhue described the plan of St. Bartholomew's as "the traditional cruciform one, although the length of the transept arms will be much less than would have been the case in the past" (fig. 38). That the specific source for this plan was San Marco is made clear by Goodhue's urging Parks to visit "the church whose plan undoubtedly inspired Perigueux and, as undoubtedly, the one I am now working on for you."[54] Keeping in mind that the nave of St. Bartholomew's was originally one bay shorter and the plan therefore more nearly centralized, one sees a remarkably close relationship between the New York church and its Venetian prototype (fig. 39). Resemblances not only are of general contour and proportional relations among the spatial parts, but also include specific structural qualities. For example, one of the distinctive features of San Marco is its four-footed piers: four square masonry supports linked by archways and merging at gallery level to form a miniature dome. This arrangement is at St. Bartholomew's, where, however, the domical vault is below the gallery (fig. 40). Above, the pier shaft constitutes an internal-buttressing system that divides the elevation into bay compartments (figs. 30, 41; pl. XVI). A careful examination of the plan of St. Bartholomew's reveals four pairs of these piers: at the western end of the nave, at the eastern and western sides of the crossing, and at the opening of the apse.

The narthex of San Marco is composed of domed compartments, and it

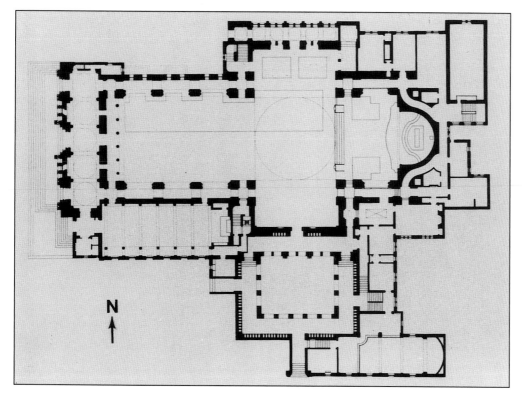

38 · St. Bartholomew's
Church, plan.

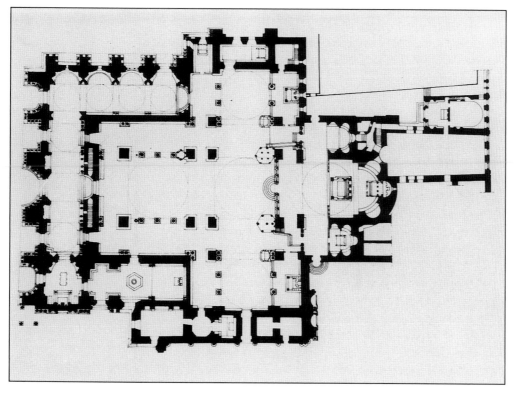

39 · San Marco, plan.

40 · St. Bartholomew's Church, domical vault in a four-footed pier.

projects beyond the west façade and along the north flank of the church; this arrangement is repeated at St. Bartholomew's. Along the south flank of San Marco is a series of subsidiary structures: treasury, baptistery, and Zen chapel. At St. Bartholomew's, the chapel sacristy, chapel, and chapel vestibule are in this location.

The Exterior

San Marco faces the enormous Piazza San Marco and the Piazzetta di San Marco, the smaller square between the Doge's Palace and the Sansovino Library. Thus it has two main views: straight on (fig. 19) and from the southwest. A similar arrangement was repeated at St. Bartholomew's, which fronts on broad Park Avenue (pl. 1) and may be viewed from the southwest, across the terrace (fig. 25).[55] The north flank of both churches must be seen close up because of the adjacent street and tall buildings (fig. 1), and the apses of both are entirely hidden from view by surrounding structures. Thus the churches are similarly related to their immediate surroundings.

The exterior massing of these churches is entirely different, however. San Marco is characterized by the profiles of its five domes and by a great deal of exceptionally rich Late Gothic ornamentation. The exterior volumes of St. Bartholomew's are pure geometric forms that were to have culminated in a tower. The general effect may remind one of Pisa Cathedral, which has a similar geometry, or of Florence Cathedral, which is dominated by a great dome, but these resemblances are of a hypothetical and generic nature.

THE FAÇADE The west façade of St. Bartholomew's is composed of two parts: the horizontal rectangle of the Vanderbilt portal, and the vertical rectangle of the upper portion (pl. 1). The combination—a projecting portal zone with rich sculpture, and a recessed upper portion with a great glass panel—repeats the façade arrangement of San Marco (fig. 19). The portal was a "given" of the design, but the upper zone had to be invented.

The skeleton of the design for the west façade of St. Bartholomew's is English Gothic, although the constituent parts were recast in a Romanesque, or at least Italian, style. It therefore has much in common with Renwick's High Victorian Gothic façade for St. Bartholomew's II (fig. 6).

The upper portion is a rectangular whole, instead of tripartite, because the main body of the church has one roof instead of separate roofs for the nave and side aisles. Such unification is found in many English Gothic cathedrals, such as Salisbury, Lincoln, and Peterborough, and it also characterizes Lombard Romanesque structures, such as Sant'Ambrogio in Milan, San Michele in Pavia, and Parma Cathedral. Angle buttresses of brick with white stone trim, such as those of Hereford, Exeter, and Lincoln cathe- 41 · San Marco, interior.

drals, enclose a central panel filled with glass. This layout has ample precedent in English Gothic cathedral façades: Durham, York Minster, Lincoln, Bath, Exeter, Hereford, Lichfield, Rochester, Salisbury, Worcester, and Southwell (fig. 42). The masonry treatment may also be related to Tudor examples. However, the buttresses are less salient than their English models and, perhaps, more Italian (reminiscent of the campanile of Florence Cathedral). Moreover, the enclosure of the window panels by massive, sculpted arches and the filling of the panels with dense geometric-tracery designs strongly recall the similar treatment of another Italian model, Troia Cathedral in Apulia (fig. 43).

42 · Southwell Minster (ca. 1130).

43 · Troia Cathedral, west façade rose window (thirteenth century).

The four over-life-size figures placed against this tracery also represent the Italianization of a northern Gothic motif (pl. III). For while their ultimate inspiration must be the gallery-level statues of French Gothic façades, such as those of Notre Dame in Paris, the figures of St. Bartholomew's are not free-standing but are flush with the plane of the wall, as are the niche figures of the campanile of Florence Cathedral.

Finally, the gable and dwarf gallery crowning the central panel may be derived from English Gothic precedents, such as Salisbury, Lincoln, Peterborough, and Durham (fig. 44). But the gallery has the low, broad proportions of those of Lombard and Apulian Romanesque churches—for example, Sant'Ambrogio in Milan, San Michele in Pavia, Bitonto Cathedral, Bari Cathedral—and it runs around the exterior (figs. 2, 45; p. IX).

THE MASONRY Goodhue planned a most unusually colored and textured exterior wall, which a lack of funds prevented him from executing. The lower parts of the building were to have been entirely of Indiana limestone; at a certain height, some courses of salmon-colored brick, irregular in height and width, were to have been introduced; and the uppermost parts of the building, at gallery level and in the tower, were to have been entirely of brick. This treatment was so novel that the Building Committee asked the architect to construct a sample wall in his office and to paint the colors of the exterior on the exhibition model.

44 · Durham Cathedral (1093–1278).

45 · Bitonto
Cathedral (twelfth
century).

46 · Santo Stefano, Bologna, masonry detail (eleventh–twelfth centuries).

There seems to be no specific model for this treatment, although the effect of random masonry of mixed materials does, in general, recall that of some Italian Romanesque churches (on which, however, it is the result of successive restorations more than the will of the architect). That Goodhue had examples of Italian medieval masonry in mind is demonstrated by the marble inlays on the south transept (pls. VI, VII). They so closely resemble the eleventh- and twelfth-century work in Santo Stefano in Bologna that a specific relation between these buildings may well exist (fig. 46).

If the inlays on the south transept are Emilian Romanesque, the stone disks set into the wall of the north transept in a cross pattern surely derive from Venice (figs. 47, 48). This treatment is quite common in Venice, although it is more often seen on house façades than on churches.

The Interior Elevation

The elevation of the nave of St. Bartholomew's reveals a limited dependence on that of San Marco (figs. 30, 41; pl. XIII). In both churches, light and heavy supports alternate. At San Marco, the light supports are columns, whereas at St. Bartholomew's, they are rectangular piers with addorsed columns. They recall the piers at Norwich Cathedral (fig. 49), although some resemblance to the lighter piers at Sant'Ambrogio in Milan may also be noted.

47 · St. Bartholomew's Church,
north transept detail.

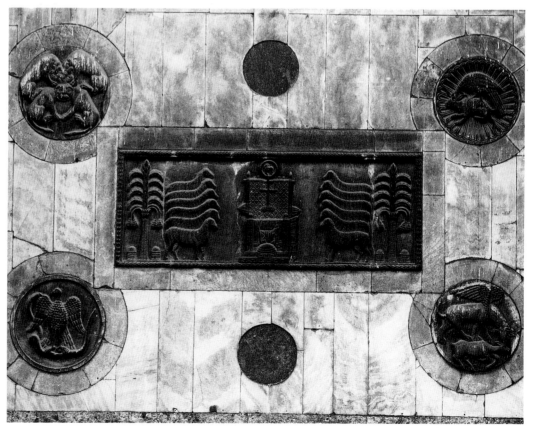

48 · San Marco,
north flank detail.

The heavy piers are almost exact copies of those in San Marco (although they reverse the proportions of the openings above and below), and they would have concealed their muscle behind a shining marble revetment, as do those in San Marco. However, the slender colonnettes fitted into the pier corners, softening their edges and emphasizing their verticality, are reminiscent of those at Norwich Cathedral or perhaps Chichester.

49 · Norwich Cathedral, nave piers (ca. 1145).

At San Marco, as at St. Bartholomew's, the nave wall between the major piers was omitted, creating high, arched openings at the boundary of the nave volume. The openings are blind at San Marco, so that a continuous wall surface is viewed through the arches, whereas at St. Bartholomew's, windows in the recesses of these niches let in the main source of light for the nave. The effect is not unlike that at Sant'Andrea in Mantua, where the high side chapels constitute well-lighted subsidiary volumes at the periphery of the main space (fig. 50). The form of the windows at St. Bartholomew's, however, derives from those at San Marco (for example, the windows over the west façade portal) (figs. 2, 51). The barrel vaults at St. Bartholomew's also recall Sant'Andrea, not San Marco. Although Sant'Andrea is a Renaissance church, its structure and layout belong to the functional group that Goodhue chose for St. Bartholomew's.

Sant'Andrea does not have galleries, which are found (in skeleton) at San Marco.[56] Further, the western arm of San Marco has a gallery area. Seen from the nave, the west façade window appears to be recessed behind the intervening gallery and framed by a barrel vault, just as it does at St. Bartholomew's (pl. XVIII).

Although Goodhue claimed that the rose window in the south transept

50 · Alberti. Sant'Andrea, Mantua (1470–72).

51 · San Marco, west
façade window.

derived from Italian examples, such as San Francesco in Assisi (fig. 21),
this was not precise. In Italian Gothic buildings, the rose window is almost
always on the west façade, not in the transept, and it has stained glass.
Goodhue's transept window, designed for uniformly tinted glass, would
be unique, were there not a very similar one in the south transept of San
Marco (fig. 52; pls. v, xxiv); Trinity Church in Boston also shares this
feature. Of course, the Venetian window is an addition to the original
structure, and it imitates the great transept windows of French Gothic
cathedrals.

The Crossing Tower

Goodhue claimed that the crossing tower he had designed was Lombard,
and he gave two specific examples: Santa Maria delle Grazie in Milan (fig.
22), and the Certosa di Pavia (fig. 23). While both churches are certainly

in the heart of Lombardy, they are of the Renaissance rather than the Romanesque period. Analogous forms do exist in Lombard Romanesque, at Sant'Ambrogio, for example (fig. 53), but Goodhue did not refer to them.

The exterior housing for the tower shown on the medal struck to commemorate the foundation of St. Bartholomew's (fig. 17) has some general relation to the lantern tower built by Bramante at Santa Maria delle Grazie, and its interior, known from a drawing still at St. Bartholomew's (fig. 54), resembles, to a limited extent, the dome of the Certosa di Pavia, executed by Giovanni and Giuniforte Solari. But the closest source for Goodhue's design, particularly for the interior dome, is neither Lombard nor Romanesque. The tower is a reworking of the octagon at Ely Cathedral (fig. 55).

52 · San Marco, south transept rose window.

53 · Sant'Ambrogio, Milan, apse and crossing tower (ca. 1100).

The design of Goodhue's "ciborium" may be described on the basis of two drawings (figs. 15, 54) and the foundation medal (fig. 17). The base of the tower is square, rising directly from the crossing. Squinches, at the next vertical stage, smooth the angles of the square and provide an octagonal base for the tower. This first zone is capped by a corbel table. The second zone, about 8 feet in height, is articulated by slender colonnettes and terminates in a corbel table. The third zone, almost 30 feet tall, supports the arches on which the dome was to rest. Double lancet windows between the colonnettes in this zone admit light into the tower. The dome, which caps the multiple-staged, interior structure, is eight-sided, and from its oculus a lantern projects upward. This whole structure, which was to rise 100 feet above the nave vaults, and 200 feet above the pavement of the church, was to be housed within a polygonal tower, rising above it.

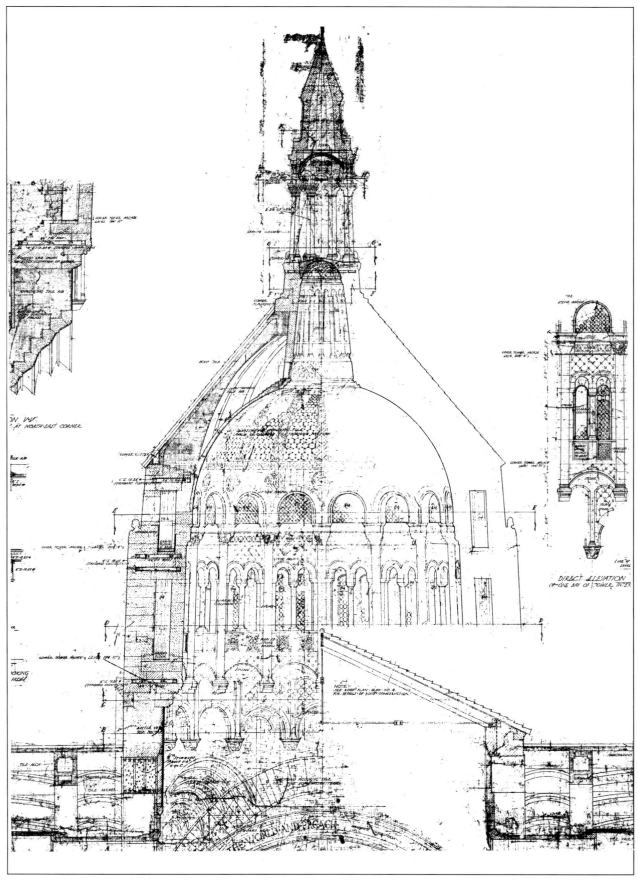

54 · Goodhue. Drawing of the "ciborium," St. Bartholomew's Church (1916).

55 · Alan de Walsingham. Central octagon, Ely Cathedral (1328–40).

The apex of the interior lantern corresponded in height with the base of the lantern of the exterior housing.

Although its corbel tables and eight-sided dome relate this tower to Lombard Romanesque precedents (fig. 53), the design as a whole is closer to the multiple-staged polygonal towers of Late Gothic architecture, such as the Ely octagon. Other examples may have contributed to the details: the squinches are like those of San Juan de los Reyes at Toledo; the corbels below the colonnettes recall those of Coutances Cathedral; and a relationship with the Torre del Gallo at the old cathedral of Salamanca might also be considered. The culminating feature of Goodhue's design, then, was certainly Gothic in inspiration.

Analysis of Goodhue's sources reveals a wide variety of borrowings from Byzantine; Italian and English Romanesque; French, English, and Italian

Gothic; and Italian Renaissance models. The influence of Lombard Romanesque is either indirect, such as the "ciborium," or confined to details, such as the dwarf gallery. A strong Gothic, particularly English Gothic, current underlies the design of some of the most prominent and important features: the west façade and the crossing tower. The single most important example is undoubtedly the eleventh-century San Marco, whose plan, layout, structural system, and materials inspired St. Bartholomew's. The addition of mosaics and a hemispheric dome, after Goodhue's death, strengthened this Byzantine influence, but it was already present and intended in the architect's original design.

GOODHUE'S UNDERSTANDING OF THE ROMANESQUE

Although the style of St. Bartholomew's was declared to be Romanesque by its architect and patron, the principal source for its plan and elevation was byzantinizing San Marco. There are three possible explanations for this apparent ambiguity. First, neither the patrons nor the architect of St. Bartholomew's had a clear idea of what Lombard Romanesque architecture looked like, and thought of it simply as a non-Gothic medieval style. Second, until the third decade of the twentieth century, the distinction between Romanesque and Byzantine architecture was often blurred, not only by patrons, architects, and critics, but even by scholars. Finally, San Marco itself is both a Romanesque and a Byzantine structure.

Although some of the parishioners may have noted a disparity between the style of the Vanderbilt portal and that of Goodhue's church,[57] few would have been in a position to judge whether this difference was one of Italian Romanesque versus French Romanesque or French Romanesque versus Byzantine. That Parks consistently referred to St. Bartholomew's as Romanesque is evidence that this was its official style; that he twice mentioned Byzantine and Romanesque architecture almost in the same breath indicates that he did not draw a firm boundary between these styles.[58] The parishioners, accustomed to consider the High Victorian Gothic St. Bartholomew's II as Lombard Romanesque, presumably because of its dwarf gallery and polychrome masonry, may have assumed that the repetition of these features in the new church classified it, too, as Lombard Romanesque. Indeed, judged on this level of stylistic criteria, Goodhue's church represents a step toward archaeological accuracy, if only because it is less overtly Gothic than Renwick's. It is also more Romanesque than the portal, which, despite its Romanesque layout, has sculpture that is clearly inspired by fifteenth-century Florentine art, particularly that of Luca della Robbia.

It was, after all, only in the first quarter of the nineteenth century that Romanesque had been distinguished from Gothic as an earlier architectural style, and clear definitions of the style were only slowly acquired in the course of the century.[59] Although some architects, such as Richardson, owned many of the new scholarly works on Romanesque and Byzantine architecture, the majority of these texts were in French and German and therefore not readily accessible to the American reading public. Even Richardson seems to have thought that some features of Romanesque architecture could be explained as further developments of Byzantine innovations, thus assuming evolutionary continuity between the styles.[60]

The influential works of John Ruskin, widely available to the English-speaking public, were unlikely to clarify the question of Romanesque's stylistic identity. Whereas in *Val d'Arno,* he describes the exterior apse arrangement of Pisa Cathedral as Byzantine, in *The Seven Lamps of Architecture,* he discusses the façade of the cathedral as Romanesque. All hope of understanding Italian medieval architecture in terms of coherent stylistic categories is crushed by Ruskin's analysis of it: "The noblest buildings of the world, the Pisan-Romanesque, Tuscan (Giottesque) Gothic, and Veronese Gothic, are those of the Lombard schools themselves, under its close and direct influence; the various Gothics of the North are the original forms of the architecture which the Lombards brought into Italy." In a final contribution to this already hopeless confusion, Ruskin conflates Romanesque and Byzantine art: "Perhaps the most solemn roofs in the world are the apse conchas of the Romanesque basilicas, with their golden ground and severe figures."[61]

Serious historical study of Romanesque and Byzantine architecture really got under way in the last decades of the nineteenth century. At the same time, a vivid interest in the history of the Middle Ages manifested itself in the United States, where the seminal decade was probably the 1880s and the key location, Harvard University.[62] Charles Eliot Norton, a personal friend of Ruskin and mentor to Goodhue, who referred to Norton as "my old friend," taught the course "History of the Arts of Construction and Design and Their Relations to Literature."[63] Charles Moore, author of three important works on medieval and Renaissance architecture,[64] was Norton's colleague there, as were the historians Henry C. Lea and Henry Adams. The importance of the Harvard circle for medieval studies is dramatized by the fact that when the Medieval Academy of America was founded in 1925, almost half the founding fellows had Harvard degrees. Goodhue, who worked in Boston during his partnership with Cram (a founding fellow of the Medieval Academy), had contact with the circle through his "old friend" Norton. He certainly knew Norton's *Historical Studies of Church Buildings in the Middle Ages* (1888).

Like Ruskin, Norton investigated the past from a moral point of view, convinced that morality and aesthetics were inseparable. Although he claimed that the "moral import" had been the chief concern of the Romanesque architect, Norton did analyze Romanesque style. This style, he said, had derived its main elements from late Roman architecture, but it had also been "a new thing, the slowly matured product of a long period and of many influences." Romanesque architecture could be defined in terms of its constructional elements: columns or piers supporting round arches, and broad expanses of solid walls, both of which had come from Roman architecture. Unique to Romanesque was the strongly plastic treatment accorded these forms. In Norton's view, San Marco was both Byzantine and Romanesque, and neither. The Venetian architect had borrowed elements from both Constantinople and Rome "which he fused into a composition neither Byzantine nor Romanesque, unexampled hitherto, only to be called Venetian."[65]

Another of Goodhue's friends from this early period, the critic Montgomery Schuyler, also considered Romanesque to be a late stage in the evolution of Roman architecture.[66] For him, the term covered all European architecture between the fall of the Roman Empire and the rise of Gothic style (fifth through thirteenth centuries, by his account). Byzantine and Romanesque had been parallel developments in the East and the West, Byzantine exploring the formal potential of the dome and Romanesque, that of the arch and vault. Like Norton, Schuyler stressed the analogies between these two styles in his definition of them.

Goodhue's partner Cram confirmed the validity of this connection, relating that the choir vault designed by Heins and La Farge for St. John the Divine was intended to be covered with "Byzantine mosaics . . . quite consonant with the first design,"[67] elsewhere acknowledged to be Romanesque.

Thus in Goodhue's circle of friends and professional associates, Romanesque and Byzantine, while thought to be somehow different, were usually paired and considered to be complementary. Although they were intellectual and even scholarly, these scholars, critics, and architects do not seem to have been abreast of the latest developments in research. There is no hint, for instance, that they knew N. P. Kondakov's *Histoire de l'art byzantin considéré principalement dans les miniatures* (1885–91), R. Cattaneo's *L'Architettura in Italia dal secolo VI al mille circa* (1888; English translation, 1896), G. Dehio and G. von Bezold's *Die Kirchliche Baukunst des Abendlands* (1892), F. De Dartein's *Etude sur l'architecture lombarde et sur les origines de l'architecture romano-byzantine* (1865–82), and E. Molinier's *Histoire générale des arts appliqués à l'industrie* (1901), to name but a few of the most prominent publications in this field.

From this point of view, Goodhue's study of W. R. Lethaby's publications demonstrates a move toward a more informed and scholarly view of the material than his friends possessed. Of great importance were Lethaby's book *The Church of Sophia* (1894), on Hagia Sophia, and, as we have seen, his article on Westminster Cathedral. But his surveys—*Medieval Art from the Peace of the Church to the Eve of the Renaissance: 312–1350* (1904), *Architecture, Mysticism and Myth* (1892), and *Architecture: An Introduction to the History and Theory of the Art of Building* (1911)—occupied a special place in Goodhue's esteem.

Although in 1915, Goodhue claimed that he and Lethaby were friends, the evidence of other letters suggests that they did not become correspondents until 1920 and close friends until the last years of Goodhue's life. However, Goodhue had read enough of Lethaby's works by 1915 to declare him "the greatest living theorist on matters architectural" and "the very greatest—indeed perhaps the only great—writer on the theory of architecture." This admiration increased over the years, and by 1924, Goodhue considered himself to be Lethaby's disciple, trying "faithfully to have my work reflect the theories that, from reading your books, I think you hold."[68]

Lethaby regarded architectural development as an evolution of forms. The art of the Byzantine Empire had evolved from the art of ancient Greece; it was paralleled in the West by Romanesque, which had grown from the ruins of ancient Rome. These two currents were closely related; Eastern influence on Western art had been so pervasive that until the year 1000, the latter might be better called "Byzantinesque than Romanesque."[69] The chief characteristics of Byzantine architecture were the use of brick for construction; a preference for broad, rather than high, vaults and domes; the use of marble for columns, lintels, and door jambs; the sheathing of the interior with marble paneling and mosaic; and the absence of bay divisions. San Marco was discussed as part of Byzantine architecture, for Lethaby correctly recognized it as a copy of the Church of the Holy Apostles in Constantinople, which no longer exists.[70]

For Lethaby, Italian medieval art had very little independent character, and he was able to define Lombard Romanesque architecture only as "the more barbaric element found associated with the current Italo-Byzantine style of Northern Italy." At this point, distinctions between Byzantine and Lombard become extremely difficult to draw. Lethaby declared himself content, however, "to have tried to suggest the unity in diversity of the stream of art which flowed down the centuries, every age showing a different manifestation of one energy as the old tradition was ever new shaped by the need and experiment of the moment."[71]

Goodhue's definition of Romanesque architecture reveals the imprint of Lethaby's Eastern bias; he considered the center of pre-Gothic medieval Christian civilization to have been Constantinople. Western Europe merely "strove to produce as well as they might the effect given by the great church in the capitol of the Eastern Empire [Hagia Sophia]," and San Marco was evaluated in comparison with Hagia Sophia as "a very much later and architecturally considered, a rather less important structure." Romanesque was seen as a sort of preparatory, or formative, stage in the evolution toward that "veritable burgeoning . . . of faith, intellect, and art that we call Medievalism," or Gothic.[72] As part of the "Dark Ages," Romanesque had no clear physiognomy.

In the first two decades of the twentieth century, there was an extraordinary outpouring of English-language scholarship on the Byzantine and Romanesque periods. The most important works included A. van Millingen's *Byzantine Constantinople* (1899), G. T. Rivoira's *Lombardic Architecture: Its Origins, Development, and Derivatives* (1901; English translation, 1910), O. M. Dalton's *Byzantine Art and Archaeology* (1911), J. B. Bury's *History of the Eastern Roman Empire from the Fall of Irene to the Accession of Basil I* (1912), T. G. Jackson's *Byzantine and Romanesque Architecture* (1915), and the great and influential study by H. O. Taylor, *The Medieval Mind: A History of the Development of Thought and Emotion in the Middle Ages* (1911).[73]

In particular, the second decade produced two eminent American historians of medieval art: Charles Rufus Morey, whose *Lost Mosaics and Frescoes of Rome of the Medieval Period* (1915) was followed by *Studies in East Christian and Roman Art* (1918), written with W. Dennison; and Arthur Kingsley Porter, author of *Medieval Architecture* (1908), *The Construction of Lombard and Gothic Vaults* (1912), and *Lombard Architecture* (1915–17). And in 1914 George Gray Bernard opened in New York a museum of medieval sculpture and architectural elements, which was bought by the Metropolitan Museum of Art in 1925 and reopened as The Cloisters. Later in his life, Goodhue became acquainted with works by Jackson and Kingsley Porter, but there is no evidence that when he designed St. Bartholomew's in 1914, he had read the most recent publications in the field.[74] If the scholarly work of the late nineteenth century took a broad cultural approach and desired to achieve a unified overall view of architectural evolution, and the studies of the early twentieth century were more detailed, then Goodhue's knowledge of Romanesque architecture was molded by the earlier work.

When asked to comment on Lucian Smith's "Lombard Romanesque" design for the First Methodist Episcopal Church in Asbury Park, New Jersey, for example, Goodhue noted that he was "engaged on a similar though larger church."[75] Yet Smith's design, a Greek cross church with a saucer dome on pendentives, was evidently inspired by the Byzantine Hagia Sophia. It would seem, then, that Goodhue, rather than deceiving his patrons by calling St. Bartholomew's Romanesque, really believed that it was. His comment that Clarence Stein, the chief draftsman for the project, had become, "thanks to St. Bartholomew's, a very excellent Italian of about 900 A.D."[76] suggests that Goodhue's knowledge of Lombard Romanesque chronology was almost nonexistent. He may have arrived at the dating of Lombard Romanesque churches simply by placing them several centuries earlier than the Gothic structures whose dates he probably knew. Since Goodhue had never been to northern Italy or even north of Rome when he designed St. Bartholomew's,[77] he had not seen those buildings that he urged Parks to visit in 1914 and, even more important, had not seen the church that actually did inspire his design—San Marco.

Goodhue reveals himself to have been a man of culture, but not a scholar. Thus judged by the standards of modern scholarship, his notion of Lombard Romanesque was neither clear nor detailed. He was led by the scholarly literature that he had read to consider such architecture as lacking strongly defined character, merely a pre-Gothic style rooted in Roman arch-and-vault construction, and as subject to a pervasive Byzantine influence. And the links between Byzantine and Italian Romanesque architecture—which, although different in some respects, were not entirely distinct styles—were clearly demonstrated by San Marco, which drew on both currents. Was Goodhue, by modern standards, wrong?

Classifying San Marco as Byzantine, and thus implicitly denying a definition for it as Lombard Romanesque, oversimplifies a matter that is in reality complex and subtle, for it is difficult to determine the style of San Marco. The eleventh-century basilica was intended to be a copy of the sixth-century Church of the Holy Apostles in Constantinople. From this point of view, San Marco is a Byzantine building. But Venice is in northern Italy, and San Marco is contemporary with such classic Italian Romanesque structures as Pisa Cathedral, Sant'Ambrogio in Milan, and San Miniato al Monte in Florence. The Venetian church was built by Italian workmen with Italian materials, and it incorporates a number of specifically Western features in both plan and elevation, such as the crypt, raised choir, and rose window. In important ways, it constitutes a part of that western European movement called Romanesque.

Goodhue's difficulty in distinguishing Romanesque from Byzantine was not merely a sign of insufficient knowledge, for in the case of San Marco, the two are almost impossible to separate. While modern scholars may tend to agree that St. Front at Périgueux is rather more Romanesque and San Marco rather more Byzantine, it is equally true that no survey of Italian Romanesque art that omitted San Marco could be considered complete.[78] On balance, then, Goodhue had a fair amount of justification for describing St. Bartholomew's as Romanesque in style.

By contrast, the virtual consensus of modern critics in describing St. Bartholomew's as Byzantine has to be challenged. Were this attribution made on the basis of its links to San Marco, it would have some merit. But that relationship had not been recognized. Instead, the Byzantine label was chosen largely because of the profile of the dome, the brick exterior masonry, and the absence of exterior buttresses. The dome was not part of Goodhue's design, and its sources, in any case, are not Byzantine. The brick masonry is one of the most purely Romanesque features of the building and has specific precedents in northern Italian models. The absence of exterior buttresses is a structural device copied from the Gothic Albi Cathedral in southern France. Goodhue was not a scholar, but his awareness of historical style has not been surpassed by the critics of his church.

56 · Antelami. Prophet, Fidenza
Cathedral (ca. 1200).

5 · THE DECORATION

THE FURNITURE and decoration of St. Bartholomew's include furnishings brought from St. Bartholomew's II, elements designed by Goodhue, objects designed and executed by Lee Lawrie in association with Goodhue, and additions made after Goodhue's death.

ST. BARTHOLOMEW'S II: VANDERBILT PORTAL AND FURNISHINGS

Leighton Parks promised the parishioners, in a sermon delivered on April 19, 1914, that the new church would incorporate the best of the old.[1] This referred above all, of course, to the Vanderbilt portal, but it extended to a substantial part of the old church's furnishings. When money for the project eventually ran short, additional material from St. Bartholomew's II was slated for reuse. Almost all the objects added to St. Bartholomew's II in the 1890s are in the present church, although in different locations.[2] Francis Lathrop's huge painting, *The Light of the World,* for example, had filled the apse of the old church. In November 1916, Goodhue informed the rector that it could not be placed in the same position in the new church, and he accommodated it in the north transept, where (before it faded into illegibility) it must have made a splendid effect (pl. XXIII). Goodhue also banished the old retable, a loose copy in Caen stone of Leonardo's *Last Supper,* from the sanctuary; it now forms the altar in the baptistery. The font in the baptistery, a colossal marble angel by James Redfern, is also from the old church.[3] The mosaic floor of the old chancel was taken apart, and its tesserae form the pavement of the present chancel of the church (pl. XXII). The choir stalls in the chancel are adaptations of the old ones, and some of the pews in the church are from St. Bartholomew's II.

The altar rails in both the church and the chapel seem to come, at least in part, from St. Bartholomew's II. On stylistic grounds, the rail in the chapel, with gilt bronze vine leaves, must be nineteenth century and therefore from the old church. It may have been the altar rail until 1892, when a new rail, of "colored marbles and mosaic,"[4] was installed. More difficult to determine is whether this second rail forms part of the communion rail in the present church, which also is of colored marbles and mosaic (pl. XXVI). The marble frame and ornamental panels of the communion rail, probably designed by Lee Lawrie in the 1920s but not executed until 1935, harmonize with the style of all the sanctuary furnishings. But a contract signed on June 11, 1918, says that the chancel rail of St. Bartholomew's II is to be recut and reset. It may be that the mosaic panels of the present rail come from the old church, while the marble panels between and around them were added.

Other materials transferred to the new church included the stained-glass windows once in the west façade[5] and the windows in the north transept vestibule and the mortuary chapel, the memorial plaques in the south transept corridor, the altar in the mortuary chapel, and the liturgical furniture in the chapel.[6]

By and large, Goodhue sought to place these furnishings in positions of secondary importance in his church. None of the furnishings from the sanctuary of St. Bartholomew's II were retained in the sanctuary of the new church, unless they were entirely recomposed, as were the communion rail, choir stalls, and pavement. Thus Goodhue satisfied his patrons' desire to retain these objects, without permitting the furnishings to intrude on his own scheme.

GOODHUE: ARCHITECTURAL SCULPTURE, ORGAN LOFT, APSE, AND PAVEMENT

For St. Bartholomew's, Goodhue designed all the architectural sculpture, the west organ loft, the intarsia pavement in the sanctuaries of the church and chapel, and, perhaps, the marble revetment in the apse.

Most of the architectural sculpture was executed, with varying degrees of success, by the Piccirilli Brothers firm, and much of it is of cast rather than natural stone. The architectural sculpture includes the figures on the west façade and the south transept; the capitals in the narthex, church, and chapel; the reliefs on the north transept of the church and south flank of the chapel; the tracery for all the windows; and the narrative relief panels in the crossing.

Taken as a whole, the stone sculpture is based on twelfth- and thirteenth-century Italian models, with occasional influences from other sources. Although the standing saints on the south transept have the elongated proportions of French Gothic statues, the bold generalization of their form and sense of compressed mass recall the sculpture by Benedetto Antelami at Parma Bapistery and Fidenza Cathedral (fig. 56; pl. VI). The isolation of the figures is reminiscent of the placement of the statues on the façade of Siena Cathedral, designed by Giovanni Pisano, and their position atop

57 · St. Bartholomew's Church, chancel capital.

58 · Monreale Cathedral, Sicily, cloister capital (twelfth century).

tall colonnettes repeats the arrangement of figures in the crossing of Siena Cathedral and of San Marco.

The capitals also have Italian Romanesque sources, but within a wider chronological range. Some of them are close to the compositions on the capitals in the cloister of Monreale Cathedral, near Palermo (figs. 57, 58). Classicizing elements are the starting point for curvilinear inventions: acanthus leaves form scrolls and volutes in an almost infinite number of variations. Some of the capitals at St. Bartholomew's have human heads; those in the narthex were inspired by Pisan Romanesque sculpture and closely resemble the work of Nicola Pisano (fig. 59; pl. XII). The historiated double capitals in the nave draw on several sources (fig. 60). Double capitals are found in twelfth-century cloister decoration, but it is not possible to determine whether the specific source is Monreale (fig. 61), St. Trophime at Arles, or another monument. The figural style and narrative mode of the nave capitals are not particularly close to Romanesque examples, which Goodhue may have felt lacked clarity in these respects. Indeed, at least one pair was inspired by Egyptian reliefs (fig. 60).

The reliefs on the north transept also have Italian sources. The decorative arrangement of separate relief disks has precise precedents in Venice, where Byzantine and Romanesque plaques are so placed on church and house façades (fig. 48). The arrangement of the symbols of the Evangelists around a lamb of God is a design common in Umbria, although it is also seen in Campania (figs. 47, 62).

While the frieze and the window arches on the south flank of the chapel (fig. 63) seem to return to the model for the west portal—St. Gilles-du-Gard (fig. 20)—similar scroll ornament is found on Italian buildings, particularly framing the portals of San Marco (fig. 64).

59 · Pisano. Pisa Cathedral, façade capital (ca. 1250).

60 · St. Bartholomew's Church, side aisle with double capital of nave pier.

61 · Monreale Cathedral, cloister capital (twelfth century).

62 · Assisi Cathedral, façade detail (thirteenth century).

The variety of window types and tracery at St. Bartholomew's—carved stone screens; vertical lights beneath a tracery tympanum; a wheel, or rose, window—is paralleled at San Marco. Yet it is difficult to point to any specific precedents for the tracery patterns of these windows. The tracery on the west window, for example, has an interlace of lines and surface textures (pls. III, XVIII); the myriad voids and solids create a subtle play of light and dark, enlivening the façade and contrasting with the planar quality of the wall. The interlace has affinities with the curvilinear designs of Italian Romanesque portals, Celtic manuscripts, and Islamic carved screens. The relative density of the tracery produces an effect closer to that of Byzantine than of Gothic examples. Considering all the various characteristics of the tracery, the closest comparison is with tracery on the west window

63 · St. Bartholomew's Church,
south flank, chapel exterior.

of Troia Cathedral in southern Italy, in which Byzantine, Romanesque, Gothic, and Islamic sources were synthesized (fig. 43).[8]

The wheel structure of the window of Troia Cathedral may have served as a model for Goodhue's south transept rose window (pls. v, xxiv), although its placement, design, and (originally) uniformly tinted glass bring it close to the rose window of San Marco (fig. 52).

The unusual combination of vertical lancets beneath a heavy, tracery tympanum on the windows of the west façade and the nave also recall San Marco, where such windows occupy the tympana of the west façade portals (fig. 51).

The wooden, west organ loft belongs to a cultural tradition different from that of Italy (pls. xviii, xix). While its overall structure—a carved screen resting on columns—recalls Italian Romanesque choir screens, such as that at Modena Cathedral (fig. 65), and the placement of free-standing figures along its upper edge copies the choir screen at San Marco, designed by Jacobello and Pierpaolo dalle Masegne (fig. 66), the style of its figural carving is northern Late Gothic and of its interlace, Islamic. Since most

64 · San Marco, archivolts over right portal, west façade (thirteenth century).

65 · Modena
Cathedral, pontile
(twelfth–thirteenth
centuries).

66 · Jacobello and
Pierpaolo dalle
Masegne. Choir
screen, San Marco
(1394).

67 · Bramante. Santa Maria delle Grazie, crossing.

Italian decorative carving is in stone rather than wood, Goodhue may have preferred to follow the acknowledged masters of wood carving. Despite this mixture of styles, the general effect of the interior west wall is neither Italian Romanesque nor northern Gothic, but Byzantine. The view over the gallery toward the west window repeats the arrangement at San Marco, and the superimposition of columnar arcades of differing luminosities recalls the elevation of Hagia Sophia. The implied dissolution of the wall into lacy patterns is similar in principle, at least, to the handling of the nave wall at Hagia Sophia.

A drawing by Goodhue shows the conch of the apse divided into segments by bands of ornamental tile (fig. 18). This design recalls Bramante's patterns for the crossing of Santa Maria delle Grazie in Milan (fig. 67). But Goodhue's conception for the apse was not realized. In January 1918, the Building Commitee, having decided to omit all ornamental tile in order to save money, was debating whether to leave the conch of the apse in plain brick or to paint it. This is clear evidence that Goodhue never intended a mosaic to be placed in the apse, and it explains why the apse was considered to be in need of decoration in the 1920s.

The lower walls of the apse were to be sheathed in marble. But on November 15, 1916, the Building Committee decided to omit the marble revetment in order to economize, and in January 1918, the committee was

68 · San Lorenzo fuori le mura,
Rome, bishop's throne (ca. 1254).

considering whether to face the apse with Akoustolith or with a heavy
fabric. Deciding that neither of these solutions was acoustically as desirable
as marble sheathing, which had been found very satisfactory at St.
Bartholomew's II, the committee reversed itself on January 29. The marble revetment was installed in 1929, five years after Goodhue's death. The
apse design of vertical marble panels separated by ornamental borders recalls Goodhue's drawing for the apse conch and may be his (pls. XXI,
XXVI). While the use of beautifully veined marble revetment recalls San
Marco (among other churches), the combination of such panels with geo-
metrically patterned borders derives from Cosmati work in thirteenth-
century Rome (fig. 68).

The marble intarsia for the pavements of the chancels in the church and
chapel also have Italian sources (pl. XXII). All the pavements of San Marco
are of colored stone intarsia, and the tesserae are large, as they are at St.
Bartholomew's (fig. 69). However, the pavement designed by Goodhue
for the church chancel is of a specific type, Cosmati, more closely associated with Rome and the Rome area than with Venice (fig. 70), although

69 · San Marco, pavement detail (twelfth century).

70 · San Clemente, Rome, pavement detail (ca. 1200).

the large Cosmati pavement in Canterbury Cathedral may have determined the choice made for St. Bartholomew's. That the tesserae for this pavement came from St. Bartholomew's II suggests that their size, if not their present arrangement, was a given of Goodhue's design. The figural mosaics in the pavements of the church apse and the chapel chancel are more difficult to trace. They have analogies with ancient Roman work, such as at the Basilica of Junius Bassus, which certainly was not known to Goodhue. They are also similar to Florentine *pietra dura* work, although there are strong stylistic disparities between them.

Goodhue, then, drew on a large number of specific sources for the design of the ornamentation of St. Bartholomew's. Most of the source material is in northern Italy and dates between 1100 and 1500. While the integration of Egyptian, Classical, Byzantine, Romanesque, Gothic, and Renaissance elements at St. Bartholomew's leads to the definition of its style as eclectic, this should not obscure a very real coherence of reference in terms of essential features. The model for St. Bartholomew's was San Marco, reconceived with the aid of Lombard and Emilian Romanesque examples.

LAWRIE: LECTERN, PULPIT, AND COMMUNION RAIL

Goodhue believed that architecture represented a collaborative effort of specialists:

> I should like to be merely one of three people to produce a building, i.e. architect, painter, sculptor. You see what I mean: I should like to do the plan and the massing of the building; then I should like to turn the ornament . . . over to a perfectly qualified sculptor, and the color and the surface direction . . . to an equally qualified painter.[9]

One of the most important members of Goodhue's *équipe* was the sculptor Lee Lawrie. At the time of Goodhue's death, Lawrie asserted that they had worked together for twenty-nine years (that is, since 1895),[10] although the first documentation of their association known to me is for the chapel at West Point (1904).[11] In either case, their relationship spanned almost all of Goodhue's career. Lawrie was a sculptor of importance in his own right; he taught sculpture at both Yale and Harvard. Yet his stylistic development so closely paralleled Goodhue's that it is legitimate to regard his work for St. Bartholomew's as an extension of Goodhue's thought.

Lawrie reached the apex of his career as a neo-Gothicist, together with Goodhue, in the reredos for St. Thomas Church. With St. Bartholomew's, both men entered a phase of transition. Lawrie's earliest pieces for St. Bartholomew's, such as the grotesques for the chapel sedilia, are still

71 · San Ambrogio,
Milan, pulpit detail
(ca. 1100).

Gothic in style and were executed while he was completing the reredos at
St. Thomas.[12] But by 1923, when the lectern was installed in the church,[13]
his style had become far more abstract (pl. XXV). In his later work, the
density of the masses is emphasized, and the design centers on bold, geometric forms with exquisitely etched surfaces—exactly the stylistic formula of St. Bartholomew's. The sources of the new style are partly Romanesque (fig. 71) and partly Assyrian and Egyptian. The lectern and pulpit
of St. Bartholomew's should be seen in relation to Lawrie's contemporary,
similar work on the late Goodhue buildings: the Nebraska State Capitol
and the National Academy of Sciences.

The pulpit of St. Bartholomew's, completed in 1925, was Lawrie's favorite of his works (fig. 72; pl. XXVII). Although Parks claimed, at its
dedication, that it would "forever remain a significant part of that realization of the dream of Romanesque which sprang from the brain of Bertram Grosvenor Goodhue,"[14] the work has little to do with the Romanesque style. While the fluted shape of the pulpit recalls the pulpits of San
Marco (fig. 66), its circular stairs and suspension from the wall suggest
that, typologically, it may owe something to fifteenth-century Florentine
pulpits, especially Il Buggiano's for Santa Maria Novella (fig. 73). The
classicizing cornices, decorative borders, and epigraphy of the inscription
that circles the lower edge could have been drawn from the same source.

72 · Lawrie. Pulpit, St.
Bartholomew's Church (1925).

Like Italian Romanesque pulpits, Lawrie's rests on columns and includes
frontal, full-length figures. Yet comparison between Nicola Pisano's pulpit in Pisa Baptistery and Lawrie's in St. Bartholomew's reveals Lawrie's
to be consciously archaizing in style (fig. 74).

Renaissance influence all but disappears from Lawrie's latest works, those
for the sanctuary (pls. XXI, XXVI). Although a variety of source material is
still evident, the strands are more effectively amalgamated. The pierced
panels of the communion rail, for example, are of a type common in early
medieval Italy, such as at Sant'Apollinare Nuovo in Ravenna (fig. 75),
although the design of their interlace was also influenced by pre-
Columbian patterns.

In general, Lee Lawrie's style moved in the direction of pure geometric

73 · Il Buggiano. Pulpit, Santa Maria
Novella, Florence (ca. 1440).

74 · Pisano. Pulpit, Pisa Bapistery
(1259).

75 · Sant'Apollinare Nuovo, Ravenna, choir screen panels (sixth–seventh centuries).

masses and delicately incised surfaces. The style was consonant with the ideals of Italian Romanesque sculpture, even though Egyptian, Assyrian, and archaic Greek art contributed to its stylized, linear forms. More important, this style was in line with Goodhue's and the sculptural ornamentation of the interior thus completes and enhances the stylistic qualities of the architecture. The same cannot be said for the decoration done by other of Goodhue's associates after his death.

MOSAICS, DOME, AND STAINED-GLASS WINDOWS

Concerns of taste and economy caused a fundamental alteration of the character of St. Bartholomew's after Goodhue's death. The most important additions made after 1924 are mosaics in the apse and narthex, the dome, and the stained-glass windows.

On March 14, 1922, Goodhue wrote to Robert Brewster, the chairman of the Building Committee, about completing the interior of the church and adding the crossing element. But before anything could be done, Goodhue died and Parks resigned as rector.

In January 1927, Robert Norwood, the new rector, asked the vestry to reassess Goodhue's drawings for the interior. They must have been rejected immediately, since in February, F. L. S. Mayers and O. H. Murray of Goodhue Associates were requested to make new sketches. At the same time, Alvin Krech, the chairman of the Art Committee, prepared a report that recommended the sort of decoration that should be added to the church. As a result of this study, it was decided "to adopt the Byzantine primitive type of mosaics for the embellishment of the apse and sanctuary of St.

Bartholomew's Church."[15] Preliminary drawings were prepared by Goodhue Associates and Hildredth Meiere.

Meiere was, like Lee Lawrie, a member of Goodhue's *équipe*. She may have come to his attention through her work at St. John the Divine, where Lawrie was also active,[16] and she collaborated with Goodhue and Lawrie on Goodhue's late works, including the National Academy of Sciences and the Nebraska State Capitol. At these buildings, her strongly stylized natural forms are consonant with Lawrie's figural style and with Goodhue's architecture.

Goodhue had not planned any large-scale figural decoration for the interior of St. Bartholomew's. He intended to enliven the upper parts of the wall with inlaid geometric designs, but not to conceal the wall behind glass sheathing. Some idea of the effect he sought may be gained from the north transept, whose decoration was largely carried out according to his plans (pl. XXIII). A comparison of the north transept with the apse (pl. XIV) dramatizes the degree to which the mosaics represent a divergence from his style. While it is true that San Marco has mosaics (fig. 41), as do many Byzantine churches, Goodhue did not plan to follow this model at St. Bartholomew's, preferring instead to emphasize its hard, clear, Romanesque qualities. Thus the decision to add byzantinizing mosaics shifted the scales on which Romanesque and Byzantine elements had been balanced, in the direction of the latter. Indeed, the last time the building was referred to as Romanesque was at the dedication of the pulpit in 1926; thereafter, it has been perceived as Byzantine. This change in stylistic designation signals a real break with Goodhue's project on the part of Norwood, the vestry, and Goodhue's followers.

Why did Krech recommend that byzantinizing mosaics be installed? Obviously, he recognized San Marco to be the most important source for St. Bartholomew's, and San Marco is famous for its mosaics. Several important works in English had been published on Byzantine art, above all by Charles Rufus Morey, of Princeton University, and by O. M. Dalton.[17] Krech seems to have known Morey personally. Also, Goodhue's church, devoid of any large-scale figures or narratives, was probably fairly difficult for the layman to accept, and Krech sought a style that could remedy this "defect" while remaining in harmony with the architecture. From this point of view, the only possible post-Classical and pre-Gothic figural art was Byzantine.

There was also the larger context of a growing enthusiasm for the modern use of mosaics—an enthusiasm shared by Goodhue himself in his last works; both the Nebraska State Capitol and the National Academy of Sciences have tile-mosaic domes. An important impetus for this revival was given by the massive restoration campaigns of the nineteenth century: at Charlemagne's Palatine Chapel in Aachen; at the monuments in Ravenna; at San Marco and Santa Maria dell'Assunta in Torcello; at San Paolo fuori le mura in Rome; and at the Baptistery in Florence, to name but a few well-known examples. Many of these restorations were accompanied by large-scale additions (particularly at Aachen), which provided a training ground for mosaic artists.

The Friedenskirche in Potsdam (1845–48), designed by Ludwig Persius, was one of the first modern churches to house a mosaic. By the late nineteenth century, some English and American architects were projecting mosaic schemes for their buildings. Edward Burne-Jones decorated G. E. Street's St. Paul's Within the Walls in Rome with some very beautiful and original mosaics; St. Matthew's Cathedral in Washington, designed by C. Grant La Farge has an apse mosaic; and McKim, Mead, and White sheathed the vaults of the Boston Public Library with mosaics. In New York, Heins and La Farge's design for St. John the Divine called for a mosaic in the apse (fig. 28), but the only New York church in which mosaics were actually carried out in the 1890s was St. Michael's Episcopal Church (Ninety-ninth Street and Amsterdam Avenue).[18] Cass Gilbert was to demonstrate their utility for office buildings in his Woolworth Building (1913), while York and Sawyer applied mosaics to the Bowery Savings Bank (1921–23). Enthusiasm reached a high pitch on an international scale in the early twentieth century when Westminster Cathedral in London was decorated with mosaics, as was the Sacré-Cœur in Paris. That this medium was particularly favored for large-scale religious sanctuaries is suggested by the

76 · Sant'Apollinare in Classe, Ravenna, apse mosaic (ca. 549).

77 · San Lorenzo in
Lucina, Rome,
drawing of lost apse
fresco.

design for the shrine of the Immaculate Conception in Washington (Maginnis and Walsh, 1922).[19]

Seen against this background, Krech's choice of mosaic for St. Bartholomew's attests, once again, to the high ambition of the project and to its participation in recent developments in taste.

The choice of subject for the apse mosaic, the Transfiguration, also demonstrates the modernity of the decorative program. For only in 1892 had the General Convention of the Episcopal Church voted to include the Feast of the Transfiguration as one of the holy days of the church calendar.[20] The collect for the day that was composed at the time suggests that, above all, the theme of immanence inherent in the event urged its new importance,[21] and as the liberal current won its inclusion as a feast day, so the parish of St. Bartholomew's selected this event, above all others, for the apse of its church. Immanence was, as we have seen, the central theme of Goodhue's architecture for St. Bartholomew's. The apse mosaic clarifies and makes more easily accessible the conceptual core of the building.

In terms of composition and style, the mosaic represents a conflation of prestigious medieval models (pl. xx). The pose of the central Christ figure (frontal, orant) recalls that of St. Apollinaris in the Transfiguration apse at Sant'Apollinare in Classe, near Ravenna (fig. 76). But the composition as a whole is less reminiscent of Ravenna than of Rome: the apses of SS. Cosma e Damiano and of Santa Prassede, or the lost fresco in the apse of San Lorenzo in Lucina (fig. 77).[22] Ravenna furnished elements for the ornamental panels elsewhere in the apse.

The choice of a Creation cycle for the narthex domes (pls. x, xi) demonstrates an awareness that the narthex was modeled on the vestibule of San Marco, whose domes carry a Genesis cycle (fig. 78).[23] If the apse is overtly derivative in style and composition, and perhaps too close to its

78 · San Marco,
vestibule (ca. 1200).

medieval models, the narthex is a triumph of modern religious art. Particularly felicitous is the reordering of the sequence of the days of Creation in order to place the creation of man, made in God's image, over the main entrance to the church. The mosaics sparkle like a ceiling of sapphires, in which stylized forms are embedded, as in amber. The dark luminosity of the mosaic domes unifies the narthex space and renders it intimate, while inviting the spectator to probe the mysteries of the stylized symbols it contains.

Although the mosaic decoration of St. Bartholomew's was not foreseen by Goodhue and, indeed, goes against the kind of aesthetic effect he wanted to create, it is at least a seriously considered and well-executed addition. For many, the mosaics are perhaps the most impressive and memorable feature of the interior, and they should be considered as positive from that point of view.

The merit of the dome is more problematic (pl. VIII). On April 16, 1919, Goodhue informed Parks that the cost of building his "ciborium" would be $273,000. This high cost effectively eliminated his design from further consideration, although the present, much more modest, dome cost $350,000 in 1929. The design for the dome as built was furnished by Goodhue Associates, which while overseeing the decoration of St. Bartholomew's, was completing the Nebraska State Capitol and supplying bells to St. Thomas Church. As heir to Goodhue's workshop, the firm inherited many of his drawings, enabling it to show the Building Committee Goodhue's original drawings for the crossing tower. After they were rejected, another of Goodhue's designs, for the dome of the California State Building at the San Diego Exposition (1911–15), was adapted to the St. Bartholomew's project (fig. 79). While the profile of the dome and its division into eight exterior faces reflect Goodhue's conception, the inlay decoration on the exterior was added for the commission, perhaps using some of the patterns that Goodhue had intended for the interior of the church.

Of course, the abandonment of the great central tower as the culmination of the exterior composition drastically altered the character of the building. The tower was to have been as tall as the body of the church, and far richer in windows, buttresses, and sculptural ornamentation than any other part of the exterior (figs. 15, 54). The planar, box-like arms would have contrasted with and served as the solid base for the polygonal, pierced tower. Moreover, the massive horizontal west portal would have been effectively countered by the richly articulated, vertical tower. The upper parts of the west, south, and north façades, sharing some of the design motifs of the tower, would have become transitional planes between the low, horizontal base areas and the high central focus. Of all this, only the square base, marking the point from which the tower would have risen, was built.

The dome performs an entirely different visual function. It serves as a cap for the lower volumes, whose importance is thereby unduly empha-

79 · Goodhue. California State Building, San Diego Exposition (1911–15).

sized. The dome concludes, rather than extends, the structure; it diffuses, rather than concentrates, the massive volumes of the lower parts, sustaining a centrifugal instead of centripetal dynamic. The inlaid marble and tile decoration of the surface contrasts with the sculptural character of the lower parts of the building without heightening its effect, and the decoration's overall planarity offers no expression of the grandeur, and little enough of the monumentality, that Goodhue wished.

The interior of the dome is also entirely different from Goodhue's design, which was based on the Ely octagon. It belongs to an entirely different cultural sphere. The vault, ingeniously constructed of wooden boxes, counterfeits an interlaced dome of Islamic type (pl. xv). Such vaults appear in Spanish Romanesque buildings, such as Santo Sepulcro in Torres del Río (fig. 80) and Saragossa Cathedral. The gilding of the wooden dome and its squinches makes indirect references to the Arab-influenced architecture of Monreale Cathedral and the Palatine Chapel in Palermo (fig. 81). Since in these churches such ceilings appear in conjunction with by-

80 · Santo Sepulcro, Torres del Río, Spain, dome detail (thirteenth century).

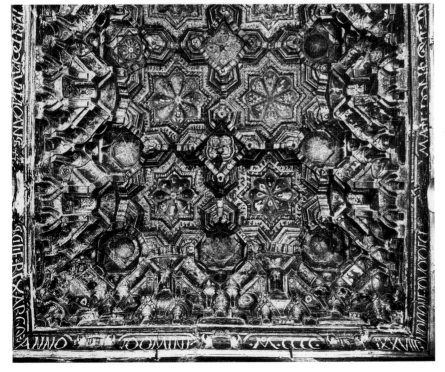

81 · Palatine Chapel, Palermo, wooden ceiling detail (ca. 1150).

zantinizing mosaics, it may be that the design concept of St. Bartholomew's developed under Goodhue Associates was inspired by Sicilian models.

The change of the crossing element has obscured St. Bartholomew's connections with Italian medieval art. Rather, the resultant combination of a dome sustained by barrel vaults recalls Hagia Irene in Constantinople and the Stag's Basilica in Pirdop (near Sofia, Bulgaria)—in short, Justinianian architecture of the sixth century.[24] This has evidently reinforced the belief that St. Bartholomew's is a neo-Byzantine building.

The mosaics and the dome do not go as far in masking Goodhue's original design as do the stained-glass windows. Goodhue intended to use clear or uniformly tinted glass for all the windows, including the rose. Thus he never mentioned the possibility of a commission to his brother Harry, who usually executed the stained glass for his churches,[25] and it was decided on December 6, 1915, that the Pittsburgh Plate Glass Company would supply the material.

As early as 1917, however, the Art Committee was indicating its desire for stained glass. Some undated sheets filed in the archive under March 14, 1917, proposed subjects for stained-glass windows throughout the church, and in August of that year William Field, a member of the Building Committee, was looking into the matter of stained glass. Yet at this point, only glass from the old church was slated for the new. The west window was composed of some of that glass, augmented by new glass painted by G. Owen Bonawit. This window was replaced in the 1960s.

No sooner had the church been opened than the parishioners urged the installation of stained glass. Although the building fund could not cover the cost of windows for the nave, at $420 each, private donations were received to commission windows for the north transept. These windows, to be designed by Henry B. Young, were not executed. Thus at the church's consecration in 1923, only the west window had stained glass.[26] Parks's remarks on this subject were probably intended to soothe his parishioners' disappointment.[27] Only in 1929, as part of the program that included the installation of mosaics and the erection of the dome, were stained-glass windows commissioned from John Gordon Guthrie for the north and south transepts.[28] Shortly thereafter, Guthrie added the six "Te Deum" windows in the north aisle of the church.

The rose window in the south transept was filled with uniformly tinted glass (fig. 82). But in 1942, as a memorial, Emily Vanderbilt White donated its stained glass (pl. XXIV). It was executed by Reynolds, Francis, and Rohnstock, who had been trained by Charles J. Connick and had apprenticed at St. John the Divine in the early decades of the century. Their association with Cram continued when they executed the glass for the Princeton Chapel. Thus their experience was in neo-Gothic design and explains their supposed suitability for the rose window commission. They also executed the six windows in the chapel and those in the narthex.

In the 1960s, the parish consulted the noted medievalist Albert M. Friend

82 · St. Bartholomew's Church,
south transept rose window in the
1920s.

regarding an iconographic program for the gallery windows in the nave. Four windows were designed by Hildredth Meiere, and the remaining two were installed later in the decade. The west window was redesigned, to have a modern composition.

Thus some thirty years after the consecration of the church, almost all the clear- or tinted-glass windows had been replaced by stained-glass ones.[29] This measurably darkened the church interior and reversed the aesthetic effect that Goodhue had intended. Had the same money been spent on the marble sheathing of the lower walls, on the slate floor, or on carving inscriptions in the crossing—all features planned by Goodhue but not executed because funds were short—the interior would be rich, luminous, and colorful. Instead, a conservative backlash on the part of the parishioners and the rectors did what was possible to Gothicize Goodhue's interior.

The placement of stained-glass windows in the church represents a negative judgment on Goodhue's design. The parish was not prepared for the architectural expressiveness of spatial volumes and articulated surfaces; they were too abstract, too remote. The parishioners desired the comfort of the human figure, the charm of narrative, the Gothic aura of holiness. Those who have criticized Goodhue's architecture as reflecting a conservative, even reactionary, current in twentieth-century design might consider the influence of clients' taste and architectural awareness on design. Goodhue failed not because his architecture was too conservative, but because it was too innovative for the parish.[30] That he failed to persuade the vestry to build the tower and sheath the interior in marble suggests that the vestrymen did not grasp, or did not accept, the premises of his design concept. Thus his original architectural proposition, in all its extravagance and splendor, was not altogether convincing. Whether the parishioners would have judged the church more favorably had Goodhue's original design been carried out can only be surmised, but they probably would have. Goodhue asked his patrons to spend a good deal of money to achieve aesthetic effects that they were entirely unprepared for and could not envision. Wary of extending themselves, they truncated the project. Its resulting barrenness then had to be remedied with well-tried solutions, such as stained-glass windows.

CONCLUSION: THE RHETORIC OF ECLECTICISM

L IKE SPEECH, architecture is a form of communication: it aims to evoke a response from its audience or to express an idea or attitude. This expressive intent likens architecture to rhetoric—the art of eloquence, the art of persuasion, the science of speaking well. In classical oratory, different styles of eloquence were considered suitable for different sorts of discourse or for different audiences. So, too, in architecture, formal vocabulary varies in relation to the function and purpose of a building and to the taste, culture, expectations, and understanding of its patrons and audience. One rhetorical mode is eclecticism. Eclectic architecture is particularly characterized by a concern with rhetoric, although all buildings may be said to have some rhetorical content. The Modern Movement in architecture was, by and large, involved in grammatical pursuits and in the attempt to devise a universal vocabulary and syntax for architectural form. Its achievements were, accordingly, primarily structural (in both the mechanical and the conceptual sense) and formal. But eclecticism considers grammar to be secondary in importance, and eclectic architecture is not ordered by a single linguistic system. Instead, it seeks to charm, to persuade, or to impress through many expressive devices unified by their relation to the essential content of a building.

Quintilian, in *Institutio oratoria,* declared that "it is not without good reason that memory has been called the treasure house of eloquence. For our whole education depends on memory, and memory alone provides us with the facts, precedents, examples, and sayings which we draw upon when addressing an audience" (Book XI, ii, 1–2). Since the purpose of eloquence is to charm, persuade, or impress the listener, good speech must be judged on the basis of its content, although its form is also of great importance. Quintilian's conviction that the art of persuasion rests on memory implies that no argument can be convincing unless it includes what is already known. The epistemological consequences of this are far-reaching, and cast doubt on our capacity to understand or find significance in something entirely new. For St. Augustine, nothing can be known purely for itself: "just as beauty of language is achieved by a contrast of opposites . . . , the beauty of the course of this world is built up by a kind of rhetoric, not of words but of things, which employs this contrast of opposites" (*De Civitate Dei,* XI, 18). Both thinkers posit memory and the associations that memory enables us to make as necessary to the acquisition of knowledge.

Memory is an explicit part of the design of an eclectic building, for, as we have seen, historical models play a central role in the creation of such buildings. The architect culls his own memory for those forms from which he will construct his discourse. Whether or not his argument is original, his points will be made with the help of examples from the past, lending it authority, enlarging its resonance, and augmenting its cultural importance. Topoi (such as San Marco), in particular, serve to clarify his meaning, for as clearly recognizable analogues, they help to define the new concept.

An eclectic building communicates on two levels. If the design is successful, it transmits its meaning directly to the spectator, who responds by feeling charmed, being persuaded, or acknowledging himself impressed. Thus the quality of eclectic architecture is assessed by the degree to which it wins the assent of its audience, which is the purpose of its rhetoric. But those who remain unswayed may yet appreciate the skill with which the architect devised his argument, if they have sufficient knowledge to understand the historical references that are being made by the building.

Given Leighton Parks's belief that the task of ecclesiastical architecture was to suggest the old, and thus carry on the tradition to which not only the Episcopal church, but also the American people is heir, it was inevitable that the eclectic mode would be chosen for St. Bartholomew's. The building aimed both to express and, even more, to define the continuity between past and present. Thus the nature of the project necessitated a style of rhetoric dependent on memory, and the problems it posed were not problems of inventing architectural forms, but of defining just what tradition had been inherited. The task of the architect—no easy one—was to establish the nature of this inheritance and to embody it in a formal language that would, at once, persuade spectators of its continuing validity and impress them with its importance. This language had to be modern, in order to speak clearly in the modern age, as well as traditional, since the past was part of its meaning.

What was the core of this tradition? In its simplest formulation, it was the belief in the immanence of God. For Goodhue, as for Parks, the history of the world was the history of the progressive revelation of God on earth. Both the progress of science and the social gospel of Liberal Protestantism bore witness to the truth of this interpretation: the great Parousia described in Revelation was being realized in the world. Just as John's vision was at once a revelation of the future and a real experience in the present, so the kingdom of heaven to be revealed at the end of time was a reality in the here and now. This mystery lay at the heart of Parks's ministry. Its truth had been expressed in Hagia Sophia of sixth-century

Constantinople and in San Marco of eleventh-century Venice. This tradition, which Goodhue reaffirmed in St. Bartholomew's in New York, asserted that God dwells among men and that his presence can be perceived by each individual.

For Goodhue, as for Parks, the idea of immanence gave meaning to all of human life. But how was this idea understood? Certainly, neither thought that the concept had been definitively expressed in the past, and they believed that the past had represented its understanding of immanence in terms analogous to but not identical with the terms of the present. By the twentieth century, the idea of immanence comprised a complex web of associations and connotations in part woven from disparate cultural experiences in the past, and in part reflecting a new consciousness. In the modern mind, the equality and purity of Romanesque and the mysticism of Gothic coalesced with the quality of becoming of Byzantine architecture as characteristics of immanence. That is, the notion itself was eclectic. Its specifically modern quality is perhaps clearest in the importance given to preaching, in the importance of people sharing their understanding through public, verbal communication.

But while the socially oriented aspect of spirituality is central to the design of St. Bartholomew's, its rhetoric is directed primarily to the individual imagination, activated by the senses. By addressing both the social and the personal, Goodhue's design attempted to reconcile the public and the private, the intellectual and the emotional, the rational and the irrational. In the church of St. Bartholomew's, eclecticism serves as a brilliant rhetorical device, enabling the architecture to express, in an articulate and eloquent fashion, modern civilization's belief in the perfectability of the world.

APPENDIX I

MEMBERS OF THE VESTRY, 1914–1930

Biographical information is from obituaries in the *New York Times,* from A. Johnson and D. Malone, eds., *Dictionary of American Biography* (New York, 1931), and from Vestry Minutes of St. Bartholomew's Church. The biographies are in the order of the members' election to the vestry.

Henry Lewis Morris (1845–1917) Vestryman, 1877–99; Warden, 1899–1917. Appointed to the Building Committee March 1, 1915.

A New York lawyer, Henry Morris was a patron of the Metropolitan Museum of Art and of the American Museum of Natural History. He was a trustee of the Cathedral Church of St. John the Divine and of the diocesan Home for Old Men and Aged Couples, and was on the board of trustees of the Estate and Property of the Diocese of New York. A lay vice president of the Seaman's Institute, Morris was also active on the boards of the New York Life Insurance and Trust Company, the Fulton Trust Company, and the Westchester and Bronx Title and Mortgage Company. He was governor and treasurer of the Metropolitan Club. (Obituary, *New York Times,* November 1, 21:4)

William Butterworth (1843–1921) Vestryman, 1888–1908; Warden, 1908–19.

A graduate of Columbia Law School, William Butterworth was a prominent New York lawyer particularly noted for his patience, order, and sense of duty. A quiet and conservative man, he served as clerk to the vestry for many years, and was therefore responsible for overseeing and recording the procedures by which decisions about the construction of St. Bartholomew's were made. The originals of the documents discussed in the Appendix of Documents are in his hand. (Obituary, *New York Times,* November 25, 15:4)

William Worthen Appleton (1845–1924) Vestryman, 1899–1918; Warden, 1918–24. Appointed to the Building Committee December 14, 1914.

A partner in the publishing house of D. Appleton and Company, William Appleton was a political activist, working for the success of the Copyright Act (1891) and serving as president of the Publishers' Copyright League. As chairman of the Committee on Circulation for the New York Public Library, he was instrumental in setting up branch libraries throughout the city. He was also a director of the Bank of Savings and of the Institute for the Blind. (Obituary, *New York Times,* January 28, 15:3)

William Armstrong Greer (1870–1939) Vestryman, 1906–37. Appointed to the Building Committee March 1, 1915.

The son of Bishop David Greer, the former rector of St. Bartholomew's, William Greer was a governor of the New York Stock Exchange and a partner in the banking and brokerage firm of Greer, Crane and Webb. He served as treasurer to the Parish House on Forty-second Street and to the present Community House. (Obituary, *New York Times,* February 19, 39:3)

James Warren Lane (1864–1927) Vestryman, 1908–19; Warden, 1919–27. Appointed to the Building Committee December 14, 1914; appointed chairman of the Building Committee September 30, 1915.

James Lane was president of the E. W. Bliss Company and of the West Boylston Manufacturing Company. He was a director of the Importers and Traders Bank and of the Equitable Trust Company. (Obituary, *New York Times,* May 23, 21:3)

William B. Osgood Field (1870–1949) Vestryman, 1910–30. Appointed to the Building Committee December 14, 1914; appointed to the Art Committee October 25, 1929.

William Field was a mechanical engineer, educated at Stevens Institute of Technology and Columbia University. A lover of literature, he published several volumes of literary criticism. He served on the board of directors of the Sloane Hospital and of the House of Refuge in New York. He also directed the Metropolitan Opera Association. (Obituary, *New York Times,* November 7, 28:4)

Alvin W. Krech (1858–1928) Vestryman, 1912–27; Warden, 1927–28. Chairman of the Art Committee, 1914 and 1927–28.

Alvin Krech was a self-made man and one of the most remarkable members of the vestry. Born of German parents, he first entered the flour-milling business. Soon he was more profitably involved with the reorganization of the Union Pacific Railroad. In 1903, he became president of the Equitable Trust Company. A director of the City Investing Company, the Federal Sugar Refining Company, the Manhattan Railway Company, the Norfolk and Southern Railroad, the Wabash Railroad, the Western Maryland Railroad, the Denver and Rio Grande Railroad, and the American Ice Company, he was also a trustee of St. Bartholomew's Hospital and Clinic and of St. Luke's Hospital, and treasurer and director of the Permanent Blind Relief Fund. He was on the board of directors of the Metropolitan Opera Association and of the Philharmonic Society. He received the medal of the Legion of Honor (France) and was named Commendatore of the Crown of Italy and Officer of the Rumanian Crown.

As chairman of the Art Committee in 1914, he was involved in the hiring of Goodhue, and as treasurer of the vestry from 1915 to 1922, he played an important role in the financing of the project. His research, in 1926, into church decoration led to the adoption of the "Byzantine primitive type of mosaics" for the apse and narthex of the church.

Krech was the principal patron of another New York landmark, the Equitable Trust Building, at 120 Broadway. Designed by Ernest R. Graham and finished in 1915, the office skyscraper (forty stories, 1.4 million square feet of office space) was one of the largest structures yet built in New York. (Obituary, *New York Times,* May 4, 25:1)

Robert S. Brewster (1875–1939) Vestryman, 1915–27; Warden, 1927–39. Appointed chairman of the Building Committee, 1918; appointed chairman of the Art Committee October 25, 1929.

Robert Brewster was president of the New York Orthopaedic Dispensary and Hospital and of the Northern Westchester Hospital in Mt. Kisco. He was a trustee

of the Seaman's Bank for Savings, the Title Guarantee and Trust Company, and the New York City YMCA. He served on the board of directors of the Western Pacific Railroad, the Metropolitan Opera and Real Estate Corporation, the National Fuel Gas Company, and the Church Life Insurance Company. He was clerk of the vestry from 1925 to 1927. In the 1930s, Brewster became director of the Metropolitan Opera Association and president of the Metropolitan Opera and Real Estate Corporation. (Obituary, *New York Times,* December 25, 23:5)

Albert Goodsell Milbank (1873–1949) Vestryman, 1912–24; Warden, 1924–49.

A New York lawyer and senior partner in the firm of Milbank, Tweed, Hope and Hadley, Albert Milbank was a director of the Chase National Bank and a trustee of the Title Guarantee and Trust Company, Princeton University, the Pierpont Morgan Library, and Barnard College. President of the Milbank Memorial Fund, Milbank was a trustee and vice president of the New York Association for Improving the Condition of the Poor. He also served on the board of the Welfare Council of New York and was vice president of the Community Service Society. As a result of his activities in war relief during the First World War and the Second World War, he was decorated with the Order of St. Sava (Serbia) and awarded the Order of the British Empire. He was clerk of the vestry from 1919 to 1925. (Obituary, *New York Times,* May 8, 29:1)

J. Morgan Wing (1880–1930) Vestryman, 1915–22. No information available.

Philip Albright Small Franklin (1871–1939) Vestryman, 1915–39.

Philip Franklin was president of the International Mercantile Marine Company and of the Atlantic Transport Company of West Virginia and chairman of the United States Lines. He was on the board of directors of the Engineers Public Service division of the New York Indemnity Company, the National City Bank, the National Surety Company, the Terminal Warehouse Company, the Western New York Railroad, the Pennsylvania Railroad, and numerous other companies. He was a trustee of the Seaman's Bank for Savings and of the Atlantic Mutual Insurance Company. Franklin was awarded the Distinguished Service Medal of the United States, was decorated by the Legion of Honor (France), and was made Commander of the Order of

Leopold II (Belgium). (Obituary, *New York Times,* August 15, 19:1)

Elgin Ralston Lovell Gould (1860–1915) Vestryman and Treasurer, 1905–15. Appointed chairman of the Building Committee March 1, 1915.

Known primarily as an economist and a social reformer, Elgin Gould lectured at the University of Chicago, Johns Hopkins University, and Columbia University. His concern for the condition of the laboring class led him to organize the City and Suburban Homes Company of New York, whose aim was to provide low-cost housing. He was instrumental in creating the Citizens Union and served as chairman of the board for the League for Political Education. His books include *Housing the Working People, Popular Control of the Liquor Traffic,* and *The Social Condition of Labor.* (Obituary, *New York Times,* August 19, 9:1)

John Clinton Gray (1834–1915) Vestryman, 1905–15.

A graduate of Harvard Law School, John Gray served as a lawyer in New York and, from 1888 to 1913, as a judge on the New York Court of Appeals. He was a member of the New York Academy of Design, the American Museum of Natural History, the New-York Historical Society, the New York Bar Association, and the Metropolitan Club. (Obituary, *New York Times,* June 28, 9:6)

William Douglas Sloane (1844–1915) Vestryman, 1898–1915.

William Sloane was a partner in the firm of W. and J. Sloane, a vice president and director of the City and Suburban Homes Company, and a trustee of the United States Trust Company and of Columbia University. He was on the board of directors of the Central and South American Telegraph Company, the Guaranty Safe Deposit Company, the Guaranty Trust Company, the Mahoning Railroad, the National City Bank, and many other companies. Active as a philanthropist, Sloane, with his brother, established a physics laboratory at Yale University and, with his wife, erected and endowed the Sloane Hospital for Women. (Obituary, *New York Times,* March 20, 13:3)

Anson Wales Hard (1840–1917) Vestryman, 1894–1915.

Anson Hard was a director of Hard and Rand and of the Bank of New York, vice president of the Chamber of Commerce (1897–1901), and a trustee of the Atlantic Mutual Insurance Company, the Norwich Union Fire Insurance Society, the Seaman's Bank for Savings, and the American Museum of Natural History. Hard was a member of the board of managers of St. Luke's Hospital and of the Home for Aged Men and Women at St. Johnsland. (Obituary, *New York Times,* January 21, 13:15)

William Williams (1862–1947) Vestryman, 1916–47.

A graduate of Yale Law School, William Williams became United States Commissioner of Immigration (1902–5, 1909–13) and Commissioner of the Water, Gas and Electricity Supply of New York City. He was a trustee of the Presbyterian Hospital and of the Seaman's Church Institute. (Obituary, *New York Times,* February 9, 63:3)

Carll Tucker (1881–1956) Vestryman, 1919–56.

A vice president of the Westchester County Emergency Work Bureau, Carll Tucker was also chairman of the Westchester County Children's Association and of the board of trustees of the Presbyterian Hospital and a director of the Seaman's Church Institute. (Obituary, *New York Times,* January 30, 21:3)

James Blackstone Taylor (1871–1956) Vestryman, 1922–39; Warden, 1939–50; Honorary Junior Warden, 1947–56. Appointed to the Art Committee October 25, 1929.

A New York stockbroker, James Taylor served as treasurer of St. Bartholomew's from 1921 to 1939, and was president of the Community House. He was a director of the American Can Company and of the Fifth Avenue Bank. (Obituary, *New York Times,* March 27, 35:3)

Edward Ridley Finch (1873–1965) Vestryman, 1924–28; Warden, 1928–40; Senior Warden, 1940–65.

A graduate of Columbia Law School, Edward Finch was a member of the New York State Legislature from 1901 to 1903. He became a justice of the New York Supreme Court in 1915, an associate justice in the Appellate Division in 1922, and an associate justice of the Court of Appeals in 1934. In 1922, President Harding chose him as envoy to Brazil. He founded the Child Welfare Committee and the Honest Ballot Association. Finch was named Chevalier of the Legion of Honor (France) and Commendatore of the Crown of Italy. He served as a trustee of the Cathedral Church of St. John the Divine and was a member of the board of the Washington Square Home for Friendless Girls, the YMCA, and the Judson Health Center. (Obituary, *New York Times,* September 16, 47:1)

Edward Henry Harriman Simmons (1876–1955) Vestryman, 1927–50; Warden, 1950–54; Honorary Vestryman, 1954–55.

A member of the New York Stock Exchange, Edward Simmons was its president from 1924 to 1930. He was chairman of the finance committee of St. Luke's Hospital. (Obituary, *New York Times,* May 22, 88:8)

George B. Post (1864–1937) Vestryman, 1927–37.

George Post, son of the architect of the same name, was a senior partner in the brokerage firm of Post and Flagg. He was a trustee of the Association for the Improvement of the Condition of the Poor, the New York Orthopaedic Dispensary and Hospital, and St. Bernard's Farm School. (Obituary, *New York Times,* May 26, 25:2)

William Nelson Davey (1874–1954) Vestryman, 1928–54. Appointed to the Art Committee October 25, 1929.

William Davey was a member of the advisory board of the Bureau of War Risk Insurance and insurance commissioner for the U.S. Shipping Board. He was chairman of the board of Johnson and Higgins, an insurance-brokerage firm. (Obituary, *New York Times,* January 9, 31:3)

APPENDIX II

DOCUMENTS

ABBREVIATIONS

ALA   Avery Library Archive, Columbia University. The Avery Library Archive has 3,500 letters, stored in 10 manuscript boxes, written by or addressed to Bertram Goodhue between 1903 and 1924.

SBA   St. Bartholomew's Archive. The St. Bartholomew's Archive stores financial statements from the 1880s to the present and, in five metal tubes, fifty-nine drawings of the church and forty-two drawings of the church complex, many of which were prepared by Goodhue's office and all of which are listed in an inventory at the church.

VM   Vestry Minutes. Nine volumes of Vestry Minutes, from 1835 to the present, are stored in the St. Bartholomew's Archive.

VMM   Vestry Memorandum. Two boxes of correspondence and memorandums relating to the construction of the present church are stored in the St. Bartholomew's Archive.

YB   *Year Book of St. Bartholomew's Parish.* Yearbooks, published from 1889 to 1937, are stored in the St. Bartholomew's Archive.

Chorley   E. C. Chorley, *The Centennial History of St. Bartholomew's Church, 1835–1935.*

April 19, 1914   Leighton Parks delivers the sermon "At the Commandment of the Lord." (SBA)

April 29, 1914   Letter, Bertram Goodhue to Arthur C. Jackson. Goodhue is aware that he is being considered for the commission of designing St. Bartholomew's, and he has made several rough sketches: "I walked over the other day and examined the new site and it seems to me that the opportunity offered is phenomenal, also I think there can be no question but that the style of the new building is already fixed, and that any design which disregarded the present beautiful triple portal would merit no consideration whatsoever on the part of the committee." (ALA)

May 15, 1914   Letter, Goodhue to Edward Goodhue. The vestry has asked Goodhue to present sketches, and he believes that the commission, "the most important ecclesiastical project now before the world of architecture," is his. (ALA)

May 28, 1914   The vestry is authorized to buy land from the Schaefer Brewing Company. The lot measures
> Park Avenue: 200 feet, 10 inches
> Fiftieth Street: 225 feet
> Fifty-first Street: 250 feet

A purchase price of $1.4 million is agreed on. (VM)

June 4, 1914   Alvin Krech reports for the Art Committee that having seen Goodhue's outline sketches for the proposed building, the committee is impressed by his ability "and peculiar qualifications for the work," and it recommends that he be hired as architect. This recommendation is accepted by the vestry, and the senior warden is authorized to prepare a contract.

Goodhue is instructed to make two drawings: showing the church occupying the entire Park Avenue frontage, and showing it on 125 feet of Park Avenue on the corner of Fiftieth Street (the southern half of the site). (VM)

June 30, 1914   Letter, Goodhue to C. Matlock Price. Goodhue has put Gothic design aside for the moment in favor of the style "Byzantine, Romanesque or whatever you call it—of the new St. Bartholomew's." (ALA)

July 10, 1914 Goodhue has signed the contract. (SBA)

August 12, 1914 Letter, Goodhue to Leighton Parks. Parks is vacationing in Europe. Goodhue reports on the progress of the "exhibition drawings" and assures Parks that "while the structural principle underlying the design is the same as that of Westminster Cathedral, the sentiment of the whole is quite different and the zebra effect so noticeable at Westminster entirely done away with." He recommends that Parks visit the following churches in Italy, which, although "none of them [is] altogether ideal or to be regarded as models for St. Bartholomew's . . . each contains wonderful bits of the style McKim, Mead and White had in mind when doing your triple portal: San Zeno at Verona; St. Ambrose, Milan; St. Michael's, Pavia; Cathedral of Borgo San Donnino; Cathedral of Parma; Cathedral of Placentia [Piacenza]; Cathedral of Cremona; Cathedral of Ferrara; Cathedral of Modena. The Churches of Bari and Bitonto are also of interest, but difficult of access." Most important of all is San Marco, "the church whose plan undoubtedly inspired that of Perigueux and, as undoubtedly the one I am now working on for you." (SBA)

October 20, 1914 Letter, Goodhue to Harry Eldredge Goodhue. "I am frantically busy with the drawings for St. Bartholomew's which, between you and me, I have a terrible fear may be rejected." (ALA)

November 6, 1914 Letter, Goodhue to Edward Goodhue. The cost of the new church may be about $750,000. Things are not going smoothly. Parks is unfriendly to Goodhue, and the vestry is strongly critical of his designs: "they are quite frank in saying that while the plans are perfect they hate what I have done in the way of design but they find it impossible to give the least hint of what they want, so I think I may lose this job." (ALA)

November 19, 1914 Letter, Goodhue to E. D. Robb. The watercolor rendering of the interior of St. Bartholomew's that Robb furnished made a bad impression on the Building Committee: "It seems impossible to suit them, try as I may." Goodhue is about to present a new set of designs for consideration. The new elevation "I think quite dreadful—so they will probably like it," and a third design is "an attempt to embody some of Dr. Parks' rather vague expressions of his wishes." (ALA)

November 23, 1914 Letter, Goodhue to E. D. Robb. "As things stand now, I guess I have got it [the commission] unless I deliberately and wilfully throw it away myself—not an impossible happening." (ALA)

December 14, 1914 Parks appoints the Building Committee, whose members are William Appleton, James Lane, and William Field. They will be responsible for the new building project. At the same meeting, Parks summarizes the results of two meetings held with Goodhue and Wallace Sabine, an acoustics expert and professor at Harvard University. Parks has also discussed the project with another architect, Charles Mathews.

Goodhue has been instructed to build a small wall in his studio, using the materials he has proposed for the exterior of the church. (VM)

December 18, 1914 Letter, Wallace Sabine to Goodhue. Sabine answers Goodhue's questions about the relative acoustic properties of a dome and a tower. While both would create acoustic difficulties if built of ordinary building materials, with the use of a strong absorbent material, the tower would create "but an imperceptible difficulty" and would be better than a dome. (SBA)

December 19, 1914 Letter, Goodhue to Leighton Parks. Goodhue reports what Sabine has written and updates his own progress with the plans. Although he has prepared several drawings showing the whole Park Avenue frontage being used, none of them is satisfactory. He is preparing two new perspective views of the exterior of the church, one of which shows "the north side of the front of the church, the little garden and the corner of the apartment house." He is having difficulty getting the right sort of brick to construct the sample wall. (SBA)

January 6, 1915 At a meeting of the vestry held in Goodhue's office, at 2 West Forty-seventh Street, Parks, as chairman of the Art Committee, reports that the sketches, drawings, and plans submitted by the architect are unsatisfactory. The wall constructed in Goodhue's studio was also found unsatisfactory.

The vestry examined the sketches and other materials and suggested changes that are communicated to Goodhue in the form of instructions: to introduce "a more ecclesiastical character" into the ground floor of the Fiftieth Street façade; to redraw the lantern; and to consider using more decoration for the narthex.

From the nature of other parts of the discussion, it is clear that, at this point, the building is to occupy the southern half of the lot (125 feet on Park Avenue, and 225 feet on Fiftieth Street). On the northern portion of the lot, an open area of 75 feet on Park Avenue and 32 feet on Fifty-first Street is planned. No buildings are to be erected on this strip. (VM)

January 7, 1915 Letter, Goodhue to Edward Goodhue. The vestry, which he describes as "the gravest, most dignified body but absolutely the most whimsical and petulant children in matters architectural," has just examined "an enormous quantity of drawings" and has selected the last design: "I have no doubt if they will stop bothering me—but that I will be able to make a good thing of it." (ALA)

January 22, 1915 Goodhue presents drawings and sketches to the vestry, who then discuss them: "The question of the desirability of building the particular kind of church shown in the drawings or any other kind was thoroughly discussed and after each member of the vestry had expressed his individual views it was moved, duly seconded, and unanimously resolved that sketches I and I [sic] be accepted."

Goodhue is instructed to prepare working drawings. The estimate for the cost of the church is $500,000. (VM)

February 3, 1915 Letter, Goodhue to J. C. M. Keith. St. Bartholomew's may cost $600,000 or $700,000. (ALA)

March 1, 1915 Parks announces the names of the members of the Building Committee: Elgin Gould (chairman), Henry Morris, William Greer, James Lane, and William Field.

Permission is granted to the Schaefer Brewing Company to extend its occupancy of the site until May 1, 1916. (VM)

March 5, 1915 Letter, Goodhue to several brick manufacturers. Goodhue asks for samples. He needs a hard brick of salmon color, not too even in shape. He intends to use bricks of several heights and of different lengths of each height. (SBA)

March 8, 1915 Letter, Goodhue to Elgin Gould. The engineer W. D. Saunders estimates that it will take approximately six months to lay the foundations, and

Saunders's fee is $2,000. Goodhue presses Gould to make a decision in the near future regarding the hiring of Saunders and Henry C. Meyer, Jr., an engineer, as "working drawings are proceeding rapidly and we would be very glad of the presence of both in the office immediately." (SBA)

April 30, 1915 Letter, Goodhue to Leighton Parks. Parks has stopped by the office and approves "in the main" of the designs that Goodhue's draftsman, Clarence Stein, is working on. The matter of the sample brick is less satisfactory, but Goodhue promises that "we are straining every nerve to have more brick for you in the immediate future." (SBA)

May 7, 1915 Henry C. Meyer, Jr., has been hired on Goodhue's recommendation to design the heating and ventilating systems of the church.

The Art Committee is still not satisfied with the brick sample presented by Goodhue. (VM)

May 17, 1915 Letter, Goodhue to Arthur Molesworth. St. Bartholomew's is "an enormous low church sort of conventicle for the Rev. Leighton Parks." The style of the new church is determined by the "Southern French or possible Italianate Romanesque" of the Stanford White portal. The church will be "of brick with a considerable admixture of stone and may cost almost anything—certainly $800,000 or $900,000." (ALA)

June 10, 1915 Letter, Goodhue to Leighton Parks. Piccirilli Brothers has submitted an estimate of $1,550 for making the half-inch scale model of the exterior of the church. The model will have "all stone and brick courses carefully lined off and colored," and samples of the stone and brick will be displayed alongside the model. (SBA)

June 15, 1915 Another set of brick samples has been rejected by the Art Committee.

Charles Mathews has advised the committee that in order to select the materials, they must have made a model showing the interior and the exterior of the church. Goodhue is instructed to make this model, which will cost "several thousand dollars."

Elgin Gould proposes (and the motion is carried) to eliminate the west gallery planned by Goodhue and to put the organ in its place. The seating capacity lost in that location will be made up by increasing the number of seats in the body of the church. (VM)

July 14, 1915   Letter, Horace S. Ely Real Estate Company. The firm estimates the value of the northern part of the lot at $575,000. The piece assessed measures 91 feet on Park Avenue and 250 feet on Fifty-first Street. However, the first 32 feet back from Park Avenue are restricted in use; the area may be landscaped or used for an entrance, but not built up. (SBA)

August 30, 1915   Letter, Goodhue to William Field. The northern portion of the lot may not be occupied by an apartment house, and the model of the church is coming along very well. (ALA)

September 15, 1915   Letter, Goodhue to Leighton Parks. The project of making the Racquet and Tennis Club adjoin the church is making progress. The model will not be finished on October 15, as promised; it will not be ready for exhibition until December. (SBA)

September 30, 1915   In the summer, Elgin Gould died. James Lane becomes chairman of the Building Committee. (VM)

October 22, 1915   The parish is willing to grant a sixty-day option at $600,000 to the Racquet and Tennis Club for the purchase of the northern side of the lot. However, the parish will retain title to the strip of 91 × 32 feet along Park Avenue. The club must design an exterior for its building that will resemble the church in style and material. (VM)

October 27, 1915   Parks tells James Lane of Goodhue's opinion about the advantages and disadvantages of using the northern section of the lot for the church.

The advantages are that the additional 25 feet of depth would "very greatly enhance the beauty of the building" and would permit 150 to 175 more seats in the church and 50 or 60 more seats in the chapel. Goodhue favors this sitting, even though "the Church will get practically no sun, the chapel no sun at all, neither will the work-rooms."

The increase of cost for the building will be $100,000. (SBA)

November 18, 1915   Letter, Goodhue to William Field. The Building Committee has not authorized the $1,000 extra needed for painting the interior of the model. (ALA)

November 24, 1915   Letter, William Field to Goodhue. "You know there is a strong undercurrent, and this is confidential, to keep the whole block! Don't throw a fit when I tell you this. It may not come through, but it has already gone far enough to hold up giving the option to the Club." (ALA)

December 6, 1915   The glass in the new church will be furnished by the Pittsburgh Plate Glass Company. (SBA)

January 11, 1916   The vestry has seen and approved the model of the church. Parks asks the vestry to use the whole frontage on Park Avenue for the church, as it "should without doubt add greatly to the beauty of the church and be a glory to the city." The vestry is attracted to the idea, but doubts that the necessary $1 million can be raised. (VM)

n.d.   Unsigned memorandum, a member of the vestry. He reports on a conversation with Goodhue. The estimated cost of the building is $650,000: "That does not include elaborate decoration in the interior but does include sufficient decoration to make the church presentable. It also includes all the ornaments on the outside with the exception of the freestanding figures on the South transept."

Goodhue agrees that it would be necessary to raise $1 million in order to occupy the full lot with the plan suggested.

Engraved invitations have been sent to the congregation to view the model at Goodhue's office beginning on January 17. (SBA)

February 9, 1916   Letter, Goodhue to James Lane. The clearing of the Park Avenue site is scheduled for July. Goodhue needs a list of everything to be saved from St. Bartholomew's II. (SBA)

February 11, 1916   Letter, Goodhue to John D. Moore. Although the model, as exhibited, showed only one-half of the lot being used, Goodhue hopes that the parish will decide to use the whole lot, thus eliminating the apartment building and giving greater opportunity for the development of the subsidiary church buildings. (ALA)

February 11, 1916   Letter, Goodhue to Peake Anderson. "The Parish is trembling on the verge of using the whole Park Avenue front, and I am pushing each member from behind as hard as I can." (ALA)

February 14, 1916   The Building Committee has studied three schemes (A, B, C) proposed by Goodhue.

Scheme A makes use of the southern half of the lot (as originally planned) and releases the northern half (assessed on July 14, 1915, at $575,000) for sale. Scheme B makes use of the whole lot and leaves nothing for sale. Scheme C uses the whole Park Avenue frontage, but not the entire depth of the lot, and releases two lots for sale on Fiftieth and Fifty-first streets.

In scheme B, the church is not placed on the center of the lot, but on the northern portion, to take advantage of the 25 feet of additional depth on the northern side of the property as compared with the southern. This greater depth will permit the lengthening of the nave of the church by one bay; that is, the addition of one window. The longer nave will allow additional seating, which is a major—perhaps the major—criterion in the design process.

St. Bartholomew's II sat 1033, whereas scheme B offers 1,275 seats (and, using folding chairs, about 1,500). The chapel of St. Bartholomew's II had a capacity of 175, whereas scheme B accommodates 210.

Scheme B, further, offers a Sunday school facility on the ground rather than the basement level and a rectory building.

Goodhue recommends scheme B (which is the scheme actually built), saying that the parish will thereby obtain "an architectural group that, if we may be permitted the use of such a term in connection with a design of our own, may be regarded as a monument among the churches of America, something that will take its place beside Old Trinity, Grace, the Brick Church, the new Cathedral and the Chapel of the Intercession as a permanent, not a temporary landmark in New York."

Attached to these proposals are cost estimates from two construction companies. Marc Eidlitz and Son, which eventually won the contract, estimated the cost of the church itself at $714,000, the organ at $75,000, the architect's fee at $72,700, and the rectory and Sunday school at $152,000. The total cost, including commissions and fees, will be $1,194,900.

The response of the vestry is emphatic; scheme B is chosen as superior "in point of excellence of design, architectural beauty and serviceability." Indeed, unless a way is found to finance this scheme, the vestry prefers to abandon all three proposals and start again from scratch.

Parks is asked to solicit funds for the project from the congregation. (VM)

February 27, 1916 Leighton Parks delivers the sermon "The House of Martha and Mary." (SBA)

February 28, 1916 Letter, Goodhue to William Field. Goodhue has heard about Parks's sermon and does not feel optimistic: "I have reached the point where if the Parish wishes me to go ahead and do as well as I can for them I will be delighted, while if they decide to throw over the whole project . . . . I shall be regretful but not despairing." (ALA)

March 6, 1916 Letter, Goodhue to Charles Mathews. Goodhue thanks Mathews for sending the message "keep up your courage," but wonders why it was sent. (ALA)

March 31, 1916 Letter, Goodhue to Leighton Parks. Goodhue gives a breakdown of the prices of certain portions of the church complex, since the parish is contemplating the temporary omission of some elements: "Although the Rectory, Sunday School, and Cloister might be built at a later time without any additional expense, the building of the Chapel, as a separate feature [that is, not attached to the church] would cause an increase in expense; but above all we wish to emphasize the fact that if the Church is built now with only two bays in the nave it would be impossible at a future time to add the third." (SBA)

April 7, 1916 A form to be used for subscriptions to the building fund is ready. The goal of $1 million must be reached by December 1, 1916. (VM)

n.d. At least four gifts of $100,000 each have been made by James Lane, Henry Clay Frick, Mr. and Mrs. Charles Harkness, and Mrs. William Douglas Sloane. (Chorley, p. 260)

April 14, 1916 Letter, Goodhue to Leighton Parks. Goodhue answers Parks's questions: the contractor has estimated that the church will cost $684,700 or, if the whole lot is used, $888,700. Goodhue reminds Parks that he never agreed that the building could be constructed for $500,000: "In fact, I distinctly remember, and feel sure you and the other members of the Art Committee will agree with me, that when this sum first was put forward, I smiled and said that you never could build such a building for such a sum; but that we might call it that for the time being."

Further, although Parks accuses Goodhue of being unwilling to design anything other than what the model shows, the architect claims that "this unwillingness extended only to making a design for a church in the Colonial style." (SBA)

April 18, 1916 Parks finds Goodhue's letter unsatisfactory and asks him to resign. (SBA)

April 24, 1916 Letter, William Field to Goodhue. "I have had a long talk with him [Parks] and, if you give me a little time, perhaps everything will be all right." (ALA)

April 27, 1916 Parks informs Goodhue that he intends to lay charges before the vestry that Goodhue has failed in his duty. (ALA)

April 29, 1916 Letter, Goodhue to William Field. "I regret deeply the offence that, it is quite evident, I have given Dr. Parks. Just what this offence may be, however, I am wholly at a loss to comprehend." (ALA)

April 29, 1916 Parks has visited Goodhue in his office, and they have discussed Parks's complaints. Goodhue is accused of having openly criticized his patrons, having made confidential information public, having withheld information from the parish, and having refused to meet with his clients. He apologizes and makes assurances for the future. (SBA)

April 29, 1916 Letter, Goodhue to Leighton Parks. Goodhue suggests ways to reduce the building cost from $888,700 to $763,700. He reports that the new acoustic tile that he used in the First Congregational Church, Montclair, New Jersey, will be ideal for St. Bartholomew's, and he invites Parks to see for himself. (ALA)

May 1, 1916 Letter, Leighton Parks to Goodhue. Parks accepts Goodhue's apology and reestablishes cordial relations. (SBA)

May 1, 1916 Letter, Leighton Parks to Goodhue. Parks reiterates that the chapel must seat 200 and that he would like to make the trip to Montclair to test the acoustic tile. (The trip is made on May 16.) (SBA)

May 8, 1916 Letter, James Lane to Albert Milbank. Lane comments on the organization of the work at St. Bartholomew's. Whereas his own experience of building "has been largely without the services of architects or of experts from outside," at St. Bartholomew's, a clerk of the works has been appointed, heating and acoustics experts have been engaged, and the vestry is about to sign a contract with an engineer. (SBA)

May 25, 1916 Goodhue informs Parks that he will proceed with the working drawings for the church (approved by the Art Committee on May 24) on receipt of written authorization from the vestry. In order to make cost estimates by August, he has to probe the area where the foundations will be laid.

He urges the committee to hire W. D. Saunders for the foundations, since this engineer helped the New York Central Railroad with its tunnel beneath Park Avenue and "is now employed on the various apartment buildings going up opposite your site." (SBA)

June 6, 1916 An account for the project has been opened at the Equitable Trust Company of New York. The Art Committee has instructed Goodhue to design a cross that will go on the lantern of the dome. (VM)

June 7, 1916 Letter, Goodhue to William Field. A new set of drawings has been prepared, and they show "a very much better thing than any that has gone before." (ALA)

June 7, 1916 The final drawings and plans for the project have been approved. Goodhue is told to proceed with the drawing up of the details and to make working drawings. (VM)

June 9, 1916 Letter, William Field to Goodhue. Parks is no longer angry, and Goodhue should continue work on the drawings: "I do not think there is much danger of the unpopular builders being thrust upon you. However, they tried to put over a very clever scheme." (ALA)

June 13, 1916 Letter, Goodhue to James Lane. Bids are being solicited from wrecking companies to clear the Park Avenue site during August. (SBA)

June 16, 1916 Goodhue informs Parks, the wardens, and the vestry that the contract that they propose, which seems to have been prepared by the construction contractors, is inadequate and will lead to "an endless series of difficulties that might and certainly should have been avoided." He has sent along his own version for them to consider. (SBA)

July 3, 1916 Letter, Goodhue to George Wilberforce Horsfield. St. Bartholomew's is "a wholly different performance from anything that ever emanated from this office." Clarence Stein is in charge of the project, and the office members have "converted themselves most successfully into Italians of the Romanesque period." (ALA)

July 3, 1916 Letter, Goodhue to John D. Moore. "Our last troubles are over with regard to St. Bartholomew's and work is to begin, I believe, the first of September." (ALA)

July 6, 1916 Decisions have been made about the new church, largely concerning which portions of the building are to be entirely finished and which left in a temporary state.

The interior of the church is to be entirely finished with a veneer of marble and stone; its upper portions are to be covered with Guastavino tile mixed with stone, colored marbles, and colored and gold tile. Both the reredos and the marble floors of St. Bartholomew's II are to be reused in the new church. The balcony fronts are to be carved and inlaid.

The walls of the vestibule are to be covered with marble; the vaults, with Guastavino and other tile.

The chapel will eventually have marble walls, but temporarily will be left with plaster only. (VMM)

July 21, 1916 Letter, Equitable Trust Company to James Lane. A model of the new church has been paid for. The cost was $3,970.18. (SBA)

August 11, 1916 The vestry has prepared a memorandum listing ten contractors and four buildings by each firm. Marc Eidlitz and Son is represented by the headquarters of Banker's Trust Company, Western Union Company, and Morgan Guaranty Trust Company, and by B. Altman department store. (VMM)

August 23, 1916 Letter, Goodhue to Harry Eldredge Goodhue. Bids for the construction of St. Bartholomew's will be opened on September 5. (ALA)

September 12, 1916 The Building Committee meets with Goodhue at his office. Eidlitz has been hired as building contractor over Goodhue's opposition. The price estimate of the building has risen, and the vestry informs Goodhue that unless the building can be executed at a price the parish can pay, the whole scheme will be abandoned. Goodhue replies that he can bring the cost down by eliminating certain parts and by substituting less costly materials in some places. (VMM)

The proposed reductions are enumerated in a memorandum. They consist of eliminating all decorative marble columns, bronze grilles, sculpture, wall veneers, and window tracery. The height of the church is to be reduced by 2.5 feet; cast stone will replace natural stone at about the height of 125 feet; and the length of the nave is to be reduced by one bay. (VMM)

September 14, 1916 Letter, Goodhue to James Lane. The list of reductions has been given to Eidlitz. However, the vestry does not understand that the price of labor and material has risen 15 to 20 percent all over the country since the estimates were made in the spring. It seems, complains Goodhue, that the church does not have full confidence in him.

Further, why must he work with a contractor whose bid was $100,000 higher than that of others as good? (SBA)

September 15, 1916 Letter, James Lane to Goodhue. Goodhue will have to work with Eidlitz, "and I can think of nothing better than their friendly rivalry with you in an effort to furnish the Church with the best services obtainable anywhere."

In a parting shot, Lane reminds Goodhue that since he had previously claimed that costs had risen 30 percent and now is claiming that they have risen 15 percent, Lane has reservations about the reliability of even this second figure. (SBA)

September 21, 1916 Letters, James Lane and Goodhue. Lane instructs Goodhue to inform all the construction contractors that submitted bids that their estimates have been rejected and that the parish has hired Marc Eidlitz and Son. (SBA)

September 21, 1916 Goodhue notifies the Globe Indemnity Company that the Northern Wrecking Company is in default of its contract, since it has not cleared the Park Avenue site for the excavations within the time limit provided by the contract. (SBA)

September 21, 1916 Lane tells Goodhue that he is impressed with the "manufactured stone" of the Emerson and Norris Company and hints that if it is used, the construction cost of the new church can be reduced. (SBA)

September 22, 1916 James Lane has also suggested this to Robert Brewster, who is familiar with the manufactured stone and has told a representative of the company to call on Goodhue and Eidlitz. (SBA)

October 3 or 6, 1916 Six schemes are proposed for reducing the estimated cost of the church: lower the height of the church by about 4 feet, omit marble veneers on the interior walls, eliminate stone floors in the church and chapel, use cast instead of natural stone for trim, leave sculptural ornaments in a rough state, and omit the tower over the crossing. (VMM)

October 11, 1916 Letter, Goodhue to Clarence Stein. "St. Bartholomew's has by no means yet ceased from troubling. I wish now I hadn't said I would make rough sketches for another scheme." (ALA)

November 1, 1916 Letter, Goodhue to James Lane. Goodhue asks that Henry Meyer be paid for drawings related to the discarded plan.

The new plans are almost ready: "Let me confirm my verbal offer that in case the cost of the new design proves too high or in case it does not meet with the approval of the Building Committee, I will make no charge to cover the cost to me of these new drawings." (SBA)

November 9, 1916 Goodhue submits a bill to Parks for $5,000 for working drawings of the new building. (SBA)

November 10, 1916 Sheet with comparison and estimates. Whereas in February 1916, the construction was to cost $968,600 and the architect was to receive $79,685, by September 7 construction was estimated at $1,203,550 and the architect's fee was $90,000. Thus the total cost of the project in September ($1,544,550) was $260,505 higher than it had been eight months earlier. All the schemes suggested on October 3 or 6 had pared back the cost by approximately $260,000, as the vestry had requested, and these reductions concerned the construction cost (reduced to about $920,000) and the architect's fee (now about $80,000)—precisely those areas where the biggest price jumps had occurred.

The latest estimate, of November 10, pulls the cost down to $1,110,577—below the estimate made in February. In this estimate, the cost of the building is reduced by an additional $130,000, and the architect's fee has dropped to $70,117. (SBA)

November 15, 1916 Memorandum describing scheme H. The height of the church is reduced by 3 feet, 9

inches. All marble work in the interior is replaced by Guastavino non-acoustic tile; all interior stonework is of cast stone, although the exterior stonework remains limestone. The church floor is of tile instead of blue slate (except for the chancel, which is marble). The chapel interior (walls, floors, roof) is left unfinished. The narthex floor is of tile, the walls are plastered, and the ceiling has Guastavino tile. The cloister arches and roof are omitted. In the subsidiary buildings, the floors and wood trim will be of hard pine, instead of oak. The mortuary chapel is left unfinished. The walls of the interior stairways are plastered, instead of faced with stone. Sodding in the garden is omitted. The four figures of the west window are left in the rough, to be carved later. The crossing tower is omitted, and a gilded coffered ceiling closes the lower portion of the tower. (SBA)

November 20, 1916 Letter, Eidlitz. Eidlitz will construct the church for $800,609, with an additional $76,300 allotted for ventilation, plumbing, and electricity. (SBA)

November 20, 1916 List of approved modifications. The tower is omitted, and the height of the church is lowered by 3 feet, 9 inches. The cloister and chapel sacristy are eliminated. Thinner slabs of stone facing on the exterior and a less expensive finish are to be used. The decoration of the north and south transept façades has been simplified in design. Marble veneer for the interior and for the apse, most bronze grilles, and stone trim at the windows are omitted. The floor of the church will be of tile instead of blue slate. All stonework in the interior will be of cast instead of cut stone. Trim will be of hard pine instead of oak. (SBA)

November 23, 1916 The vestry votes to adopt the revisions. Parks reports that Goodhue has informed him that it will not be possible to place the painting now over the altar in the same position in the new church. (VM)

December 12, 1916 Contract: R. Guastavino Company, to supply timbrel tile vaulting at a cost of $97,000. (SBA)

December 13, 1916 Letter, Goodhue to Wallace Sabine. The crossing will be temporarily closed with a colored, coffered, and gilded ceiling "instead of our very beautiful contraption (that is, a dome inside and a ciborio outside)." (ALA)

December 20, 1916 The Building Committee cannot accept some of the reductions approved on November 23. It is decided to restore the originally proposed height of the building and the chapel sacristy, and $10,000 has been added to the budget for this purpose. (VM)

January 4, 1917 Contract: Northern Wrecking Company, to clear the site. (SBA)

January 5, 1917 Contract: Post and McCord, to supply the structural steel. (SBA)

January 6, 1917 Goodhue suggests revisions to the contract that is being prepared for signature by the parish and Eidlitz. He wants the changes that have been made in the design included in the contract and the drawings signed by Eidlitz. (SBA)

January 7, 1917 Leighton Parks delivers the sermon "The New Church." (SBA)

January 10, 1917 The White Fireproofing Construction Company will erect the four crossing piers and their arches. (SBA)

January 22, 1917 The brick samples are approved by the vestry, although the members were not entirely satisfied ("as the vestry made no criticism of them, approval was inferred"). (VM)

January 23, 1917 Letter, Goodhue to James Lane. Goodhue opposes reusing the columns from St. Bartholomew's II in the new chapel, as this will not save money in the long run. He wants to use new granite two-piece columns, which will cost $3,900. (SBA)

January 26, 1917 Contracts: Piccirilli Brothers, for the modeling and carving; Charles P. Galardi, to supply the rubble masonry. (SBA)

January 30, 1917 Letter, Goodhue to Henry J. Hardenbergh. Goodhue thanks Hardenbergh for sending him the copy of Parks's January 7 sermon, and comments on it: "that the changes made in the plan are an improvement in the opinion of the architect is true if, that is, you use the word 'Plan' in its technical sense; but, of course, I cannot be expected to consider as an improvement the deletion of a lot of beautiful material." Goodhue expresses his satisfaction with Eidlitz, which has brought the cost of the building down significantly "by dint of frightening sub-contractors." (ALA)

January 31, 1917 Letter, to William Greer. Total payments made for the church between June 1 and December 13, 1916, are $1,004,219.66. (SBA)

February 3, 1917 Letter, Goodhue to James Lane. The new granite columns for the chapel are to be monolithic instead of two-piece. He has referred Lane's request for ample heating in the narthex to Henry Meyer. (SBA)

February 3, 1917 Contracts: William Angus Incorporated, to set all cast and cut stone; R. W. Hunt and Company, to test cement. (SBA)

February 8, 1917 Contracts: George Brown Company, to execute the cut stone, granite, and exterior marble for $114,136; Concrete Steel Company, to furnish steel reinforcing rods for $10,127. (SBA)

February 14, 1917 Eidlitz receives his first payment, $12,116.71. (SBA)

February 15, 1917 James Lane and Goodhue discuss whether it is necessary to lay acoustic material in the foundations to prevent sound or vibrations from trains passing under Park Avenue from entering the church. (SBA)

February 15, 1917 O. W. Ketcham has received $418 for supplying "Tygart" Fire Brick. (SBA)

February 16, 1917 The Gladding, McBean Company has received $4,750 for supplying roofing tile. (SBA)

March 5, 1917 Letter, James Lane to Robert Brewster. In excavating the lot in order to lay the foundations, Eidlitz has found that in one place the stone is soft, and in another, a large crevice full of earth extends 35 feet below sidewalk level. It has been necessary to blast out the soft stone in the places where the piers will go, and to fill the holes with concrete. These unforeseen complications will cost an additional $4,000 to $5,000. (SBA)

March 7, 1917 It has been decided not to install any insulating or acoustic material beneath the foundations. (SBA)

March 7, 1917 The Art Committee, meeting in the rectory, takes resolutions on subject matter for the sculptural ornamentation on the interior and exterior of the building and of the texts and inscriptions. The resolutions are cast in the form of recommendations to Goodhue, subject to the approval of the vestry. (VMM)

March 8, 1917 If the parish wishes to be granted the full fireproof allowance of 40 percent on the contents and 60 percent on the building, in its insurance contract, more fire doors will have to be installed and wooden trim eliminated. (SBA)

March 14, 1917 The vestry is informed about the fireproofing regulations and new difficulties encountered in laying the foundations of the building. The task will cost an additional $6,000 to $10,000. (VM)

March 14, 1917 The vestry resolves that the cornerstone will be laid on May 1 and that a medal will be struck to commemorate the occasion. A motion is passed to have a coat of arms designed for the church. The iconographic program is submitted for approval. Several changes have been made since March 7, particularly regarding the saints to be portrayed on the west front and on the capitals in the narthex.

WEST FRONT

March 7	*March 14*
Martin Luther	St. Paul
John Calvin	Martin Luther
Ulrich Zwingli	St. Francis of Assisi
Thomas Cranmer	Phillips Brooks

NARTHEX

St. Clement of Alexandria	St. Clement of Alexandria
St. John Chrysostom	St. John Chrysostom
St. Francis of Assisi	St. Athanasius
Pope Gregory I	Pope Gregory I
Hugh Latimer	John Wycliffe
Richard Hooker	Thomas Cranmer
John Wesley	John Wesley
Bishop William White	Bishop William White
George Williams	George Williams
Phillips Brooks	Louis Pasteur
General William Booth	Florence Nightingale
William Augustus	William Augustus
Muhlenberg	Muhlenberg

(VM)

n.d. Some undated sheets contain measurements and proposed subjects for the windows. It would seem, then, that there was an intention to make narrative stained-glass windows. This question was never discussed in a vestry meeting; hence the sheets may be work sheets belonging to the Art Committee. (SBA)

n.d. An undated sheet lists subjects chosen for the windows in the church. The west window will have scenes from the lives of the prophets whose emblems are in stone. The nave clerestory windows, of which there are five, will have scenes from the Passion of Christ. The apse windows will contain the life of Christ. The two narthex windows will depict symbols of the sacraments and other symbolic images. (SBA)

March 26, 1917 Letter, Goodhue. The "contemplated temporary wood roof over the dome" will not be a fire hazard, since it will hang 150 feet above the pavement level. There is no need to construct it of "incombustible material, such as very light steel members covered with corrugated iron." (SBA)

March 28, 1917 Letter, Goodhue to James Lane. Eidlitz had hoped to save $72,000 by substituting artificial for real stone. But the "cut stone people of New York" have been willing to reduce their estimate to $31,373, and thus the church could have the real stone and still save $40,627 from the original estimate. In order to use real stone in the interior of the church, Goodhue has simplified the drawings and is willing to waive his 7.5 percent commission on its cost. (SBA)

March 30, 1917 The Piccirilli Brothers will carve the interior stonework for $10,085. The Bluestone work will be executed by Best Brothers for $2,500. The George Brown Company will supply the exterior marble and limestone for $7,041. (ALA)

April 11, 1917 Contract: George Brown Company, to supply Tammany Buff stone with a sand-rubbed finish for the interior at a cost of $81,509, and limestone for the arches and cornices over the arcades and for the apse and nave columns at a cost of $97,730. (SBA)

April 23, 1917 Letter, Goodhue to Peake Anderson. "Thanks to a combination of wicked labour union methods and trade rivalries directed against Wheeler's concrete stone, only the other day we managed to change all of the interior from this material into real yellow Ohio stone." (ALA)

April 26, 1917 Letter, Goodhue to George Horsfield. "St. Bartholomew's, P.E. and Italian Romanesque . . . is going to be good I think, even though the style is so strange to us here; but St. Vincent Ferrer . . . is going to be a corker." (ALA)

April 26, 1917 The medal commemorating the foundation ceremony has been designed by Piccirilli Brothers, and it is hoped that it will be ready by May 1. It is also hoped that Pierre La Rose of Cambridge will have finished the design for the coat of arms.

The Skinner Company has offered to furnish the organ for $36,500.

The Building Committee has decided to yield to the recommendations of Goodhue and Eidlitz to use natural instead of artificial stone on the interior of the church.

It has been decided to place three brass crosses in front of the church in relatively the same position they are in at St. Bartholomew's II. (VM)

April 30, 1917 The additional cost of preparing the foundations, because of the soft stone, is $11,901. (VM)

May 1, 1917 St. Philip and St. James Day. The cornerstone is laid by David Greer, former rector of St. Bartholomew's and now bishop of the Diocese of New York. (YB)

June 6, 1917 An accounting of payments made to Eidlitz, $57,519.17. Payments have also been made to Goodhue ($5,000), Henry Boak ($1,000), and W. D. Saunders ($500). (VM)

June 22, 1917 Letter, Goodhue to Peake Anderson. "St. Bartholomew's is not yet in reproducible shape and I don't dare say whether it is going to be good or not, certainly some things about it are quite wonderful." (ALA)

June 25, 1917 Additional reinforcing rods for the four arches have cost $17,595. The concrete piers will be enclosed in wooden forms, onto which composite wire lath will be stapled. Guastavino tile will be laid on the wire lath. (SBA)

June 25, 1917 The Art Committee has been told to proceed with the decoration of the chapel, using $50,000 of the Harkness fund. (SBA)

June 27, 1917 Letter, Goodhue to James Lane. A clerk of the works has not been appointed to oversee the project. In the case of St. Vincent Ferrer, which is now under construction, a supervisor from his office was appointed. Although money was budgeted for someone in this position at St. Bartholomew's, nothing has been done. Perhaps the vestry is trying to cut corners? (SBA)

June 29, 1917 Letter, James Lane to Goodhue. Goodhue's letter calls for neither a response nor action. (SBA)

July 1, 1917 The church has been roofed over. (SBA)

July 5, 1917 Payment to Eidlitz, $62,339.94. (SBA)

August 13, 1917 William Field has been looking into the matter of stained-glass windows.

The George Brown Company will supply Tammany Buff stone for the chapel for $6,160. Best Brothers will lay a Bluestone floor in the chapel for $1,665. (SBA)

August 17, 1917 Contract: George Brown Company, to execute the marble work at a cost of $37,100. (SBA)

September 10, 1917 Total disbursement for the project to date:

New building	$ 278,453.75
Land	782,802.18
Mortgage	210,562.50
Total	$1,271,818.43 (SBA)

September 20, 1917 Payment to Eidlitz, $67,243.37. Payment to Pierre La Rose for designing the coat of arms of the church, $30. (SBA)

October 8, 1917 The Madison Avenue property and the buildings on it have been assessed at $1,337,500, while the cost of the new church and its land is valued at $2,400,000. Hence the parish has to increase its revenues, and it has been decided to charge 10 percent more for pews in the new church.

The commemorative medals struck in honor of the foundation ceremony are ready, and have been distributed to the members of the vestry. Four of the medals have been struck in gold. Three are to be presented to David Greer, Goodhue, and Eidlitz. The fourth will remain in the archive of the church. (VM)

October 18, 1917 Payment to Eidlitz, $65,869.29. (SBA)

November 19, 1917 Piccirilli Brothers has submitted a bill for $1,380 for modeling and carving.

Lee Lawrie has been paid $275 for executing models for the figures in the chapel. (SBA)

December 11, 1917 A memorandum details what is owed to Goodhue so far ($61,851.07) and what has been paid to him ($53,836.70). (SBA)

December 13, 1917 Payment to Eidlitz, $65,862.58. (SBA)

December 20, 1917 Payment to Goodhue, $8,014.37. (SBA)

January 2, 1918 Letter, Marc Eidlitz to Goodhue. The costs break down as follows:

Original estimated cost of church	$887,940
Extra for cut instead of cast stone in the interior	31,373
Extra for foundation work	11,901
Extra for the finish of the chapel	41,550
Total	$972,764

The area south of the chapel and west of the Sunday school is to be left in a rough state. It will be graded, but not sodded or planted. (SBA)

January 11, 1918 Eidlitz plans to begin the transfer of the Vanderbilt portico to the new location on March 1. (SBA)

January 11, 1918 Wallace Sabine advises Goodhue that for acoustic reasons, the ceiling over the crossing should be covered with felt or a porous fabric to avoid echoes. Since Akoustolith (acoustic tile) is not to be used for the lower part of the apse, this wall should be covered "with folded fabric of some heavy texture." (SBA)

January 16, 1918 The Building Committee has decided to omit all ornamental tile in order to save $14,650. It has not yet been decided whether to leave the conch of the apse in plain brick or paint it. (SBA)

January 25, 1918 The vestry authorizes Goodhue to provide a temporary ceiling over the crossing, which will not be entirely of wood, as originally planned. This will save $2,455. Further, all ornamental tile is to be omitted, saving $14,650.

Goodhue is instructed to accept bids for the organ casing from at least two firms besides Irving and Casson.

It is decided to ask Goodhue about the feasibility of reusing the present pews for the new church, thus saving the cost of new pews.

The parish intends to vacate the Madison Avenue premises within ninety days after March 1, 1918. (VM)

1918 Leighton Parks delivers the sermon "St. Bartholomew's Church, 1835–1918." (SBA)

January 29, 1918 The Building Committee is grateful for Wallace Sabine's advice regarding the crossing, but has decided not to follow his advice for the apse. (SBA)

January 29, 1918 Letter, Goodhue to Wallace Sabine. Goodhue clarifies the decision of the Building Committee. The sanctuary in St. Bartholomew's II is sheathed in marble, which has been found to be acoustically very favorable. It is felt that a porous fabric would absorb the sound of the choir and speaking voice and that it is necessary to have some reverberating surface to act as a sounding board. (SBA)

February 13, 1918 Payment to Eidlitz, $19,210.21. (SBA)

March 18, 1918 Payment to Eidlitz, $16,444.40. (SBA)

March 22, 1918 It has been decided to send one of the commemorative medals to the American Numismatic Society.

Permission is granted to Eidlitz to enter St. Bartholomew's II on May 1 and remove those materials that will be reused in the new church.

The Art Committee is empowered to decide, together with Goodhue, where to place the following items, which will be transferred from St. Bartholomew's II: altar painting, reredos, chancel furniture, and stained-glass windows. The old pew cushions will be remodeled for reuse. (VM)

April 10, 1918 William Grey is hired to decorate the ceiling of the chapel. (SBA)

April 16, 1918 Payment to Eidlitz, $31,283.25. (SBA)

April 25, 1918 Payment to Goodhue, $8,662.74. (SBA)

May 17, 1918 Payment to Eidlitz, $53,041.91. (SBA)

May 29, 1918 Letter, Goodhue to Ethel Parsons. Goodhue hopes that she will show him "more of your beautiful drawings for St. Bartholomew's" and is glad that she is "not so shocked by the decoration of the ceiling of the chapel as some other people." (ALA)

June 4, 1918 Contract: G. Owen Bonawit, to transfer stained glass from the old to the new church and to make new windows according to the sketches. (SBA)

June 11, 1918 Contract: George Brown Company, to execute the marble work and stonework for the floor of the chapel chancel and floors of the church chancel and apse, "using the present marble in the Old Church with necessary new marble." The present chancel rail will be recut and reset. (SBA)

June 17, 1918 Payment to Eidlitz, $43,947.27. (SBA)

July 17, 1918 Letter, Goodhue to Robert Brewster. Alvin Krech has broken the integrity of the side aisles by placing extra pews in the transepts: "A church building should be built to fit around the proper location of the pews. St. Bartholomew's was built to fit around the pews as arranged by us and approved by the Building Committee." (SBA)

August 5, 1918 Payment to Eidlitz, $53,054.41. (SBA)

September 12, 1918 Payment to Goodhue, $4,378.80. (SBA)

October 3, 1918 Eidlitz's estimate of the cost of painting the stained glass is $1,019. (SBA)

October 15, 1918 Letter, Goodhue to Leighton Parks. Flagpoles have been ordered for flags to hang in front of the church. The Moller Organ Company has promised to have the instrument ready for the opening of the church, on October 20. A sidewalk awning has been ordered. A flagpole for the chancel is being installed. Black and gold fabric will be hung in the sanctuary for the opening.

Further, the portraits on the narthex capitals follow the March 14, 1917, list and do not include Hildebrand. (SBA)

October 20, 1918 First service held in the new church. Leighton Parks delivers the sermon "Remarks of the Rector." (SBA)

n.d., but probably October 20, 1918 Bishop David Greer says that at a time like the present (referring to the First

World War), it is not right to complete the church: "your energy and substance must now be expended on a more immediate work, the work of defending and trying to maintain inviolate and safe that great and growing temple of our modern civilization." (Chorley, p. 267)

October 23, 1918 Letter, Goodhue to Edward Goodhue. Goodhue suggests that he has had a falling out with Parks. (ALA)

November 4, 1918 Private donations for the new church have been received.

The old premises have been leased at $500 a month. (VM)

November 11, 1918 Letter, Goodhue to Oscar Murray. "St. Bartholomew's was opened in a blaze of very low church glory and the rector expressed himself very prettily from the centre of the chancel steps. We had an awful row about a month ago but this was settled finally." (ALA)

November 11, 1918 Letter, Goodhue to Clarence Stein. The acoustic tile is slowly being installed, and the west organ case is now being put into place: "I wish myself that the ceiling had been a little livelier in design than it is. The shimmer of gold is altogether too diaphanous and the joint forms too strongly marked to suit me." Perhaps it will look better when the soffits of the crossing arches are in place. (ALA)

November 12, 1918 Letter, Goodhue to Peake Anderson. Goodhue describes the opening of the church: "Of course the whole thing is by no means finished, the principal feature of all, the 'ciborio' over the crossing being left until happier days. . . . The acoustic tile for the interior largely failed to put in an appearance . . . and its place had to be taken by felt covered with burlap. . . . The interior in its proportions and dimensions is pretty satisfactory, in somewhat the same fashion as Westminster Cathedral though, of course, not so big." (ALA)

December 7, 1918 Goodhue receives $40.02 for traveling expenses. (SBA)

December 21, 1918 Beginning on this date, all vestry meetings are held in the "Rector's Room in the church building, 51st and Park." (VM)

December 28, 1918 Payment to Eidlitz, $31,032.43. (SBA)

January 10, 1919 Payment to Goodhue, $1,437.17. (SBA)

February 3, 1919 The total amount received by Goodhue from August 27, 1914, to February 3, 1919, is $83,829.78. (SBA)

April 16, 1919 Letter, Goodhue to Leighton Parks. Prices of labor and materials have risen. The estimate for the completion of the tower over the crossing is, therefore, $273,000. (SBA)

May 27, 1919 Letter, Leighton Parks to the rector of St. Luke's Church, Norfolk, Virginia. Although Goodhue has designed a building "destined to be one of the most beautiful churches in the country," he would advise no one to sign "a contract with him drawn by his lawyer without the most careful attention to details," and "even for the advantage of his artistic gifts I should be unwilling to enter into any undertaking again of which he was to be the architect." (SBA)

June 3, 1919 Letter, Robert Brewster to Goodhue. The landscaping is nearing completion. (SBA)

June 27, 1919 Goodhue's estimate for the cost of a new lectern and pulpit is $2,300.
Goodhue suggests using the ten columns from the interior of the old church "in the proposed cloister." (VMM)

July 8, 1919 The building fund is insufficient to cover the cost of the windows proposed for the nave, which will cost $420 each. (SBA)

November 6, 1919 The vestry meetings are from now on held in the office of the rector, at 107 East Fiftieth Street.
The Building Committee authorizes the placement of three stained-glass windows in the north transept. Designed by Henry W. Young, the windows will be paid for through private donations. (VM)

December 8, 1919 In a report from the treasurer, the vestry is informed that $47,667.38 is left in the building fund. (VM)

1919 The Madison Avenue property is sold for $1,525,000. (YB)

March 14, 1920 Parks is requested to ask the congregation for $136,000, which is needed to meet the deficit in the building fund. (VM)

May 17, 1920 The building fund has received $35,000 in contributions as the result of an appeal. The vestry is asked to help raise funds. (VM)

August 3, 1920 Parks is authorized to have the windows in the chancel darkened. (VM)

January 9, 1921 The building fund has received $98,272.99. (VM)

April 10, 1921 The memorial tablets from the old church will be placed, temporarily, in the narthex of the new church. (VM)

May 23, 1921 The John Polachek Bronze and Iron Company estimates a charge of $320 for the removal of memorial tablets from storage and their installation. (SBA)

November 1921 Parks informs the vestry of his desire to resign, but he is persuaded to postpone this action. (VM)

March 14, 1922 Letter, Goodhue to Robert Brewster. "A while back, just how long I forget, Dr. Parks spoke of the necessity of doing something to complete St. Bartholomew's in some fashion or other. I take it that by this he meant the completion of the interior and the putting on of the feature (or a feature) over the crossing. Naturally, I am in sincere sympathy with any such idea for the church as it is, is in some ways a good deal of a barn and, with the exception of the Chapel, doesn't redound at all to my credit. . . . If you want me to, I'd be glad to ask Eidlitz to re-figure the completion of the church in accordance with the present drawings." (SBA)

January 7, 1923 The vestry decides that parishioners will be permitted to place memorial tablets on the walls of the church. (VM)

April 11, 1923 The consecration date for the new building is set: May 1, 1923.

The cost of a pew in the new building is about $1,000, and the cost of installing a memorial tablet is about $5,000.

The vestry thanks Parks for having raised the full amount ($155,000) of indebtedness for the new church. (VM)

May 1, 1923 St. Bartholomew's Church is consecrated.

May 6, 1923 Leighton Parks delivers the sermon "The Spiritual Significance of the Romanesque." (SBA)

December 5, 1923 The lectern designed by Lee Lawrie has been installed. (VM)

February 3, 1924 Thirteen memorial tablets have been placed in the church. (VM)

April 23, 1924 Goodhue dies.

November 3, 1924 Parks again tenders his resignation, and it is accepted by the vestry. (VM)

1925 In the preface to the *Year Book*, Parks urges the congregation to complete the church and establish an endowment fund. (YB)

May 3, 1925 Robert Norwood succeeds Parks as rector of St. Bartholomew's.

January 10, 1926 The vestry is considering preliminary sketches for a new Parish, or Community, House. (VM)

April 23, 1926 The budget for the Community House project is $575,000, and the architectural firm in charge will be Goodhue Associates. (VM)

June 8, 1926 The contractor for the new building will be Cauldwell-Wingate Company, whose bid of $609,026.20 is the lowest received. The buildings now on the site will have to be demolished. (VM)

January 12, 1927 Norwood intends to call a meeting of the vestry in order to discuss the completion of the church edifice and the decoration of its interior. Decisions will be made on the status of Goodhue's designs and drawings of the decoration. (VM)

February 17, 1927 F. L. S. Mayers and O. H. Murray of Goodhue Associates are requested to furnish new sketches. (VM)

April 21, 1927 The building fund has $87,905.54. (VM)

October 20, 1927 Alvin Krech reports that Charles Mathews has been appointed to the Art Committee.

The committee has decided "to adopt the Byzantine primitive type of mosaics for the embellishment of the apse and sanctuary of St. Bartholomew's Church." Goodhue Associates, in cooperation with Hildredth Meiere, will submit preliminary designs for the mosaics.

A vote of thanks is offered to Krech "for his earnest and most painstaking efforts in studying the matter of Church decoration and making such a complete and satisfactory report." (VM)

November 14, 1927 Alvin Krech reports for the Art Committee that Hildredth Meiere will receive $10,000 for her work. (VM)

November 29, 1927 The Community House is dedicated.

May 16, 1928 Mourning the death of Alvin Krech, who served on the vestry since 1912, the vestry recalls that "the decoration and embellishment of the church he took up with energy and enthusiasm, giving to the study of this subject profound thought and intense application. The beauty of the picture which will soon glorify the walls and dome of the sanctuary is due largely to this study, and it will serve as a worthy monument to his last service to the Church he loved so well."

A model of the mosaic is exhibited in the narthex. Charles Mathews has advised the vestry that some parts of it are unsatisfactory. Also under discussion is whether the Ravenna Company or another Italian firm should be hired to execute the mosaic. (VM)

October 31, 1928 The installation of the mosaics has begun, but work has been delayed because some marble deliveries had to be rejected. (VM)

November 26, 1928 Four windows, costing $2,500, have been donated for the narthex. Another gift of $750 will pay for one of the small windows beneath the rose window. (VM)

January 10, 1929 The cartoons for the apse mosaic have been attached to the wall surface, and scaffolding is being constructed.

Dr. Macon (assistant minister) informs the vestry of the following estimates for work in the church:

Dome	$350,000
Decoration of the narthex	55,000
Covering the four crossing arches with mosaics	100,000
Covering the rest of the exposed interior stone	50,000

The vestry decides to try to raise this money. (VM)

April 4, 1929 All future work of decoration must be approved by Charles Mathews. (VM)

October 25, 1929 During the summer, the apse mosaic was installed.

The Art Committee is asked to prepare a plan for the completion of the decoration and for the construction of the dome. The members of the committee are Robert Brewster (chairman), William Field, James Taylor, and William Nelson Davey. (VM)

December 16, 1929 The Building Committee is dissolved. Its remaining tasks will be taken over by the Art Committee.

The model for the bronze doors of the chapel has been approved. (VM)

December 16, 1929 The Art Committee makes its report. Detailed plans have been prepared for the dome. A celestial organ has been given. There is enough money to proceed with the mosaic decoration of the four crossing arches. Donations of $55,000 have been made toward the decoration of the narthex, whose walls and windows are already finished. Sketches for the narthex mosaics have been made. Designs for stained glass and windows in the north and south transepts are being prepared. (VM)

February 14, 1930 Baird Company's bid of $360,000 for the construction of the dome has been accepted. (VM)

December 2, 1930 The Art Committee is composing inscriptions for memorials to past vestrymen. (VM)

December 9, 1930 The decoration of the church interior and the construction of the dome are celebrated in a dedication ceremony.

1930 Robert Norwood celebrates the church decoration in the preface to the *Year Book:* "What were formerly brick surfaces have now given way to marble facings, mosaics and great stone arches. Stately bronze doors adorn the entrances to the baptistery and chapel, a number of stained glass windows appear in the transepts, a beautiful altar and altar rail have been installed and a celestial organ is the means of adding further beauty to our music. Last but not least there has been erected a dome which is outwardly appropriate to its surroundings and inwardly a work of art." (YB)

October 22, 1931 Bills totaling $795,802.59 have been paid from the Church Completion Fund.

The fund has collected $744,733.97 on pledges made, leaving $51,068.62 still to be collected. (VM)

September 28, 1932 Norwood dies.

November 14?, 1932 The proposed memorial tablet for Robert Norwood will cost $437. (VM)

December 20, 1932 All the bills for the completion of St. Bartholomew's Church have been paid. (VM)

APPENDIX III

TEXTS

AT THE COMMANDMENT OF THE LORD

"At the commandment of the Lord they rested in the tents, and at the commandment of the Lord they journeyed."

NUMBERS ix:23.

From time immemorial the journeyings of the children of Israel have been used as a parable of the history of the Church. That which distinguishes the migration of the Hebrew people from all other migrations is the consciousness of God's presence and the purpose to fulfill God's will. Our text is an illustration of this spiritual experience. The host was led, we are told, by the pillar of cloud by day and the pillar of fire by night. There were times when the cloud rested and then the congregation abode where they were, and when the cloud moved the congregation journeyed.

The Church, whether in its catholic or congregational aspect, has no visible guide today. But it is led by the Spirit of God and the mind of the Spirit is learned by the exercise of the human faculties of judgment and imagination sanctified by prayer. The former are affected by the natural events of life, and as they occur the Church seeks by prayer to free itself from prejudice and self-will so as to attain a right judgment in all things. These experiences, of which men do not often speak, but by which the lives of devout men and women are being developed, influence the corporate life of the congregation. While the circumstances of life remain normal and the opportunities for good work remain, the cloud rests—at the commandment of the Lord we rest. But when circumstances change rapidly and either the old work cannot be done, or a better work is seen, the cloud lifts and at the commandment of the Lord we journey. So interpreted the experiences of Israel in the wilderness are seen to be a parable of our experience in this city today.

Sermon delivered by Leighton Parks on April 19, 1914.

I am anxious this should be borne in mind, for otherwise when you learn the subject to which I have invited your attention this morning, you may think that those who are responsible for this parish are lacking in stability of purpose.

As I drew near the end of the tenth year of my ministry in this parish it seemed wise to announce the future policy of the church, and after consultation with the vestry and acting under their advice, I stated that it was believed to be our duty and privilege to continue the work of this parish in the building which is dear by association to many of the congregation and in the place where the church has been changed from a parish church, ministering almost exclusively to its own congregation, to a metropolitan church with two distinct congregations and where from all parts of the country strangers gather so that the influence of St. Bartholomew's is felt all over the land. Believing it was the commandment of the Lord we wished to rest in this tent and I asked that steps might be taken to provide an endowment to insure the perpetuation of the work.★

But that statement had scarcely been distributed among you when my attention was called to the fact that the mechanism of the organ was in such a state that it would be necessary practically to rebuild it at a cost of not less than $25,000, and probably considerably more. The committee of the vestry to whom the matter was referred was led to look more closely into the conditions and surroundings of the church and they found that the

★See "Moral Leadership and Other Sermons." Charles Scribner's Sons, New York, 1914.

roof, which has been a source of anxiety and expense for many years, must be entirely replaced. If these things were done it seemed as if we ought to repair the damage done to the interior of the church and this meant not only the repainting of the walls but an entire renovation of the chancel where the gold had begun to chip off and what looked like marble but was plaster was badly cracked. To make the church what it was fifteen years ago would cost I think at least $100,000, but this was not the worst. The foundations of the church—whether on account of the building of the great structure opposite or because of original fault—were settling so that the floor sagged. While there is no cause for alarm it is doubtful if this building could be saved without an expenditure that would cripple our usefulness.

When these facts were reported to the vestry they wasted no time in vain regrets. Every one, I believe, had hoped to see this church continue for many years on this place and in this house. But when it was found that the house had to be practically rebuilt they considered the effect of the recent changes in the immediate neighborhood. The result of the great building opposite has been to turn this part of Madison Avenue into a canyon, and the wind, driving back from the high wall, not only sweeps into the church each time the doors are opened, making the seatings in the rear of the church most uncomfortable, but prevents the proper ventilating of the church without creating a dangerous draft and makes both entrance and exit to and from the church dangerous for delicate or elderly people. There have been times of late when in a storm no awning could be kept in place for a wedding.

These conditions are not likely to grow better, but rather worse if, as is probable, other high buildings are erected in the immediate vicinity. There was another consideration: When the bronze doors and the facade were completed Bishop Greer spoke of them as "A notable work of architectural art; an enrichment of the city." But that can hardly be said to be the fact today. When that work was put in place there was a wide plaza between the church and the Grand Central Station from which the full effect of the work could be seen. It can still be admired in detail, but there is no point from which the effect of the work as a whole can be enjoyed.

When all these things were considered, the vestry, without a dissenting voice, decided that we must abandon this building and remove from this place.

Of course the first person to inform of this decision was Bishop Greer, not to obtain his official sanction, which will be formally requested later, but that he might know what the authorities of the parish, in which he is more interested than he can be in any other church in the diocese, thought should be done. I need not tell you that no such regret as he must have felt was expressed but only his generous and hearty agreement with what the vestry had decided. This of course was, as the lawyers say, "without prejudice," and did not commit him to an official sanction which cannot be given till application has been made in the manner required by canon.

When this momentous decision had been reached the exceedingly difficult question of deciding upon a new site for the church was before the vestry. Not to weary you with details I will state that there were three possibilities before them: First, south of 42d Street; second, north of 59th Street, and third, between 42d and 59th Streets. It was agreed that Park Avenue was the best location for a new church; but there was amongst the vestry, as there will be among you, difference of opinion as to which part of the Avenue it would be best to go.

It may help you to a right judgment if you know how those who have pews and sittings are distributed throughout the city. There are fifty-eight families living below 42d Street; thirty-one north of 59th Street and west of the Park; one hundred and sixty-eight north of 42d Street east and west to 59th Street, and seventy-three north of 59th Street and east of the Park. In other words, a little more than half the present congregation live between 42d Street and 59th Street.★

The portion of the city south of 42d Street was soon eliminated from their consideration. To go much above 59th Street would have interfered with other parishes and would probably not have been approved by the Bishop and the Standing Committee. There remained, then, land a little north of 59th Street and south of it. There were advantages and disadvantages in both. But after most careful consideration the vestry decided to take an option on the northeast corner of Park Avenue and 50th Street, and, if the license of the Bishop and the approval of the Standing Committee and the consent of the Supreme Court can be obtained, and, if

★This does not take into consideration a considerable number of people who without sittings look to this church for ministrations which are gladly given.

there be no valid objection on the part of the three nearest parishes—the Church of the Heavenly Rest, the Church of St. Mary the Virgin and St. Thomas's Church—to sell the land on which this church stands and rebuild there.

To many this must I know come as a great shock. The tenderest and deepest experiences of their lives are associated with this building. Here some of them were married; here their children were baptized; here their beloved dead were laid before being borne to the grave. Some of the vestry feel that more deeply than the Rector can, because of their longer association with the church. But he has not been forgetful of it and would have spared you had it not seemed necessary to ask for the sacrifice.

But apart from sentiment, the first thought I think will be, "If we must move why go only six blocks away—why not go where the bulk of the congregation will probably be living in the next ten years?" Apart from the uncertainty involved in that word "probably" and the ecclesiastical difficulties in choosing any place that pleases the fancy, there are other questions to be considered which have had great weight in deciding this matter. If we went north of 59th Street it would not be so easy for those living to the west of the Park to come to the church as it would be if it were south of that street, whereas those who live in the Seventies and Eighties can come down the Avenue to 50th Street about as easily as they could to, say, 60th Street. But unless we are willing to become a congregational church (not in polity but in constituency), it is desirable to keep in touch with the Parish House where at least four times a year the people who gather there look forward to worshipping in what the children call the "Big Church!"—at the Confirmation, the early Communion on Easter, the annual service of the Boys' Brigade, and the annual service of the united choirs of the parish. Moreover, a good part of the great congregation that gathers here every Sunday afternoon comes through the Grand Central Terminal and the plot at 50th Street was the nearest land available to the Parish House and the station. It is also the nearest to the great hotels where every winter people come for weeks at a time not—as we sometimes think—for shopping and frivolity alone, but also because of the educational and artistic and medical advantages of the city. They need the church and the church in ministering to them ministers to the country.

Some of the advantages of that site are these: All the land to the south is restricted by the owners,★ who will not sell but only lease, to buildings of not more than seven stories in height, so that we shall not be liable to have our light shut out by such buildings as are going up around us daily. We shall have the southerly light on one side and a wide avenue in front where there will be an opportunity for a better artistic effect than can easily be found today. A practical advantage which I think had great influence with some of the vestry who otherwise would have preferred to go farther north, is that at 50th Street there is rock foundation, whereas at the only other site available the land is swampy and a brook passes beneath the surface, so that reaching rockbed—essential now for any large building—would be a precarious and most expensive experiment.

Building operations are uncertain as to time and expense and I have no authority to speak on the subject, but if my hopes are fulfilled we may be able in two years to occupy a new church without interrupting the services here—and also, I hope, to dispose of this property to such advantage that the cost of land and a new church will not exhaust our resources but leave us a substantial sum for the foundation of the endowment to which your attention has already been called.

I have spoken of a new church but what is best in this we can take with us. The bronze doors and facade to be placed in a better light, the organ which in any case must be rebuilt, the memorials in the church and chapel, the great picture over the altar and the beautiful marble in the chancel—placed in a chancel more commodious than this where the communicants are often wearied by waiting and sometimes jostled by those trying to return to their seats.

"Are there no disadvantages," it may be asked, "in this new site?" There are; and they are so obvious that I do not think it necessary to speak of them! And now, as I know you are anxious to see this place for yourselves, I will only ask you, in the words of the prologue to King Henry the Fifth, to

"Let your *imaginary* forces work,
Piece out its imperfections with your *thoughts*."

What the bodily eye now sees is an unattractive brewery backed by mean houses and flanked by the obtrusive power-house; but what the eye of the imagination sees will depend upon yourselves. It is things

★One of the subsidiary boards of the N.Y.C. & H.R.R. [New York City and Harlem Rail Road].

that are unseen you must try to see—the land to the south and west covered with stately buildings and a church worthy of the present facade lifting itself into the sunlight, and then, if we succeed in our hope, the unseen will become real in time and your faith will be justified.

It has been said that no small part of the influence of our church in this city is due to its appeal to the imagination. The man who comes out of Wall Street has before him the beautiful spire of Trinity. If he continues up Broadway he passes the charming Renaissance Church—Old St. Paul's. Still farther north he comes to the gracious group of Grace Church. Then there is a long wilderness to pass but ultimately he sees the gorgeous French Gothic of St. Thomas's. May it be our privilege to place at the beginning of the new avenue, a thing of beauty which will give joy and peace and comfort to those who pass by and the same message as has ever been given here to those who enter its doors.

To accomplish this work in such a way as to bring a blessing will require the united interest of the whole congregation. I cannot set before you a better example than your own vestry, who have given ungrudgingly of their time, who have been without "pride of opinion" and acted as brothers for the welfare of the whole family.

This spirit we will all pray to have. We will try to keep before us the Ideal Church, where the rich and poor meet together; in which the beauty of holiness is prefigured by beauty of worship; where the concentrated energies of the congregation are enlisted for every good work; where the stranger is welcomed as a member of the family and the pure word of God is preached for the saving of souls.

If our next journey brings us a little nearer that ideal, we shall know that as we too "at the commandment of the Lord had rested in the tent," so again at the commandment of the Lord "we journeyed."

THE HOUSE OF MARTHA AND MARY

"Now Jesus loved Martha and her sister Mary"
ST. JOHN 11:5.

So far as we know the house of Martha and Mary was the only place in which our Saviour really felt at home. It was there he turned when the burden of work grew very heavy and found refreshment in the service and love that were offered him. It was there he wept when Lazarus died and it was there he told of the resurrection and the life, revealing it to those who alone were ready to receive it. And in that house he passed the last Sabbath before the crucifixion and received the last testimony of faith and love. "He loved Martha and her sister Mary." And he had reason to love them both. It was due to Martha, the practical, wise, energetic, laborious, economical spirit that the house was ordered in comfort so that there was always a place for him. Everything was prepared. Economy kept out debt, the foe of hospitality, and banished extravagance which substitutes luxury for comfort. This wise, strong, laborious, clear-headed woman made possible the home to which he could turn.

Sermon delivered by Leighton Parks on February 27, 1916.

Yet Martha had what the French call "the defects of her qualities," that is her limitations. Her work, as we say, "got on her nerves." She became anxious and apprehensive and so irritable and fault-finding. Now what we call Jesus' "rebuke" was not a rebuke at all, but the most tender sympathy. He knew that without her that home could not exist, and so when he saw her troubled about many things he tried to show her how the providing God was present and would comfort and sustain and provide so that in Him she could rest. She must turn from things to God—then things would become servants instead of masters.

And he loved Mary, the mystic, the soul that dwelt in heaven, so that when he came to that house Mary's welcome was indeed a welcome home. She was the one soul on earth that understood and her perfect devotion counted no cost if only she could express the feeling of her heart. Jesus loved Mary.

Now the house of Martha without the spirit of Mary would have been efficient but without atmosphere, and the house of Mary without Martha would have tended to an extravagance that led to disorder. It was in the house of Martha and of Mary, the house where utility and idealism dwelt together, the house where wise prudence and open-handed generosity were found in harmony that Jesus felt at home. Happy the man here today who knows something about that sort of a home, where the devoted energy of some woman is providing for his comfort and making it possible for him to do his work; where the unfailing love counts no cost too great to express the understanding of the man's heart, which no man can have. And blessed is that Church where the wise spirit of Martha is united with the loving joy of Mary. This brings us to the subject which you were called together this morning to consider,—the attempt on the part of this congregation to build a new home for Jesus Christ, a house of Martha and Mary.

When you leave the Church there will be handed you a paper giving a summary of what has been done in the last two years, which I will ask you to take home with you and read with care. And now if you will have patience for a little while I should like first of all to review these last two years.

When you were called together two years ago I said that the Vestry had decided that the time had now come when this Church should remove from this place and that they had bought new land on Park Avenue to establish a Church there. You were told also that we had hope to believe that by selling this property and one-half of the new property we should have money in hand to enable us to build a new Church, Chapel, Sunday-school rooms and Rectory, without calling on this congregation for any further gift at all. And when you heard that you experienced a sort of complacent satisfaction and you were rather proud of your Vestry and in a sense of your Rector that they could carry through such a fine business transaction and give us a new home for the old one that would cost us nothing. It appealed to the practical American sense of utility. It was the spirit of Martha and it was the right spirit in which to begin. But we have come now to the point where we find that when we thought we were working altogether in the spirit of Martha sub-consciously the spirit of Mary was influencing us; for we were ever demanding of the architect not merely utility but also beauty. Well, as a result we stand today in this position: the model of the proposed building, which you all have seen and which I am sure it is no exaggeration to say that ninety-eight per cent of the congregation is enthusiastic about, has neither the utility we had hoped for nor the economy that we had intended. It has not the

utility for which we hoped. It was found that the amount of land we had intended to hold for the Church is too small to enable us to place, first of all a Rectory (which I think is of small consequence), and would also necessitate a Chapel smaller than the one we now have, and would necessitate placing some of the classrooms of the Sunday-school below the level of the street, while the building of an apartment house or a club-house or whatever it is that is erected on that land would ruin the beauty of a Church built after that model. And that is not the worst, not only the beauty and the utility of the Church will be largely marred if not ruined, but in addition it will require $325,000.00 to build a Church which, when it is done, we shall be satisfied with neither from the standpoint of utility nor aesthetically.

Now why should these things be said, and said publicly? You cannot suppose it gives me any pleasure to say then, and you may be sure that I would have been glad if it had been possible to assemble the particular congregation of which I am minister and speak to them in private. But these things cannot be done. The whole country now knows what we have planned and it is just as well they should know the position in which we find ourselves today. We began in the spirit of Martha and like Martha we find ourselves troubled about *things*.

Now it is still possible to revert to the original plan, to wipe out all that has gone in these two years,—all the labor, money, effort and thought that has been given can be written off and we can start again and erect on the southerly side of that plot, on Park Avenue and 50th Street, a Church that will be suitable for our worship and I hope will have a certain dignity, but beauty it cannot have because it will be so overshadowed by the buildings that adjoin.

Nevertheless, if it be the wish of the congregation that that should be done that can be done, but before we come to that final decision I will ask you to consider one or two things. The first is this; that however we phrase a statement to cover the smaller plan and call it "a temporary retirement to rectify our lines," the whole world will judge it is a retreat. Now this parish, from its foundation, has never taken a backward step. I am not at liberty in this presence to remind you of what was done during the Rectorship of the Bishop, but some of you who are here know that in that day this Church was changed from an excellent, valuable, efficient Parish Church into a great Metropolitan Parish known all over this country, and its work copied in some Churches abroad. During all those years you never took a backward step. During the twelve years that I have been here the parish may not have made great advance but it has not made a backward step. It may not have gained a great victory but we have held the fort. But now, if after having seen the larger and more beautiful and efficient thing, we content ourselves with something that is less desirable, we may save money but we may lose something for which the Parish exists. For first of all I fear that an inconspicuous Church and a Church having no appeal to the imagination and a Church that does not stand out in this great city will fail to draw into its doors the great multitude of people from all parts of this country who year by year settle in this city and upon whom this Church in the years to come will be dependent for the constituency that is to keep alive the benificent activities of this Parish. And more than that, I fear your children will say, as they feel more and more the call of the country, "Why should we be interested in a Church that our fathers felt was a compromise?" How can we expect their enthusiasm and their loyalty to continue unless we leave them something that will appeal to mind and heart?

Now when we think of these things we hear once more the voice of Mary, and that says, "Think how beautiful this larger plan is, a Church like the model only greatly improved, a Chapel large enough for all needs and far more beautiful than the one we now have, a Rectory where your new Rector can serve you efficiently, Sunday-schools such as the children will delight in, a group of ecclesiastical buildings perhaps unequalled, certainly unsurpassed in the United States—a great gift of beauty to the city, a great witness to our faith in the power and eternity of the kingdom of God. Why count the cost—start the work and let the next generation if need be pay the bills—it will be worth it to them. *The time has come now, and if you miss it it never can be recovered.*"

Who does not feel the force of that appeal? Surely I feel it, but nevertheless I protest and so do the Vestry and so, I believe, do you against shifting our burden to the next generation that will have its own burden, if we ourselves are able to accomplish the greater work alone. It seems, then, as if we had reached an *impasse*— a retreat or the disaster that would follow debt. No, we have tried to work in the spirit of Martha and then we have been tempted to work in the spirit of Mary separately. Now let us see if the two cannot be combined. Yes, if in the spirit of Martha, prudent, far-

seeing, economical, this congregation will *provide the means needed before we begin,* then in the spirit of Mary the work of joy and beauty can be accomplished.

Now what are those means that are required? You will see by the paper to be given you where every calculation has been made by the Vestry of the gross sum for all that we desire and more than we had expected is $1,260,000.00. Since those figures were printed I have reason to believe that that amount can be somewhat shaded, and for practical purposes we will speak of one million dollars in order to accomplish that great and beautiful work. How can it be done? It can be done in various ways. The way in which such things are often done is for the Rector to abandon his ministry and go about from house to house as a public canvasser. Well, I will say to you what I said to the Vestry when this thing was brought home to me. I am not the man to do it. Forty years this year I have been in the ministry of the Church and I never had to serve a Church in debt and I never had to ask individuals for money. If that is the way it must be done then let me do what I asked the Vestry to let me do, resign and call in some other man of different traditions, better equipped for this work, younger, more energetic—let him do the work in that way and let me step out as quietly as twelve years ago I stepped in. "But before we come to that," the Vestry said, "let us see if there is no other way of doing this thing. Let us see what an appeal to the congregation will do." That is the reason I am speaking to you today. This does not require the minister who began as a pastor and a preacher to end as a promoter! Will you co-operate? How? Well, it is evident that if this work is to be accomplished it is to be not done alone by those who can give one, five or ten thousand dollars, it must be *begun* by those who can give one hundred thousand dollars. That need not be paid today—it may be subscribed, it may be paid in three annual payments in the next three years, but unless there is a certain number of people in this congregation who can provide such large sums as that and afterwards every one of us give what we can it is useless to undertake the work and we will settle ourselves with, I hope, dignity and serenity to meet the inevitable.

But perhaps we shall not have to consider failure. Perhaps this congregation will say to itself something like this: We often speak of the utilitarian spirit of the American people and hasty travellers from Europe gain no other impression, but we know that this is the most idealistic people the world has ever seen. Why we dream, in the midst of war we dream of universal peace and no ridicule or ill advised attempts to bring about premature peace, end the dream. What we see today is not the normal, not the necessary, not the eternal condition of man upon earth, but the horrible, the abnormal, the unnecessary! The ideal life of peace and brotherhood and mutual service and loving-kindness is God's will. That idealism is expressing itself in the religious life of this country. We have more sects than any country of the world, and economically disastrous as they are, ideally they are bearing witness to man's belief that the voice of God has not yet been heard in all the fullness in which it may be heard, so that every one of those new sects is the gathering together of idealists to hear a new word of God. And we show it in our practical affairs. Some of you can remember the Hudson River Railroad station on 28th or 29th Streets, some of you can remember the New Haven Rail Road on 32d Street, some of you can remember the sheds of the Pennsylvania Railroad in Jersey City. Well, they were serviceable, you could buy your ticket and find your train and start on your journey. But now we must have great palaces built over the gates of the splendid city that is about to come. Why even our stores rival in their towers the cathedrals of old! We have private houses like Italian palaces, we are no longer content with the useful, we are insisting that in banks, insurance companies, stores, railroads, libraries, private houses there be some expression of the beauty which underlies our somewhat sordid life. Perhaps those things will be remembered and some of you will say, If the Church, whatever it may have done in the equipment which it has today which was suited for its day and generation, now begins a new move and falls below the artistic

demand of the community it will fail to do the work that it desires to do.

I spoke some time ago to one of my friends who is doing a great work for the welfare of this city and said to him, "The city owes you much"; but he very finely answered, "I owe New York a great deal." So do I and so do you—you owe New York a great deal. Would it not be fine to give the city an object of beauty that would be a joy forever?

One more word and I have done. This is a day "when men's hearts are failing them for fear and for looking after those things that are coming on the earth," when the towers of heaven are shaken, and men and women are asking, Has Christ failed? Well, this is the day to prepare for what is coming, for when this deluge of blood has subsided we must have a home for those who would return to God. In the day when Jerusalem was besieged on every side, when it seemed as if the end had come, Jeremiah the prophet bought a piece of land and handed the evidences of the sale to a trustee and said, "Thus saith the Lord of hosts, the God of Israel, houses and lands and vineyards shall again be possessed in this land." Let us in this hour of darkness and of fear, testify by this outward and visible sign that we believe that the kingdom of God is to be established on this earth and in it men will dwell. What courage it would bring to this congregation, what strength it would be to our Church throughout the land, what rejoicing in this city if I could announce that the congregation, managing wisely like Martha by providing the means, would now in the spirit of Mary proceed to this great and beautiful work of making a new home for Him who though He were rich yet for our sakes became poor!

THE NEW CHURCH

You will all rejoice with me when I tell you that the million dollars asked for the new Church has been subscribed. It is a wonderful thing that such a sum should have been raised in ten months without any private solicitation on the part of the Rector. I will not say that no other congregation could have done it. I

will simply say that no other congregation has done it. I am humbly thankful to be your minister and I thank you for making a year of deep anxiety so easy and so successful.

There are certain questions you will wish answered:

1. "When may we expect our new church to be ready?"
   I cannot answer definitely but I hope by the autumn of 1918.

Portion of a New Year's address delivered by Leighton Parks on January 7, 1917.

2. "What is our position in regard to this property? Have we sold it with the uncertainty of finding a purchaser, with the possibility of loss?" That question I can answer, I believe to your entire satisfaction. Without going into technical details, I will say that the Vestry have entered into an agreement with a syndicate which the Vestry believe will protect the church from all loss and insure a price for the property entirely satisfactory to them, leaving us in possession of this church until we are ready to move into the new one. What that means you can appreciate.

3. "Will the million dollars subscribed be sufficient for the work as planned?" To what I will give as full an answer as possible at this moment.

If the contracts for the new building could have been let on March 1st last the million dollars would have been amply sufficient to build the church according to the model, also the chapel and the Sunday school rooms and the cloister, though not the rectory. But the contractors would have lost money because of the unprecedented increase since then in cost of labor and material.

But as the Vestry had determined not to sign a contract until the million dollars had been subscribed, or at least was in sight—we could not take advantage of the favorable market. Consequently the plans had to be modified. But this modification took the form of simplification of detail, and inasmuch as there is always danger of over-ornamentation in Romanesque, I can state that in the opinion of the Architect and of the Vestry, the changes made in the plan are an improvement. Two important structural changes have been made, first, what the Architect calls the "ciborium," but what is popularly known as the "dome" will not be built immediately, nor will the cloisters. Those can be added later. But the cost of all the work contracted for can be met and more than met by the million dollars. Certain other charges such as Architect's fees and interest on the carrying charges may entail a further cost, the amount of which I cannot now state. But when the congregation considers the extraordinary economic conditions of the times and the amount of labor given by the Vestry and the wisdom of their action, I know that there will be as liberal a response for a supplementary gift, if that should be needed, as was shown in the million dollar contribution. A sketch of the church as it will appear has been made by the Architect and hangs in the chapel porch where you can all see it.

THE ENDOWMENT FUND

A question which has not been formulated but which has been in the minds of many people is this: "Shall we not be put to larger expense in the maintenance of the new church, and have we any funds for that purpose?" This question was not absent from the thoughts of the Vestry, nor, need I add, from the Rector's. But to call for an endowment at such a time seemed impossible. That question was, however, asked me by one of the largest subscribers to the Building Fund, the late Charles W. Harkness. He spoke to me very earnestly on the subject. He said: "You will get the million dollars without difficulty" (we then had but $200,000), "and as soon as that is in hand begin on an endowment,—not a small one but a big one." This, he added, "I consider very important." I answered, "It is indeed important but it must be the work of my successor, the building of this church is the end of my work." He

Year Book of St. Bartholomew's Parish, 1917.

added some words of cheer and I never saw him again. In six weeks he was dead. Soon after his death Mrs. Harkness told me that he had spoken to her on the subject, and she knew that had he lived he would have given largely for that purpose, and therefore she wished to give as a memorial to her husband three hundred thousand dollars for the endowment of the new church. By a codicil to her will, made a few weeks before her own death, two hundred thousand dollars was added, so that the church will enjoy, from the day it is finished, an endowment of half a million dollars. I will not, in this formal statement, express an opinion on this munificent gift, except to say that it was purely voluntary. It was not suggested by me, for from neither of these generous souls did I ever ask a dollar. My object is to remind you that but for this great venture of faith on your part not one dollar of this endowment would have been received.

We are not out of our troubles,—there will be days

of anxiety and perplexity, as there have been in these past two years. But if ever a congregation had reason to thank God for answering the prayer of the Psalmist, "Prosper thou the work of our hands upon us, O prosper thou our handiwork," it is I.

So we enter upon a new year of Parish life with deepened reverence because of the memory of those who labored with us in the part and are now at test—with a strong sense of personal responsibility for our own souls and the community we call the Church, and with larger hope for this parish and its influence in the city.

ST. BARTHOLOMEW'S CHURCH, 1835–1918

The removal of the congregation from its present building to the new church seems an appropriate time for a consideration of the history of this parish. The origin of parishes differs greatly. Some of the early Colonial churches were founded by missionary societies like the London Society for the Propagation of the Gospel in Foreign Parts; others were planted by bishops who were true overseers, as were Bishop Hobart and Bishop Chase; others by devoted ministers like that apostle of Orange County, Dr. John Brown; others were swarms from older hives, as was the Church of the Incarnation from Grace. But St. Bartholomew's Church was the result of the zeal of laymen who, without even consultation with the bishop, so far as we know, and led by no clergyman, decided that the time had come to plant a new church in this city, and as a result, "In January 1835, a number of gentlemen residing in the Bowery and its vicinity, having deemed it expedient to form a new Episcopal Congregation in that neighbourhood, caused publication to be given in the different newspapers that divine service would be celebrated in Military Hall, on the morning and evening of Sunday, the 11th and 18th of January. In accordance with this notice a numerous congregation assembled and the Rev. Charles V. Kelly of Ohio officiated."

This is the first record in our parish register and with it the history of St. Bartholomew's Church begins. It is not necessary to remind New Yorkers that at that time the Bowery was still the garden in which well-to-do people lived, but it is hard for us to remember that eighty years ago New York was a city of but 250,000 inhabitants, and that these "gentlemen of the Bowery" were about to take a step which must have seemed to their more conservative brethren a venturesome undertaking, for they had in mind to build a church at the very northern limit of the city.

Other churches would soon follow their example: The Church of the Ascension, Grace and St. George's all within ten years, but St. Bartholomew's was the pioneer in that northern movement of the city which has now extended to Spuyten Duyvil.

Military Hall was No. 193 Bowery, and there the new congregation first worshipped, having elected as wardens Effingham H. Warner and Joseph Fowler, and as vestrymen David W. Townsend, Frederick R. Lee, John Ridley, Moses Bedell, Edwin Townsend, William R. Cooke, John W. Meserole and George J. W. Mabie. So far as I know, no descendents of the first vestry are to be found in this congregation with the exception of the grandson of Mr. John Ridley.★ It was not until much later that we meet the names of John Parkin, J. F. Butterworth, Jacob Reese, John Q. Aymar, Schuyler Livingston, Dr. J. W. Beck, Mr. and Mrs. Banyer, Mr. dePeyster, Mrs. George Dominick, H. H. Elliott, Lewis Gregory, Alfred L. Hoyt, Mr. and Mrs. Henry, Mr. and Mrs. Irving, Judge Nathaniel Pendleton, P. S. Van Rensselaer, J. Welling, William Rhinelander, William H. Appleton, James Roosevelt, William H. Vanderbilt and Cornelius Vanderbilt, all of whom are represented today in this congregation.

It was decided to build the church to be known as St. Bartholomew's on the corner of Great Jones Street and Lafayette Place, and on June 24th, 1835, being the feast of St. John the Baptist, the cornerstone was laid by the Right Reverend George Washington Doane, D.D., Bishop of New Jersey, acting for and at the request of the Bishop of the Diocese, who was prevented by indisposition from being present.

The first act of the vestry was to elect a rector, and they chose the Rev. Charles V. Kelly of Ohio. Mr. Kelly was, however, only nominally a resident of Ohio, for he had lately come to this country from Ireland,

---

Sermon delivered by Leighton Parks in January 1918.

★Mr. Justice Edward Ridley Finch and his children.

where he was born in the year 1803, being graduated from Trinity College, Dublin, in 1816. He must have been a man of engaging personality to have attracted the attention of the new congregation. Whether on account of an enlarged congregation or for other reasons which we do not know, on July 1st Military Hall was abandoned and a church in Christie Street, corner of Delancey Street, was leased from B. Rhinelander from October 1st to March 1st, 1836. By November of the same year we find that the pew rents amounted to $350, and the collections of the previous month to $92.26. A small beginning and of doubtful augury!

By June of the following year the congregation had moved into the basement of the new church and an order is given to dig a cistern. The fearful fire which had lately swept through the city was to lead to the introduction of the Croton water, but at this date the safety of the city depended upon a precarious supply. Whether as a result of this or for some other reason, we soon read that the basement had become so damp that it was impossible for the congregation to continue its meetings there. Meanwhile the vestry contracted with a Mr. Erban for the first organ, which was to cost $3,000. They also ordered a bell for the steeple to cost $1,250, and a little later a dial to be placed on the steeple. The vestry now authorized a special prayer book to be bought for the chorister, which shows us that in that day the congregational singing was led by a precentor. This chorister was required to hold a meeting once a week for the congregation for "its improvement in sacred music."

A little later difficulties about the music arose which continued for several years. In the first place, the chorister gave notice that he would be unable to attend the meetings on Wednesday and Friday in Lent, whereupon the vestry promptly decided that his services would be no longer required, a very excellent way of dealing with such a chorister!

It was soon found that a chorister was unsatisfactory, and a choir was formed with an orchestra to accompany them. Apparently this was not altogether satisfactory, for reasons which can easily be understood by those whose memories go back to the earlier days of church services, and the vestry is soon authorizing curtains to be placed in the gallery to hide the orchestra and singers. Still later we find the vestry complaining of the cost of the music, and the rector is instructed to inform the organist that under no circumstances is the appropriation to be exceeded, all of which seems to have been in vain. Troubles with the music have existed in many parishes, and we are fortunate that the problem was solved many years ago in this parish by the formation of a choir consisting not only of skilled musicians but also of reverent and devout members of the Church, which has added greatly to the artistic beauty of the service and to the devotion of the congregation. A long line of distinguished organists and choir-masters have conducted the musical services of this church, but to none of them is the congregation more indebted than to the present organist and choirmaster, Captain Arthur S. Hyde, who has combined a high degree of artistic finish with reverent and devout spirit.

Students of American history need not be reminded of the dreadful financial condition in which the whole country found itself in the year 1837. Whether this was due, as the Whigs asserted, to General Jackson's removal of the deposits from the United States Bank, or, as the Democrats retorted, "to the folly of the Whigs in distributing the surplus in the treasury among the several States," or whether the Whigs were right in declaring that Van Buren's insistence upon the continuance of "Jackson's tyranny" in requiring specie payments for custom duties and the purchase of government land we need not now enquire. The probability is that the mania for speculation which had spread like a malignant fever throughout the whole country from 1830 was now reaching its inevitable crisis. But whatever the cause the fact was appalling. In one week an hundred merchants in this city went into backruptcy, and within a month the number was beyond computation, and what was true of New York was true of every financial center. There were bread riots in the city and the whole country was in despair.★

Possibly the members who two years before had organized the new church were not uninfluenced by the speculative craze and believed that the prosperity of '35 was to continue forever. At any rate, the frail bark of the new church was caught in the tornado and well nigh foundered. Indeed, by November, 1837, the finances of the church were in such a serious state that the vestry applied to Trinity Church for a loan of $25,000 on a second mortgage on the church, every member of the vestry becoming security for the same. This loan Trinity refused to grant. The rights of the case it is hard at this distance to judge. There was a widespread feeling that the property of Trinity Church was intended to be held in trust for the benefit of all

★ See *Martin Van Buren*, by Edward M. Shepard. Houghton, Mifflin, Boston and New York.

the Episcopal Churches on this island, but on the other hand the trustees of Trinity not unnaturally felt that they had a responsibility in deciding what sums were to be given and to whom they were to be paid out. They had already loaned to St. Bartholomew's $20,000 at 6 per cent., taking a mortgage upon the church. To be asked in the midst of a great panic to advance $25,000 more and take a second mortgage could hardly have seemed to them a justifiable undertaking. But the state of the new church was almost desperate, and in December the vestry had written to the vestry of Trinity Church that the mason or builder had obtained a judgment for $4,500 against the corporation, and "that everything in the power of man had been done to avert the scandal." But some compromise must have been made, for the suit was not brought and the parish still staggered on under its great debt.

Trinity finally comes to the aid of the parish and agrees to lend $20,000, providing that the vestry will certify that there is no floating debt after a certain date. After "a prolonged argument" the vestry decides to place a new mortgage on the church and to pay Trinity 6 per cent. on the new debt. Before this can be done they must pay off $50,000 due the treasurer and a floating debt of $2,800. No doubt the case seemed hopeless, and, what was worse, the vestry and rector were not acting in harmony. At the next parish election no member of the vestry, with the exception of Samuel Jones, the senior warden, was retained in office. A letter from Mr. Kelly to the new vestry speaks with a certain complacency of the congregation's justification of his administration by the election of a new vestry, but as always in such cases this proved a Pyrrhic victory, for the minister who divides a congregation and brings in a new vestry is not the master of the situation but the leader of a faction. Soon after Mr. Kelly, apparently hopeless of the financial future of the parish, resigns, whereupon one warden and seven vestrymen resign also, so that the organization had practically to start anew. We recall this first and only quarrel in the parish with a deep sense of thankfulness that for eighty years there has never been a disturbance in the peace and harmony of this congregation, and that however difficult the position of the vestry at times may have been the rectors of this parish have always been relieved as far as possible from financial anxiety.

In August, 1838, the Rev. J. A. Johnston is called to the rectorship but promptly declines. We can well believe that no clergyman desired to become the rector of a parish that had had the unhappy history of St. Bar-

tholomew's in its past two years. The summer of 1838 must have been a most difficult one for the new congregation and "The gentlemen of the Bowery and its vicinity" must have had many private meetings and deep searchings of heart, but in September they called the Rev. Lewis P. Balch of Philadelphia who promptly accepts. The choice was a most fortunate one and from the installation of Mr. Balch the parish sets out on a path of prosperity which has grown longer and wider as the years have passed. As one reads the records of the vestry meetings there are only hints here and there, but they are illuminative. In the first place, the records of the vestry meetings are very short, always a healthful sign. Again, frequently the vestry adjourns for want of a quorum, a thing irritating to the rector and the members who attend, but on the whole showing a healthy state of affairs, for a vestry will always come together if there is trouble and when they do not come together it is a sure sign that things are going well!

In December there is a record that $40 is given to the Foreign Missionary Society. It is the first record of any payment for missions and shows that a new spirit had come into the parish and that it had begun to think less of itself and more of the Kingdom. Mr. Balch proposed an entire re-organization of the parochial activities and is evidently bringing a new spirit into the congregation. In January, 1839, payments to various missionary and charitable organizations are authorized by the vestry.

Mr. Balch also instituted a change in the management of the collections, which is our rule at this day and cannot be improved. Instead of the rector's appropriating the money received in the collection, it is all done by and with the approval of the vestry. In the autumn of '39 a parish school is begun, showing that the congregation has a sense of its duty to the neighborhood, so this year closes with every mark of increasing usefulness and prosperity. The fourth of July 1840 must have been a joyful day for the parish, because on the previous day Trinity Church had relinquished the mortgage for $20,000, leaving only the original $20,000 on which, so far as I know, interest was neither paid nor expected and which was finally relinquished by Trinity Parish during the present rectorship.

The vestry now evidently feel themselves able to indulge a little and so order cushions "trimmed with gold lace" to be placed on the desk and pulpit. But in 1841 things were not looking quite so bright and there was the inevitable tendency to turn once more to Trinity and ask for money. This apparently was the line of least resistance for all vestries to take, but fortunately (and I hope through the influence of the rector) action was first deferred and finally laid definitely aside. That the congregation was able to meet its debts was evident because in 1842 they decided to enlarge the church and 1844 opens with new evidences of financial prosperity. In May of that year Mr. Balch makes a suggestion which is worthy of our consideration as we are about to enter into the new church. He calls the attention of the vestry to the fact that numbers of young married people find themselves unable to pay the rentals which the expenses of the church made necessary, and he suggests that those who were well-to-do become responsible for one-half or two-thirds of the rental of certain pews and allow the vestry to sublet them for the balance, thus bringing the rental of seats within the means of those just beginning to build a home.

There is one member of this congregation whose sound judgment and clear mind are in no way affected by the weight of years, who remembers distinctly the ministry of Mr. Balch.★ She has told me that he was a man of untiring energy, who worked and preached with enthusiasm. He belonged to the old evangelical school and the institution meant far less to him than did individual souls. With them he dealt and as a result the congregation grew and prospered and became a living force in the community. His burden must have been very heavy, but it would seem that he bore it with cheerfulness and great courage until failing health made it necessary for him, in 1850, to resign. While St. Bartholomew's Church was soon to become a much larger and more conspicuous parish, I think it is not too much to say that its vigor is largely due to the fostering care of that good and wise pastor who for twelve years guided and inspired it.

In the year 1850 the Reverend Samuel Cooke became the rector. Of his ministry there are not a few of this congregation who have vivid and grateful remembrance. For twenty-one years Dr. Cooke continued in the old church on Great Jones Street and crowded congregations witnessed to his ability as a preacher. There are fashions in preaching as there are in architecture, and Dr. Cooke was one of the leading sermonizers of the day. His sermons were carefully written and each was a work of art. This was possible in the middle of the last century because, in spite of the growing city where villas were being built as far away as Union Square, life was a much more serene and quiet existence than we can easily imagine. Two services on Sunday, a Wednesday evening meeting and a Sunday-school

★Mrs. Wm. B. Parsons.

were all that any minister was expected to supervise. There was time for quiet study and faithful preparation and artistic development of the subject that appealed to the preacher. That there were temptations with such leisure every one who knows human nature can understand. But to those temptations Dr. Cooke did not yield. He was a reserved and quiet man, but a faithful pastor who knew his own sheep by name and for thirty-seven years he rendered an effective ministry to this congregation.

It was my privilege when a student in the seminary to hear him preach and after all these years I can remember well the sermon. It was the story of the widow woman who went out of the city to gather faggots and was met by the prophet Elijah. It was a vivid and picturesque description and no one who heard it could fail to be inspired by the deepest sympathy for this woman in her sore distress and the glory of the prophet's faith. Picturesque preaching has not departed from the church, but it is rare to hear today such sermons as Dr. Cooke preached. That the less formal and perhaps more direct preaching which this age demands has certain advantages it is to be hoped, but nevertheless we have lost, with the quiet leisure of former days, the more scholarly, picturesque and finished sermons which the faithful men of that day gave to their congregations, in rythmic prose.

By 1879 the conditions of the neighborhood about Lafayette Square had greatly changed and possibly the proximity of the Ascension and Grace Church and St. George's was drawing away from the church, but at any rate a feeling was growing that the congregation should make a move far to the north. It was suggested that Christ Church, then on the corner of Fifth Avenue and 35th Street, might be bought by St. Bartholomew's and the records show that when a proposition was made by this church to buy that property for $200,000 it was gladly accepted by the vestry, and a committee consisting of Mr. William H. Appleton and Mr. William H. Vanderbilt was appointed to carry out the plan. But nothing came of it. After many delays the committee finally reported that it was evident that "The vestry of Christ Church had made no effort to fulfill their pledges and did not intend to fulfill their pledges and therefore that the offer of this church be withdrawn." We can well imagine the indignation of men of the strict integrity of these gentlemen when they found that the word of a vestry was not so good as their bond, but we must not hastily conclude that the vestry of Christ Church had been unfaithful to their trust. The fact of the matter seems to be that they acted hastily and in the absence of their rector and that when he returned and found that the vestry was favorable to the transfer of the property to St. Bartholomew's Church, he declined to give his consent. Probably what the committee did not know but what Dr. Cooke clearly understood, was that the brilliant rector of Christ Church, Dr. Ewer, the leader of the new so-called ritualistic party, was most unwilling to have his church used by such a low churchman as Dr. Cooke, and I suppose that the indignation of the committee was increased by Dr. Cooke's ecclesiastical prejudices! However irritating it must have been to the vestry of St. Bartholomew's Church, we of this day may be thankful that the deal was not carried through, for it would inevitably have followed that the congregation would have been obliged to make another move within comparatively few years. Mr. William H. Vanderbilt now offers the property on which this church stands, which was owned by the New York and Harlem Railroad, for $150,000 and this the vestry proceeds to buy and to erect the present church from the plans of Mr. James Renwick★ at a cost of $379,684.

In 1873 the church was completed and the vestry passed the following resolution: "Resolved, That the thanks of this vestry is hereby tendered to Messrs. Roosevelt and Vanderbilt, the building committee, for the very successful and satisfactory manner in which they have discharged their laborious and arduous duties and that the church's completion and beauty is a more eloquent tribute to their labors than any words we can embody in this resolution."

There was, however, still a debt of $146,500 on the church and the vestry authorizes the rector to appeal to the congregation for subscriptions to pay the same in order that the church may be consecrated. This is promptly done and the names of all the subscribers and the sums given are duly entered in the parish register. Among those names we find several whose descendants or relatives are still with us: William H. Vanderbilt, Cornelius Vanderbilt, Miss Pearsall, James Roosevelt, William H. Appleton, Dr. Stephen A. Main, Alfred M. Hoyt, the Rev. Dr. Cooke, Henry Lewis Morris, Mrs. Tenbroeck, Mrs. Rhoades, Henry J. Barbey, William K. Thorne, Isaac L. Kip, Jacob Reese (two subscriptions), Mr. and Mrs. George A. Crocker, A. H. Pomroy, William H. Tillinghast, Mrs. Schuyler Livingston and Mrs. Eastman Benjamin. On February 21st, 1878, the present edifice was consecrated by Bishop Horatio Potter.

Here let us pause for a moment and remember that the parish records cannot give more than certain facts. The spirit which inspired minister and people we must imagine for ourselves. But this should not be difficult. The early financial difficulties of the building of two churches means that the rectors carried heavy burdens of responsibility. Then think of all the sermons that were preached in those forty years, what study, thought and prayer must have gone into them. What disappointment and despondency must have followed as a result of their meagre results! The long record of baptisms, confirmations, funerals and weddings★ means not only time and strength but also sympathetic exhaustion, yet that must not appear in public. Think what men like Mr. Kelly, harrassed by pecuniary cares, Mr. Balch, weakened by failing health, and Dr. Cooke, saddened by domestic grief, must have endured as they tried to fulfill their solemn obligations. Some of you who are here today are better men and women because of the ministration of those men who prayed for and with your parents and helped them with problems of your early life, of which you know nothing. And what is true of the ordained ministry is true of the unordained. There is but one record of spiritual work by the laity. When Mr. Jacob Reese died the vestry records its thankfulness for his faithful labors in the Sunday-school, but there were many more men and women who kept alive the spirit of missions and taught the young and ministered to the sick and needy, without whom all the money collected would be nothing worth. We know the names of but few:

> "Many a name, by man forgotten,
>   Lives forever round Thy throne:
> Lights, which earth-born mists have darkened,
>   There are shining full and clear,
> Princes in the court of heaven,
>   Nameless, unremembered here."

Here it may not be improper to say that it would have been wise had Dr. Cooke resigned, when the new church was consecrated. He had been the rector for thirty years and the church had now reached what seemed to be the high watermark of its prosperity. The whole congregation was grateful to him for his leadership in bringing the church to its new site and in paying off the heavy debt. And not only was he himself entering into the valley of the lengthening shadows but a new era had begun. The city now had a population of 800,000. The expansion of business and especially the development of the railroads had greatly increased

★See Appendix [Gifts and Endowments].

★See Appendix [Statistics].

the wealth of the country and the tide of immigration was changing the character both of the city and of the nation. The parish must now meet the new age with new activities. The Church itself was feeling the new spirit, missions were being enlarged, and Henry George's book, "Progress and Poverty," was piercing the consciences of Christian men and women. What was needed was a mind of new vision and yet whose judgment could be trusted. It was too much to ask that a man of Dr. Cooke's age should face the problems of the new world. Before long it became evident both to him and to his friends that the congregation was falling away and therefore he withdrew. But the man needed for the new work was found in Dr. David H. Greer.

He was not a visionary, he had the gift of revelation which enabled him to show to the people the vision which had been revealed to him and as a result money was poured into his hands until he was sometimes embarrassed by the riches that were offered him. The Parish House was built and then enlarged and then endowed. The Clinic, the like of which had never been seen either in Europe or in this country, and perhaps has not been surpassed even to this day, was built, fully equipped and presented to the parish. Then this church was adorned and beautified and the new choir was organized, which soon became known throughout the whole country for its reverent and beautiful service. The Year Book began to be published, giving a record of work already done and promise of still greater activity. The sending of little children into the country, which has done so much for the health and happiness of the community, was inaugurated, then through the generous liberality and hospitality of Mr. and Mrs. E. H. Van Ingen a sumptuous house at Washington, Connecticut, was opened for the members of the Girls' Club and then still later the Alfred L. Hoyt Memorial House at Pawling was given to the parish. There probably has never been a more varied and efficient ministry than that which changed this church from a prosperous parish to a great metropolitan organization. The election of such a rector to the Episcopate was as inevitable as it was desirable.

That the parish should not have fallen back after such a strenuous sixteen years when a new rector came is cause for humble thankfulness. The last fourteen years would have been but an inconspicuous interlude in the parish history had it not come to pass that some five years ago I was convinced, by a conversation with the late Mr. William Douglas Sloane, that the foundations of this building were settling and that the cost of rebuilding would be so great and that the present site would soon become so undesirable that a new church must be built.★

The history of that enterprise is too well known to need recapitulation. That a million dollars would be given without personal solicitation on the part of the Rector seemed incredible to all except a few, among whom should be named Mr. Henry Lewis Morris and Dr. E. R. L. Gould, but it was so and as a result a church that opens a new era in American architecture is rising on Park Avenue and will, we hope, be ready for divine service early in the autumn.

Had the course of this world continued as when this work began, all that I promised could have been fulfilled, but the storm broke and the floods arose and the landmarks were swept away and as the panic of 1837 nearly wrecked the parish, so the world-wide war has destroyed many of our hopes. The church cannot be finished at this time and while it has been possible to make our new church habitable for the sum we shall have in hand, the delay in building has increased the carrying charges on the land so that there will be a deficit on that account of a little over $100,000. Those who have been familiar with the conditions in the labor market and in the abrupt and unprecedented advance in the cost of material will, I think, be astonished to know that the vestry has been able to carry out such a work practically within the sum allotted. That we should be able to occupy our new building and practically to have paid for all the construction, is due largely to the firmness of the building committee. As the work progressed the architect naturally saw new beauties which would add to the glory of the church, but the building committee saw not only the glory but the cost, and resolutely declined to allow any changes in the plan and even decided to delay such embellishments as at this time could not be undertaken without incurring a debt. So while it is sad that there should be a deficit on the cost of the land, there is no reason to despair. One hundred thousand dollars is not so large for such a congregation as this as was $40,000 for the congregation of 1837. Moreover, the interest is provided for so that it can lie without being a burden until peace comes, and with peace and renewed prosperity you will be glad to give a great thanks offering as you have done in the past. Meanwhile we will bear our disappointment with patience and courage, for indeed it will seem as

---

★That the church should be moved from its present site was the opinion of Mr. John D. Wing expressed to me in the first year of my rectorship. But when I dissented, he dryly remarked: "You will see!"

but the small dust in the balance when we remember the destruction of Louvain and the desecration of Rheims. God grant we may not have to add Amiens!

I know that many of you must be sad today as you remember the years that are past, for not only were some of you baptized in this building, others confirmed, others married here: not only have you been inspired to nobler life and comforted in great sorrows, but you are "compassed about by a great cloud of witnesses"— those who once worshipped here with you seem near as long as the church which they loved is standing. But when that is removed can you ever feel in a new church that spiritual companionship which has consecrated this one? Believe me I sympathize with you. But we must remember that we too shall soon be gone, and if by our sacrifice a church better fitted for the new generation can arise in a city of six millions of people, then our sorrows will be sanctified. In the years to come others will tell the continued story of this church's life and try to guess what sort of men and women we were. Let us hope that we leave such a record that they, remembering us, will say then, as we say today, "considering the days of old": "As God was with our fathers so may he be with us."

APPENDIX

Since this paper was written, I have had the pleasure of reading Mr. Brander Matthews' charming reminiscences. I regret that the following extract could not have been incorporated in the text where it more properly belongs:

"Another and more enduring testimony of his judgment is St. Bartholomew's Church. My father had been elected a vestryman when the congregation occupied a bare and barn-like edifice on the corner of Lafayette Place and Great Jones Street. When the movement uptown led to the purchase of a new site at Madison Avenue and Forty-fourth Street, the vestrymen had almost accepted an empty and yet tawdry design by a builder devoid of architectural training. My father in disgust went to his old friend James Renwick, the architect of Grace Church and St. Patrick's Cathedral, and agreed to pay out of his own pocket for a more seemly design if the vestry should decline it. When Renwick and Sands had prepared the plans for the present church, my father procured bids from responsible builders, who stood ready to erect the more stately building for less money than the tasteless design was estimated to cost. In view of this combina-

tion of art and business, the other members of the vestry could not but see the advantage of entrusting the new church to the architects to whom my father had gone."★

Statistics

	Baptisms	Confirmations	Marriages	Burials
Record Book 1..	688	129	176	268
Record Book 2..	828	652	373	609
Record Book 3..	971	1624	415	694
Record Book 4..	1533	3374	865	1141
	4020	5779	1829	2712

Gifts and Endowments

First St. Bartholomew's Church, Lafayette Place and
Great Jones Street (northeast corner)

Cost of property	$24,500.00	
Cost of building	33,000.00	$57,500.00

Fifty lots purchased in Greenwood Cemetery — 3,000.00

Second St. Bartholomew's Church, Madison Avenue
and 44th street (southwest corner)

Cost of property	$150,000.00	
Cost of church and rectory .	229,684.00	
	$379,684.00	
Old church sold for	120,000.00	259,684.00
In 1894: Alterations to church and rectory		102,945.59
In 1910: Alterations transforming rectory into chapel and Sunday-school (special gifts not included)		39,545.38
Purchase and repairs of rectory		59,157.00

Third St. Bartholomew's Church, Park Avenue
50th and 51st Street

Cost of building 1,126,339.55

Swedish Church, East 127th Street, between Park
and Lexington Avenues

Land and building	$33,600.00	
Rectory and parish rooms ..	6,000.00	39,600.000

Parish House, 209 East 42nd Street

Total gift of land and building 335,143.16

Clinic, 213 East 42nd Street

Total gift of land and building 320,000.00

Alfred M. Hoyt Memorial House, Pawling, N.Y.

Total gift of land and buildings valued at — 30,000.00

St. Francis Chapel, Pawling, N.Y. — 3,657.73

Endowment of new church on Park Avenue ... 500,000.00

Endowment of Parish House $3,642,102.41

Endowment of Alfred M. Hoyt Memorial
House.................................. 15,000.00

Endowment of Clinic 20,000.00

$3,642,102.41

★These Many Years, by Brander Matthews. Charles Scribner's Sons. Pages 85, 86.

REMARKS OF THE RECTOR

It is my privilege to welcome you to your new church.

It was meet and right that our service should begin with the singing of the national anthem for thereby we saluted the flag in the chancel and the one on the outer wall of the church, both gifts of two members of this congregation. But there was even a deeper reason, for today our hearts beat high with righteous pride and are filled with holy hope that this country is about to end the desolating war by the "punishment of wickedness and vice and the maintenance of true religion and virtue."

While our thanks are due to Mr. Bertram Grosvenor Goodhue, the architect, for the commodious and beautiful structure he has designed, he has our sympathy as well, for first impressions are apt to be lasting and it is hard that his work should be judged by a building as incomplete as this one is. Not only have we been unable fully to complete the design, including the dome and the cloisters, but even what we had hoped to finish has been delayed by the conditions produced by the war. The chancel is left bare, the north wall is far from sightly, the acoustic tiles for the interior walls have not been delivered, and only a small part of the chancel organ has been installed. Nor is the color of the interior what later we hope it will be. Yet the two essential things that the Vestry had in mind, in the construction of this building, I hope are entirely successful. We believe that the acoustic conditions of the church are favorable to an intelligent participation in the services of the church and that the seating of the congregation is such that each worshipper has an unobstructed view of lectern and pulpit. The walls, which later are to be encrusted with tile, are at present covered by burlap, but all that you see is genuine and we have reason to believe that in its completed condition it will be a joy and inspiration. Yet in spite of all its present disadvantages we hope that those who have eyes to see will visualize this church not as it is today but as it is becoming and agree that Mr. Goodhue has struck a new note and designed a building which marks a new era in American church architecture.

Those who took part in the laying of the cornerstone only eighteen months ago will be filled with wonder at what they see today. Those who know what the industrial and economic conditions have been will join with us in thanks to Messrs. Marc Eidlitz & Sons, but

Sermon delivered by Leighton Parks on October 20, 1918.

for whom this work could never have been brought to its present condition. But beyond what is seen there is something deeper and more valuable still. There were two unusual facts in the construction of this church. There was no formal contract, and there was no clerk of the works! We placed ourselves in the hands of the contractors and they have guarded our interests as faithfully as their own. In the Second Book of Kings there is a beautiful verse which applies if not in letter at least in spirit to our present experience. When, under Josiah, the temple at Jerusalem was reconstructed and repaired, the writer, speaking of the "carpenters and builders and masons," says, "Howbeit there was no reckoning made with them of the money delivered into their hand because they dealt faithfully."

To the Wardens and Vestry of St. Bartholomew's Church, both Rector and congregation owe a deep debt of gratitude. For four years they have given to this parish the benefit of their unflagging service and cheerful co-operation, but there are two of them to whom I am sure we all owe a special debt.

Mr. James Warren Lane was Chairman of the Building Committee from the acceptance of the design until about six months ago. By his liberality the church was tided over a critical moment in its history, and by his wisdom and indefatigable energy the construction of this building was made possible. When owing to the pressure of other duties I insisted that he lay down the burden, Mr. Robert S. Brewster became Chairman of the Building Committee, and upon him devolved the manifold details of the conclusion of this work. His serene wisdom and cheerful kindliness made the rough places smooth. It is a deep regret to us, and I am sure to Mr. Brewster, that he is not present today. Indeed, we hurried the preparations for our opening service in the hope that he might be with us, but yesterday he was summoned by the Government to proceed at once to London for important war work.

These two men are but representatives of a Vestry which has so faithfully fulfilled its duties that I am sure both Architect and Contractor will say that the work was never hindered by unnecessary delay on the part of any Committee.

There is one other whose name should be spoke today in this church; Captain Arthur S. Hyde, our choirmaster, drew the specifications for the two great organs that we hope before long to have installed. He left the pleasant paths of peace and offered his services to the country as soon as war was declared. He is now in France but we know that today, amid the roar of the guns, he is hearing in his heart the sweet sounds of the familiar service of the Church which he so dearly loves.

And now we hope that this work, planned in the days of peace, carried on amid the tumult of war, dedicated in the dawn of victory, will be an instrument of God's glory by preparing the way of the Lord in the new world which has been revealed. We have been terrified by the whirlwind; we have trembled in the earthquake and been horrified by the fire, but today we

are hearing the still, small voice that tells us that all this great sacrifice is atoning. The things which could be shaken have been removed in order that those things which cannot be shaken may remain. What deep significance today have the words of the familiar hymn:

> "Crowns and thrones may perish
> Kingdoms rise and wane
> But the Church of Jesus
> Constant will remain."

THE SPIRITUAL SIGNIFICANCE OF THE ROMANESQUE

"And look that thou make them after their pattern, which was showed thee in the mount."

EXODUS 25:40

On Tuesday last we assembled for the solemn Consecration of a Church. The first buildings which the Church occupied for public worship were temples which the heathen had built, and inasmuch as in the fourth century the belief was widespread that such temples were the abode of evil spirits, it was inevitable that the first thought of consecration should be exorcism, the driving out of the evil spirits.

But any one who listened attentively or will read carefully the Order for Consecration of a Church ★ will see that its whole meaning is summed up in the prayer which precedes the final benediction—the thanksgiving for the promise of God's sacred presence in the "assembly of His saints."

In the centuries which have passed since a pagan temple was adapted to Christian worship, many different forms of buildings have been erected for the worship of God; and in each of them, the people have been consciously or subconsciously influenced by the thought expressed by our text, for all art is the expression of the ideal religion, or man's relation to God. Whatever may have been the economic, or political, or social reasons which led to the building of certain styles of churches, each of them expressed some particular thought of God and of man's relation to Him. Without attempt-

ing to trace the course of religious architecture from the beginning, let the older members of the congregation recall the churches with which they were familiar in their youth, and this truth will appear.

I. The "Wren" Churches.
After the Reformation, when Englishmen began to build churches to express the Protestant conception of the relation of man to God, a great architect appeared whose influence was felt for centuries—Sir Christopher Wren. His abiding monument is, of course, St. Paul's Cathedral in London, but all through the ancient city there are Wren churches. St. Clement Dane's in the Strand is familiar to every American traveller. But Wren's influence was also widespread in this country in colonial days. St. Paul's Church on lower Broadway, and King's Chapel in Boston are exquisite examples of this style, and when in imagination we enter such churches, we see at once the conception of God and of man's relation to Him which was dear to the people. The square pews were to accommodate a whole family; the Communion Table was inconspicuous. It was the great, high pulpit, underneath which stood the reading desk with its sumptuous cushion on which the great Bible lay, which caught the eye. On the chancel walls were painted or engraved the Lord's Prayer, the Ten Commandments, and the Creed. The whole atmosphere of the church led to the reverence of the Bible.

Sermon delivered by Leighton Parks on May 6, 1923.
★See Prayer Book, p. 546.

Chillingworth's dictum, "The Bible and the Bible alone is the religion of Protestants," dominated the building and the worship. The profound influence of such worship cannot be exaggerated. It was solemn, sober, ethical, character-moulding; and just as long as men could believe that every word in the sacred Scriptures had been uttered by God, that worship and the buildings which typified it, remained.

II. The Oxford Movement.

But in the middle of the nineteenth century occurred what is known as the Oxford Movement. It was the religious form of that Romantic movement which swept over Europe under the leadership of Goethe and Sir Walter Scott, and later of Victor Hugo. It glorified the past and denied that the Protestant Reformation was the final expression of man's relation to God. But instead of finding a nobler expression in the present or in the future, it turned back to the mediaeval thought which was expressed by that sublime architecture which we know as "Gothic." As a result, there began to appear in this country Gothic churches. One of the earliest, and I think one of the most beautiful, is St. Mary's Church at Burlington, New Jersey, designed by the elder Upjohn, and one of the latest, the chapel at Groton, designed by the late Henry Vaughn.

As works of art, these buildings and others like them far surpass the Wren churches, but if we ask ourselves what was the thought of God which the Gothic cathedral expressed, we shall see that it not only is in direct opposition to the thought of the Reformation, but is incompatible with the larger knowledge which has come through the study of science. So supreme is the technical excellence of this style, so exquisite is it as a work of art, that the esthetic taste has been satisfied and is justified in saying that no other style of architecture can be compared with it. But it should be remembered that the most splendid examples of the Gothic architecture are cathedrals, whose very size insures sublimity; too often the small parish churches built in this style are "pretty" rather than beautiful. If we separate the esthetic from the religious, the Gothic is the final form of church architecture; but if it be the expression of a thought of God and of man which the modern mind cannot accept, so far from helping religion, it will only serve to deepen the chasm between emotion and thought.

Now, the fundamental dogma of the mediaeval theology was introduced by St. Augustine by his doctrine of Original Sin and the utter depravity of man, which led inevitably to a theory of the Atonement which satisfied the divine justice of a Transcendent God who could be brought to the altar only by the magic influence of a priest; and the result of the inexorable logic of the Augustinian theology drove Christ from the Church. And therefore, the wall of the chancel, against which the crucifix hung, was broken down, and the crown and glory of the Gothic cathedral became the Lady Chapel, where the humanity of Christ was recalled by the worship of the Virgin.

The "dim, religious light" which influences the worshipper was the proper atmosphere for the soul that felt itself alienated from God. The intricate tracery which delights the eye of the artist was the expression of the speculation in which the mind had become entangled under the guidance of the Schoolmen. All this appeals to the mystic's sense of awe. It humbles man; it reminds him of death and of judgment and leads him, in the words of the psalmist, to "lay hold upon the horns of the altar," not that he may commune with the love of God but that he may escape the wrath of God. That all this expresses an essential element in religion, no serious-minded man will deny, but that the religious soul can rest in such a thought of God is incredible and, as we are seeing today, impossible.

III. The Romanesque.

But there was an earlier form of church architecture than the Gothic, and to that I would call your attention today. It is what is known technically as the Romanesque.

There are five characteristics in the Romanesque style of architecture:

(1) The Arch.

First there is the rounded or Roman arch which was taken over by the Italian builders from the ancient Roman structures with which they were familiar. The mechanical reasons for this we need not now consider. We recognize that the pointed arch was a development which had to be preceded by an earlier and more fundamental form. The pointed arch aspires; it leads the mind to think of the God who dwells above the firmament. But the rounded arch of ancient Rome typified two thoughts which have often been forgotten: it is the meeting of two great piers or columns; and the key stone insures its permanence. It is an outward and visible sign of human brotherhood. It does not express the escape of the individual from the common conditions of life, as does the pointed window; it preaches the gospel of brotherhood. Each stone is essential in the arch, and the great pillars on which the arch rests require foundations that can not be shaken. The brotherhood of man on the foundation that has been laid by God in the character of Jesus Christ is the first thought that the Romanesque expresses.

(2) The Chancel.

The second characteristic of the Romanesque is the apsidal chancel. The straight wall can be broken down and something added beyond, but the half circle of the apse cannot be broken without its destruction. In the early Romanesque churches, the seats for the clergy were ranged against this circular wall. The middle seat was occupied by the bishop, and so, the earliest form of the Episcopate was preserved by the symbolism of the chancel. There was no throne, as in the later churches, separating the bishop from the presbyters. They all sat together. The bishop was only the elder brother of the other clergy, and as the worshippers gazed upon the pastors sitting around the Holy Table, they were led to think of them not as a special order with magical powers, but as the encircling pastorate of the Church. The Holy Table was not placed at the end of the chancel, but in the middle of what is now called the sanctuary, that ministers and people might gather around it as the family gathers around the father's table, and in the Holy Communion the bishop naturally took the place that tradition assigns to our Saviour in the Last Supper, not turning his back upon the people but facing them, as a father faces the family when he breaks the daily bread.

(3) The Dome.

The third and most distinctive characteristic of the Romanesque is the dome. As the arch had been brought from Rome, and the apse perpetuated the earlier conception of the ministry, so the dome had been brought from the East. The early builders of Christian churches were familiar with the dome, which had been used in pagan days, as in the Pantheon. Victor Hugo says that the dome came to Rome from Carthage; but the Carthaginians were Phoenicians, that is, Semitics, a part of that great people who had swarmed out of Arabia, the noblest branch of which is the Hebrew. And the earliest edifice for Hebrew worship was the tabernacle or tent which was erected in the wilderness. Now, the dome is simply the top of the rounded tent, and is the first expression of the spiritual relation between man and God,—the great Shepherd dwells amongst His flock.

But the home of the dome became Byzantium, which we know as Constantinople, and the architecture which arose in the time of Constantine is called Byzantine. That passed into Italy and gave us St. Mark's at Venice and the ancient temples at Ravenna when the Exarch represented the Eastern Empire. Therefore, the Romanesque, which arose out of the Byzantine, also crowned its temples with the dome.

The dome signifies, not the transcendence but the immanence of God, God dwelling amongst His people. Now, just as the exclusive thought of the transcendence of God made the Atonement the fundamental dogma of the mediaeval theology, so did the immanence of God make the Incarnation—God's tabernacling in human life—the foundation of the Greek theology. It is that thought of God which we sometimes call modern. It is modern in the sense that the modern mind is profoundly affected by it, but it is ancient because it was the fundamental thought of the early Church. And that is what the dome stands for. There are those to whom the transcendence of God seems more sublime than the immanence of God, and yet when you consider the great buildings which express majesty most perfectly, you will remember that they are Santa Sophia at Constantinople, St. Peter's at Rome, St. Paul's in London, Les Invalides in Paris, and the Capitol at Washington. I know of no buildings which so fill the soul with a sense of majesty as do these buildings, crowned with the dome.

But the dome emphasizes more than majesty. It is the symbol of unity. It is more than the reproduction in stone of the ancient tent. It is a symbol of the overarching firmament. It crowns and unifies all the varieties of human life that appear in the various parts of the building. The immanence of God, the majesty of God, and the unity of God, are all expressed by the dome as they can be expressed by no other form. The spire which lifts its cross into the clouds is the symbol of the sceptre of a king. Its fundamental thought is force. When the speculation which tended to heresy disturbed the peace of the Church, the teachers did not meet it with sweet reasonableness, but with force; and the spire became the symbol of the irresistible power of the transcendent King. But the dome typifies a majesty that overshadows and unifies and sanctifies human life. "Dome" means "home"—the home of God and the home of man, and under the great dome, the soul felt its sin, not as in the mediaval church as a "fall" from which man could be lifted only by magic "grace," but as a stain which could be washed out by the love of

God revealed in Jesus Christ, and as a darkness which could be banished by light.

(4) The Windows.

There is something lacking in the Romanesque churches which from an artistic point of view makes them seem essentially inferior to the Gothic, and that is the absence of the gorgeous glass which is the glory of Rheims and Chartres and Yorkminster. The natural explanation is that the discovery of glass coincided with the rise of the Gothic arthitecture, but that is not a complete explanation because the Romanesque as it is known to us in its Norman form in England might easily have been filled with stained glass, but it is foreign to a fundamental thought which animated the builders of the Romanesque. They knew the glory of color, but they preferred to get it by pictures and mosaics, and blue and golden tiles. To let in the clear light of heaven seemed to these early builders essential, for the Greek thought of the revelation of Jesus was illumination: in his light and in his light only can we see light. Therefore they kept their windows clear, that God's light might shine into the building and glorify the inner life. It was symbolical of their whole conception of the meaning of God's redemption of man. Beautiful as the stained glass windows are, they shut out God's light, but the clear window allows the light of heaven to enter, and wherever that light enters, the church is glorified. To attempt in a Romanesque church to keep the walls sombre and monotonous is fatal to the glory of the building. To fill it with pictures and mosaics and then obscure the light by painted glass is an anachronism. We shall not know what the early builders had in mind to do until our church is filled with color illuminated by the clear light of the sun. Students of theology know that in the mediaeval church, "grace" was conceived as the antidote to sin, but in the Greek Church "grace" meant illumination. It is the illumination by the light of Christ which brings out the hidden glories of the soul which the Romanesque sought to symbolise.

(5) The Campanile.

In the Lombard form of the Romanesque, which has influenced the building of our own church, there appeared a new form—the campanile, in which the bells were hung to carry the Good News across the wide plains. This was a new departure. It showed that while the Romanesque builders were profoundly influenced by the past and wished to perpetuate that sense of the brotherhood of mankind which the Roman Empire had failed to spiritualize, and that Divine Presence which the Greek Church witnessed to, and the Light which is the life of men, they did not wish to prevent progress in religious thought, and as they looked across the wide plains of Lombardy and saw the poplars with their leafy crowns towering above the olives, they built the campanile, just as the Gothic builders later built the spire in imitation of the giant fir which lifted itself above the other trees of the German forest.

When the Romanesque passed to southern France and Burgundy, and so, in what we call Norman architecture, to northern France and England, the campanile was abandoned; spires were attempted in Germany, as at Spier and Worms, and in England the square tower replaced the dome, as at Rochester and Durham. All these changes witness to the perpetual progress of religious thought.

IV. Practical Elements.

I have been speaking of the spiritual significance of the Romanesque, but there is a practical element in these buildings which should not be overlooked. The Gothic cathedral with its long aisle and noble columns, was perfectly fitted for the sort of worship which the mediaeval mind desired. The people were separated from the priest; there was no need for them to hear; there was no need for them to see; the "sacring" bell would remind them when to abase and cross themselves as the Sacred Office proceeded. But in the Romanesque, there was an entirely different thought. The wide space under the dome provided a place for the congregation to see and hear and participate in the service. It made a perfect auditorium such as no Gothic cathedral could make.

Henry Ward Beecher once said that no soul had ever been converted in a Gothic church. That is one of those extravagant statements which will not bear close examination, but which do express a modicum of truth. There have been great preachers in the Gothic churches, such as Bossuet and Massillon and Lacordaire and Pere Hyacinthe, but it is true that most of the greatest preaching has been heard in the "Wren" and the early Romanesque churches. It is significant that the man who holds the place in ecclesiastical tradition which Demosthenes and Cicero hold in the history of Greece and Rome is Chrysostom, the golden-tongued orator who preached in the Byzantine churches of Antioch and Constantinople.

For an architect to have built a church in America which when it is completed will witness to human brotherhood, the eternal presence of God, the Table about which the disciples of Jesus may gather as a family and be strengthened and refreshed by the Divinely Human Life; in which the people can participate in the service and hear the Word of God, and which has the promise of perpetual progress, is a notable achievement. Its artistic value cannot be estimated until it is completed. But even now in it the soul may hear an echo of the great words of John: "The tabernacle of God is with men, and he will dwell with them, and they shall be his people, and God himself shall be with them, and be their God."★

★Revelation 21:3.

PREFACE TO THE YEAR BOOK OF ST. BARTHOLOMEW'S PARISH, 1925

The event of most importance to the Diocese this year is the campaign for the completion of the Cathedral of St. John the Divine, at a cost of fifteen million dollars. I have found myself unable to advise the parish to take part in this work, not because of any narrow parochialism, but because of prior moral obligations which, in my judgment, should be met before any other work is undertaken.

It will be remembered that when the Harkness gift of half a million dollars was made for the endowment of this church, Mrs. Harkness was assured that an effort would be made to increase the endowment, so that when the day, foreseen by her husband, Mr. Charles H. Harkness, came, when the city churches could no longer count upon a congregation of people of large means and must either be abandoned or minister to a community unable to support them, this church would be a house of prayer for all people. But this undertaking I have been unable to keep in the way I had hoped.

A beginning was made by an effort to have all deeds of privately owned pews turned in to the Vestry, so that when the time came, the authorities of the church would be free to deal with the new problem in the way that seemed best to them. This effort has been, in a large measure, successful. There are still a few privately owned pews which the proprietors have not been willing to relinquish, but when they clearly understand that their rights will be protected as long as they live, and that at their death the pews will have no pecuniary value, I am sure they will see that by a slight sacrifice on their part a much needed work can be accomplished.

Second, we have begun to embellish the church by simple memorials bearing the names of those who have been blessed by the services of the church, and have blessed it in return by gifts and by character. Their names are commemorated and their memories will be kept alive from generation to generation. When the opportunity thus offered, of erecting a memorial at a cost of either five thousand or one thousand dollars, has been taken advantage of, the endowment fund will steadily increase. More than this I have not been able to undertake because of a still prior moral obligation, of which I shall speak in a moment. But I am not willing to leave the subject of endowment without calling attention to a duty and a privilege to be met in years to come.

We are citizens of the richest country in the world, and perhaps never in the history of mankind have such gifts been given as we note in the last ten years in this country, and perhaps nowhere more generously than in this city. Fortunes beyond the dreams of avarice have been given for the endowment of hospitals, for research work, for the better housing of the poor, for libraries and art museums, for music, and for universities and technical schools, that the highest education may be within the reach of all. All this is well; and no doubt, much of it has been given in the Name, that is, in the Spirit of Christ.

But what I think is often overlooked is that no knowledge that does not lead to the knowledge of the glory of God can be a blessing. The Great War has shown that knowledge may become a curse. The fear, the reverence, the awful sense of the majesty of God's wisdom revealed in this universe, is the beginning of wisdom today, as truly as when the words were first spoken. All the beauty in the world that does not tend to reveal the beauty of holiness will degrade. The spirit of pity, which sympathizes with the sick and the poor, was generated by the Spirit of Christ. Unless there be

Year Book of St. Bartholomew's Parish, 1925.

some institution to enshrine the Spirit of Christ, who is the glory of God, all these gifts will be in vain. If that were remembered, I cannot doubt that those who have large wealth would ask themselves whether they are not under obligation, in the drawing of their wills, to give great gifts to the church, remembering that their children too often have abandoned the Church, and that unless their wealth is left for the perpetuation of the Church, while the institution will not fail, that part of it which has blessed them may be unable to live.

I would make it more definite. The numbers of those who have great wealth is limited, and comparatively few of them are interested in the Church. But there are many people who are beyond the fear of want, who might well bequeath moderate gifts which would be a blessing from generation to generation.

I am not satisfied that I have done my whole duty in this respect. Knowing the terrible abuses that have followed from the influence of priests and ministers upon the minds of the sick and the dying, I have not only scrupulously avoided suggesting to the sick that they should give gifts to the Church, but have in more than one instance refused to give advice without the concurrence of the patient's legal adviser. For a clergyman to be called as a witness in a suit to break a will on the ground of undue influence is a scandalous thing and cannot fail to injure the reputation of the minister and prejudice men against the Church. But the quaint rubric in the Visitation to the Sick, I should like to call to the attention of my people while they are in good health: "Then shall the Minister examine whether he repent him truly of his sins, and be in charity with all the world. . . . And if he hath not before disposed of his goods, let him then be admonished to make his Will, and to declare his Debts, what he oweth, and what is owing unto him, for the better discharging of his conscience, and the quietness of his Executors. But men should often be put in remembrance to take order for the settling of their temporal estates, whilst they are in health." ★

Let me now speak of the prior moral obligation referred to above. Those of you who recall the removal from the old site and the beginning of this church building will remember that when the Vestry had bought the land on Park Avenue between Fiftieth and Fifty-first Streets, the question arose: "Shall we occupy the whole lot, or shall we use but the southern half of it, and sell the northern part for the erection of an apart-

★See Prayer Book, page 285.

ment house?" In order to learn the will of the congregation, a model of the church was made and beside it was placed a model of an apartment house, and the people were asked to express an opinion. So far as I can remember, there was no difference of opinion, and some of the largest gifts were made *with the distinct understanding that the church would be built on the whole lot, substantially in accordance with the plan of Mr. Goodhue—the nave crowned by a dome and the garden surrounded by cloisters.* To rest satisfied with what we have done, or to delay the accomplishment of our promise and divert the gifts of the congregation to any other work, however desirable, until that has been accomplished, would be, in my judgment, to fail in our duty to those who gave their money into our hands to be used for a definite purpose, many of whom went to their reward, trusting us.

At the time the decision was made to occupy the whole lot, it was believed that the money already subscribed was sufficient for that purpose and, under normal conditions, it would have been amply sufficient. But the outbreak of the Great War sent prices soaring and the Vestry, as honest trustees, felt themselves obliged to limit the work and not run into debt. But even so, they were disappointed. The delay in selling the old site, on account of unsettled conditions, led to a debt of over one hundred and fifty thousand dollars, which the congregation paid off about eighteen months ago. But now the time has come when we should set ourselves to the task of fulfilling our obligation to those who trusted us; and until that obligation is fulfilled, in my judgment, we are not justified in diverting our gifts either to Diocesan or General Church expansion.

I know that this position will be misunderstood, but I trust the congregation will be no more influenced by such a fear than is their Rector. I know also that the suggestion that one of the Bays of the Nave of the Cathedral shall be a memorial to Bishop Greer will appeal to those who knew and loved him, but I have no doubt what his judgment would have been—a consideration which has never been absent from my thoughts in any step taken in my rectorship. I know how firmly convinced he was that the strength of our Church is dependent upon the vitality of the parishes, and that any weakening of that vitality by over-centralization will weaken the whole Church. Until we have been just to those who trusted us, we cannot afford to be generous to the Cathedral.

I do not suggest that the completion of the church and the enlargement of the endowment should be immediately undertaken. That will be the happy work of my successor. But I cannot, with a quiet conscience,

refrain from reminding the congregation of the solemn obligations which I undertook with their approval.

THE PROPOSED NEW ST. BARTHOLOMEW'S CHURCH

by Bertram G. Goodhue, The Architect

Everyone who enters St. Bartholomew's Church passes through one of the three entrances of the great triple portal. This portal, by Messers. McKim, Mead & White, was incorporated some years ago in the old church. It is universally regarded, by architects and public alike, as one of the most beautiful things, perhaps the most beautiful thing of its kind in America.

Naturally, in moving to a new site, the Parish wished to retain this portal, so the question of the architectural style of the new building determined itself.

The new building, therefore, is Romanesque—a Romanesque of the Italian type rather than that of any of the French phases of this style. For although the triple portal found its original inspiration in the one at St. Gilles, in the South of France, it is in no sense a replica. Both the detail and the sentiment of the sculpture and the carving, which is essentially Provençal in the original, gave way in the modern example to something far more Italianate. In the design for the new church this great triple portal appears as the crux of the whole, and every endeavour has been made to keep the work of the present designer in harmony with that of Messrs. McKim, Mead & White. It has been felt that to compete with this triple portal would be at once impertinent and unwise, therefore, in all those portions of the new design that are near this portal, the utmost reticence has been maintained; for instance, the little doorway leading to the chapel, though of the same materials, stone and bronze, as the great one, is of the simplest type imaginable.

The full value of the great entrance, however, has never been apparent in its present position where its sturdy arches bear the whole weight of the facade above. In the original at St. Gilles the portal stands free as the front merely of the narthex, behind which comes the wall of the church proper; and so it will be in the new St. Bartholomew's. At St. Gilles, the narthex parapet terminates in the most microscopic of mouldings. Fortunately, somewhat more height has been per-

mitted the present designer and he has, therefore, ventured to introduce, in defiance of the original, an appropriate inscription carved frieze-like along the face of the narthex wall immediately beneath its coping course.

The narthex, which one will enter through the familiar portals, will be 15½ feet wide by 73 feet long and will be spacious enough to prevent undue crowding even when the church is filled to its utmost capacity. From this narthex, or vestibule, divided into three bays and ceiled with pendentive domes, one will enter through three light double doorways into as many aisles of the church.

The basic form of the church will be the traditional cruciform one, although the length of the transept arms will be much less than would have been the case in the past. And so every single individual, even though seated at the extremity of the arms, whether he be on the main floor or in either of the transept balconies, will have a full and unobstructed view of both pulpit and lectern. Besides the transept balconies, there will be a series of clerestory galleries running the full length of both nave and chancel above the side aisles. In computing the seating capacity of the Church at 1,302, no attempt has been made to take into account the hundreds of persons that may be accommodated by these galleries, which might well be used in the case of great festivals.

In the outer walls behind these passageways will be the large clerestory windows. There will be three of these to each bay excepting on the northern side of the chancel. Here will be placed the organs that are now divided between the two sides of the present chancel. The great organ that is above the main entrance of the present church will have a similar position in the new St. Bartholomew's. It will be placed in a rich new case in harmony with its architectural surroundings. The great 32-foot pipes will rise at either side of the big west window, which will be divided into five circular-headed divisions. The rest of the space that fills the circle concentric with the vault will be filled with elaborate stone tracery. The tracery is quite un-Gothic. In fact, although it will be in perfect harmony with the Romanesque architecture around it, and particularly that of the great portals, it is difficult to point to any exact precedent. On the contrary, the great rose window of the south transept, though differing in detail, is reminiscent of such Italian examples as St. Francis at Assisi. The main wall of the other transept, which can have no window, as it is a party wall of the adjoining property, will display better than ever before the great painting by the late Francis Lathrop, which, in the present Church, is placed above the altar.

Both the main body of the church and the transepts will be 44½ feet wide. They will be covered by barrel vaults. Above the crossing these barrel vaults are omitted and four piers support four arches upon which rise the walls that form the lower story of the ciborium, the scale everywhere being tremendous. This form of central tower is a very unusual feature and has always been such. The best known examples are perhaps those of the church at Santa Maria delle Grazie at Milan and the Certosa at Pavia. The transition from the square form of the crossing to the octagon of the lower part is accomplished by means of a series of concentric arches diagonally crossing the corners of the rectangular space, forming a perculiar kind of pendentive. Again from this octagon are thrown sixteen smaller arches from which rise the columns and arches of a tall gallery. This gallery opens into the church and is lighted by glazed windows in its outer wall. Above this again is a still smaller sixteen-sided gallery. Unlike the gallery immediately beneath, this passageway is glazed toward the church and open to the weather. Above this is a semi-circular dome pierced at the apex by a ring from which rises the cupola.

This, in the simplest terms, is a description of the form of the interior. Any adequate description of the materials or any attempt to realize the effect of the completed whole would require many more pages, and, since the question of materials is still somewhat undecided, would be out of place here.

One point, however, that should be mentioned since it is of the greatest importance, is the one that has to do with the covering of the greater part of the interior plane-surfaces. Of course, the structural members, piers, arches, etc., would be of stone or of marble veneer over concrete. The greater part of the plane-surfaces, however, will be covered with acoustic tile, a material of great beauty, both in colour and texture, slightly rough, and of a soft and rather warm coffee colour, whose greatest value lies not in its beauty but in its acoustic value. This tile is the result of the scientific knowledge and research of Dr. Wallace C. Sabine, Professor of Physics at Harvard University, universally accepted as the foremost authority on the subject of acoustics, and of the labour and experimenting of Mr. Raphael Guastavino, a manufacturer of clay products, whose work is well known to the world of architecture. It seems to have definitely solved the long vexed question as to how to guarantee in advance that the preacher and music will be satisfactorily heard in an as yet unbuilt church. In the past, felt has been often used to make churches and halls acoustically possible. With felt, surely a most unarchitectural material, as zero, the co-efficient of this tile is 15 while the co-efficient of the nearest natural stone is 73.

Beside the great west portal and the smaller doorway at the side leading into the chapel, there will be two other entrances to the church. The one at the northern extremity of the property leads into the north transept. An interesting feature of this entrance is that by a series of inclines all steps will be done away with, so that the aged and infirm may reach their seats in the church and their places at the communicants' rail without encountering a single step. In order to make this possible the floors of the ambulatories on both sides will be sloped in the fashion that has proved successful in the Chapel of the Intercession. The other entrance is on 50th Street, where one will be able to enter under the open porch and ascend to the south transept by a short flight of stairs.

This open porch, that is a free-standing arcade under the great rose window, is but one of the group of lower structures that give scale to the main body of the church and to the central towering mass of the ciborium. It links the parish house on one hand to the chapel on the other.

The chapel will be entered through the small vestibule at the side of the main portals. At one side of the vestibule will be a small retiring room. Although the chief use of the chapel will probably be for the younger members of the congregation, in its planning and chancel arrangement the necessities of wedding and funeral ceremonies have been recognized. To all intents and purposes it will be a separate building though connected with the main church by four doorways. The various members of the main church are large in scale on account of the great width of the nave and transepts;

but the size of the chapel will permit of a much more intimate treatment in the matter of its decoration. Here it is proposed to use the shafts of the columns of the present church with the bases omitted and with new capitals of carved stone. The chapel will be ceiled with a trussed timber roof, painted and gilt like the famous Italian Romanesque example of San Miniato 'al Monte at Florence. At one side of the diminutive chancel will be a gallery for the organist and above the west entrance will be hung a small but perfectly adequate organ. At the end of the south aisle of the chapel will be a door through which the officiating clergyman may enter from a little vestry. In the chapel may be seated 168 persons, and this number may be somewhat added to in case of necessity by placing chairs in the south aisle.

In the parish house, on the level of the main church, will be accommodations for the rector's office, that of the curate, and secretary, and behind these the various necessary vestries, choir practice rooms and the like.

Below will be the Sunday school. Since the grade of 50th Street slopes down to the east, it will be possible, using more sloping planes, for the children to enter the Sunday school without encountering any steps whatsoever. In the second story will be provision for the organist's and choir-master's office and library as well as additional vestries and Sunday school rooms.

Much study has been given both by the architect and the Art Committee of the church to the most effective material that might be used to keep the building in harmony both with the style chosen and with the atmospheric effect of New York. We too often forget that New York is blessed with the brilliant skies of Italy. And so it has been felt advisable to use materials that would give a somewhat similar effect of richness to that which one finds in the Romanesque churches of Milan and Bologna and, at the same time, to keep in perfect harmony with the portals of the present church. These, with the exception of the marble shafts of the columns and the various architraves and tympana, are

constructed of Indiana limestone. This material, the only fault of which is its familiarity, will be used for the trimming and carving. But much of the wall surface will be of brick—a brick, however, of an unusual character and quality—quite unlike the brick in common use: brick by no means regular either in size or shape—some being two or three times as high as others, and each height being made of several lengths. The wall surface will, however, not be entirely of brick. For it has been felt desirable to effect a modulation from the almost complete use of stone in the lower to the almost exclusive use of brick in the upper portions of the building. Thus the face and ends of the narthex will be wholly of stone, the walls of the chapel almost entirely so; brick will appear at first in small masses and courses and gradually increase in amount until, beneath the open gallery that encircles the church, and in the central tower, the walls will be almost wholly of brick.

By the use of these two materials, the one a warm gray in color and the other a warm and rather light salmon, it is believed that something at least of the quality and charm of the buildings of the old Italian prototypes may be achieved. If built of stone alone, even so picturesquely varied a mass as is contemplated could never obtain this effect—could never attain to this quality—for it needs the color and contrast of the various materials. To be sure, there will always be lacking one other and extremely important element. This church, like all our other churches, whatever their style, should possess more space than our great American cities permit. It should not be elbowed and jostled by great apartment houses, but should rise through the greenery of trees and flowers. To make up in some sort for this lack, it has been agreed that whatever building—club, apartment house, or whatever it may be—that shall be placed on the adjoining property, shall be set back 32 feet from the present building line of Park Avenue.

APPENDIX IV

ICONOGRAPHY

As soon as the construction of St. Bartholomew's began, Parks and the Art Committee worked out the iconographic program for the church, making recommendations to Goodhue in regard to the subjects for the interior and exterior sculpture and for the inscriptions to be incised into the stone.[1] The program was approved on May 14, 1917.

On the west façade, the portal and its doors have Old and New Testament scenes, prophets, and the Madonna and Child (pl. II). These architectural elements, transferred from St. Bartholomew's II, constituted a given for the new program. Their iconography symbolizes the life, Passion, and Resurrection of Christ, amplified by the inclusion of Old Testament prefigurations and prophecies and of the apostles. In order to strengthen the relation between this iconography and the church's dedication to St. Bartholomew, it was decided to carve the collect for his feast day along the top of the narthex: O ALMIGHTY AND EVERLASTING GOD, WHO DIDST GIVE TO THINE APOSTLE BARTHOLOMEW GRACE TRULY TO BELIEVE AND TO PREACH THY WORD; GRANT, WE BESEECH THEE, UNTO THY CHURCH, TO LOVE THAT WORD WHICH HE BELIEVED, AND BOTH TO PREACH AND RECEIVE THE SAME; THROUGH JESUS CHRIST OUR LORD. This text also emphasizes the evangelical mission of the church and its commitment to preaching.

On the upper part of the façade, against the mullions of the window, are statues of four great preachers: Martin Luther, St. Paul, St. Francis of Assisi, and Phillips Brooks (pl. III). In an earlier scheme, the statues were to be of great representatives of Protestantism; now the specific mission of St. Bartholomew's—preaching—is stressed. Symbols of Old Testament figures, recipients of heavenly revelation and grace, are woven into the tracery between the figures of their successors, the great preachers. The revealed truth—that is, the Christ and his salvation—is represented by symbols of the events of his life on bosses beneath the columnar arcade that crowns the façade. Atop the buttresses flanking the façade are the coats of arms of Canterbury (left) and the diocese of New York (right). In the center, the crowning gable is a medallion with three knives, the symbol of St. Bartholomew.

The program of mosaics in the narthex was not part of the original scheme. The first plan called for only the representation of twelve famous men and women on the capitals of the narthex (pl. XII). These are pillars of the church in both the literal and the metaphorical sense. Some are preachers; others, reformers; yet others, modern representatives of a life of Christian virtue.

The iconographic program of the church's interior was to consist of several parts, not all of which were executed. Reliefs containing scenes from the life and mission of St. Bartholomew were set into the crossing piers. The sixteen double columns of the nave carry historiated capitals (fig. 60). The Old Testament prefiguration and the New Testament event face each other across the nave. Thus the (successful) temptation of Eve is paired with the (unsuccessful) temptation of Christ; Moses giving the Law is paired with the Sermon on the Mount. Events from the life of Christ are presented as completing the work of salvation begun in the Old Testament.

A third iconographic section, which was not executed, was to have been in the south transept, where panels flanking the rose windows were to contain the Hebrew name of God and the Greek name of Christ. Very likely, these wall panels were to have been read together with the window, whose light would have symbolized the third member of the Trinity, the Holy Spirit.

This rich iconographic program of images was to have been complemented by a program of inscriptions placed on the four arches of the crossing. That on the east arch, leading into the chancel, referred to the spiritual relation between the worshipper and God: GOD IS

A SPIRIT AND THEY THAT WORSHIP HIM MUST WORSHIP HIM IN SPIRIT AND IN TRUTH (John 4:24). On the north arch, toward the entrance to the mortuary chapel and the seats for the infirm, the text referred to Christ's promise of eternal life: I AM COME THAT THEY MIGHT HAVE LIFE, AND THAT THEY MIGHT HAVE IT MORE ABUNDANTLY (John 10:10). The painting *The Light of the World,* brought from the old church and placed in the north transept, is framed by this arch. The text on the south arch, in front of the rose window symbolizing divine light, spoke of the power of the Holy Spirit to bring man into spiritual union with God: WE BEHOLDING THE IMAGE OF THE LORD ARE CHANGED INTO THE SAME IMAGE BY THE SPIRIT OF THE LORD (2 Corinthians 3:18). Finally, the text on the west arch exhorted the priest leaving the chancel for the pulpit to pursue his evangelical mission of preaching and baptizing: GO TEACH TO ALL NATIONS, BAPTIZING THEM INTO THE NAME OF THE FATHER AND OF THE SON AND OF THE HOLY GHOST (Matthew 28:19).

Interestingly, no inscriptions or imagery was planned for the apse and chancel, except, perhaps, the huge cross inlaid into the marble of the apse. Although St. Bartholomew's II had a reredos representing the Last Supper on the main altar and *The Light of the World* against the apse wall, Goodhue decided to place them in the baptistery and north transept, respectively (pl. XIII). The mosaic now in the conch of the apse contradicts the architect's aniconic decorative plan for the church.

The iconographic program is impressive in its coherence, completeness, and appropriateness. It apparently supersedes an earlier scheme, perhaps presented in conjunction with the model of the church in January 1916, which centered on stained-glass windows. An undated sheet in the church archive lists the subjects to appear in the clerestory and west windows. Since the sheet specifies that five clerestory windows are to be decorated, the list of subjects must have been drawn up before it was decided to add the third nave bay, which resulted in eight, rather than six, windows (one window in the chancel is blocked by the organ pipes, so only five or seven windows could be decorated). This plan called for the representation of the lives of the prophets "whose emblems are in stone" in the west window, scenes from the Passion in the nave windows, and scenes from the life of Christ in the apse windows. The program has an amateurish quality. The placement of the scenes does not follow traditional usages, and it is questionable whether the scenes from the life of Christ,

three to each apse window, would have been legible to someone seated in the congregation. The whole lacks both the conciseness of the later scheme and the intimate, even interdependent, relationship between iconographic content and architectural setting of Goodhue's program of sculpture and inscriptions.

The stained-glass window scheme, then, must belong to an earlier phase of the project and perhaps reflects Parks's desire to have, in this at least, a Gothic church. Goodhue's design, calling for marble revetment, sculpture, and inscriptions, necessitated the use of clear, tinted, or nonfigural windows. Historically, buildings with reveted interiors do not have stained-glass windows, whose darker, colored light obscures the beauty of the finish materials. Moreover, it is difficult to imagine that inscriptions on the soffits of the crossing arches would have been legible in such light. The church as Goodhue designed it could have had only one stained-glass window, the rose in the south transept, and even this was originally designed for clear or tinted glass.

Although the main portions of the iconographic program are on the west façade and in the interior of the church, programs for the transept exteriors and the north and south flanks were also devised.

The iconographic program of the north transept called for inset panels with the symbols of the Evangelists arranged around a symbol of Christ (fig. 47). Flanking these, other panels represent the sacraments: Baptism and Holy Communion. On the south transept, facing the cloister and Sunday school, are symbolic representations of Christian virtues (the Cardinal and Theological virtues) (pls. V, VI). Below, to the right and left of the rose window, are the emblems of the first and second Adam—that is, sin and salvation (pl. VII). At the top of the transept façade, on the corner buttresses, are over-life-size statues of St. Philip and St. Bartholomew (pl. VI).

Images related to the Eucharist were to have been placed above the ramp along the north flank of the church. These medallions would find their thematic culmination in a tympanum over the portal, representing Christ healing the sick. Free-standing statues of St. Luke and St. Dorcas were planned to go above this entrance.

The two chapels, the mortuary chapel in the crypt and the chapel along the south flank of the church, have more modest programs. A simple inscription referring to resurrection and salvation was the main iconographic element planned for the mortuary chapel, and the inscription ALL THY CHILDREN SHALL BE TAUGHT OF THE

LORD; AND GREAT SHALL BE THE PLACE OF THY CHILDREN (Isaiah 54:12) is over the main entrance to the chapel. The other elements of the chapel's iconography were established later. Finally, figural friezes were planned for the exterior of the chapel, facing the garden (fig. 63). Although Goodhue suggested a program including the signs of the zodiac, the elements, the winds, the arts and trades connected with building, and the functions of the church, this scheme was not adopted. Parks preferred to expand the theme of the functions of the church to cover the whole area. Preaching was to have been in the central arch, flanked by praise, prayer, the sacraments, and instruction in the other arches.

Taken together, the iconographic program, or rather programs, of St. Bartholomew's is remarkable for its encyclopedic content, skillful placement in relation to the architectural setting, and appropriateness to the aims and functions of this particular church. To one trained as a medievalist, it comes as a surprise that anyone in the early twentieth century was capable of devising such a program. Although much of the content is due to the erudition of Parks, the intelligence and imagination with which the iconography is adapted to its architectural setting are Goodhue's. It is one of Goodhue's most impressive achievements that, by drawing on his extensive knowledge of the vast repertory of iconographic imagery and on his considerable familiarity with sacred and secular literature, he was able to invent iconographic programs that spoke to the modern world. The challenge of designing such programs was rarely, if ever, so brilliantly resolved as in Goodhue's works.

ICONOGRAPHY OF ST. BARTHOLOMEW'S
CHURCH AS EXECUTED[2]

EXTERIOR
West Façade
Portal zone
Doors

North doors (top to bottom)
Transfiguration / Paul on the Road to Damascus

Peter and Andrew / Barnabas and Saul

Peter Addressing the Centurian's Family / Conversion of Lydia by Paul

Inscription ENTER INTO HIS GATES WITH THANKSGIVING AND INTO HIS COURTS WITH PRAISE *(Psalm 104)*

Center doors
Annunciation / Adoration of the Magi

Matthew and Luke / John and Mark

Descent from the Cross / Way of the Cross

Inscriptions HEAR THE WORD OF THE LORD DAILY, YE THAT ENTER AT THESE GATES TO WORSHIP THE LORD *(Jeremiah 7:2)*

TO THE GLORY OF GOD AND IN LOVING MEMORY OF CORNELIUS VANDERBILT, BORN 1843, DIED 1899. THESE DOORS ARE ERECTED BY HIS WIFE AND CHILDREN

South doors
Pentecost / Ascension

Philip and James / Andrew and Bartholomew

Judas's Betrayal of Christ / Peter Receiving the Keys

Inscriptions BEHOLD, I STAND AT THE DOOR AND KNOCK; IF ANY MAN HEAR MY VOICE AND OPEN THE DOOR, I WILL COME IN *(Revelation 3:20)*

LORD, I HAVE LOVED THE HABITATION OF THY HOUSE AND THE PLACE WHERE THINE HONOUR DWELLETH *(Psalm 26)*

Statues between doors (north to south)
Isaiah (sword and book) / Elijah (chariot) / Jeremiah (staff) / Moses (Tablets of the Law)

Tympana and lintels
North
Madonna and Child with Angels
Lintel   Entombment

Central
Coronation of Christ
Lintel   Crucifixion

South
Jesus and John the Baptist as Infants
Lintel   Road to the Calvary

Statues flanking central tympanum
Elijah and Moses

Frieze between arches of portals
North
Journey of the Magi / Flight into Egypt / Betrayal of Christ / John the Baptist
South
Adam and Eve / Expulsion from Eden / Murder of Abel / Moses Freeing the Israelites

Cornice level

Inscription ALMIGHTY AND EVERLASTING GOD, WHO DIDST GIVE TO THINE APOSTLE BARTHOLOMEW GRACE TRULY TO BELIEVE AND TO PREACH THY WORD; GRANT, WE BESEECH THEE, UNTO THY CHURCH, TO LOVE THAT WORD WHICH HE BELIEVED, AND BOTH TO PREACH AND RECEIVE THE SAME; THROUGH JESUS CHRIST OUR LORD *(Collect for St. Bartholomew's Day)*

Upper portion
Statues at west window
Martin Luther / St. Paul / St. Francis of Assisi / Phillips Brooks

West window tracery
Symbols of Old Testament figures
Ark = Noah
Lion = Joel
Chariot = Elijah

Turreted Gate = Ezekiel
Angel = Malachi
Temple = Zechariah
Gourd = Jonah
Wand in Hand = Jeremiah
Ram = Daniel
Shepherd's Crook = Amos
Sword = Isaiah

Bosses beneath dwarf gallery

Symbols of events of the life of Christ
Alpha = Beginning
Lily = Annunciation
Star = Nativity
Crowns = Epiphany
Doves = Presentation
Pyramids = Flight into Egypt
Dove and Monogram = Baptism
Palm = Entry into Jerusalem
Crown of Thorns = Crowning
Cross = Crucifixion
Pomegranate = Resurrection
Omega = End

Coats of arms

North buttress   Canterbury
South buttress   Diocese of New York
Gable   St. Bartholomew

North Side

Entrance ramp portal

Christ Healing the Sick

Inscription   WHO SAVETH THY LIFE FROM DESTRUCTION

North transept façade

Cross with central medallion of Agnus Dei / Symbols of Evangelists at ends of arms of the Cross, flanked by symbols of baptism (font and dove) and Holy Communion (chalice)

Entrance to crypt

Inscription   I AM THE RESURRECTION AND THE LIFE, SAITH THE LORD: HE THAT BELIEVETH IN ME, THOUGH HE WERE DEAD, YET SHALL HE LIVE; AND WHOSOEVER LIVETH AND BELIEVETH IN ME, SHALL NEVER DIE

Doorway sculpted with symbols of immortality (peacock) and resurrection (phoenix)

Choir practice room

St. Cecilia and an organ carved in relief over window

South Side

Archivolts of chapel windows

Subjects from Psalm 158 (east to west):

Angels   Praise ye the Lord from the heavens: praise Him in the heights. Praise ye Him, all His angels: praise ye Him all His hosts

Sun and the four winds   Praise ye Him, sun and moon: praise Him all ye stars of light. Praise Him, ye heavens of heavens, and ye waters that be above the heavens

Dragons intertwined   Praise the Lord from the earth, ye dragons, and all deeps: fire, and air; snow, and vapour; stormy wind fulfilling His word

Leaves, flowers, and branches   Mountains, and all hills; fruitful trees, and all cedars

Animals and birds   Beasts, and all cattle creeping things, and flying fowl

Men, women, and children   Kings of the earth, and all people; princes, and all, judges of the earth: Both young men, and maidens; old men, and children

South transept façade

Arcade
Emblems of Christian virtues in marble inlay
Sword = Fortitude
Scales = Justice
Padlock = Prudence
Cross = Faith
Anchor = Hope
Heart = Charity
Bridle = Temperance
Prayer Book = Piety

Buttress statues

Bartholomew and Philip

INTERIOR

Narthex

Dome mosaics

Genesis cycle (arranged, out of chronological order, so that the creation of man ["Let us make man in our own image"] is over the main entrance to the church)
Creation of Light
Separation of Heaven and Earth
Creation of Earth and Water / Creation of Plants
Creation of Sun and Moon
Creation of Animals / Creation of Man

Capitals
Heads representing saints or exemplars of Christian life (north to south)

West side
St. Athanasius, bishop of Alexandria
Pope Gregory I
Thomas Cranmer, archbishop of Canterbury
Bishop William White
Florence Nightingale
George Williams

East side
St. Clement of Alexandria
St. John Chrysostom
John Wycliffe
John Wesley
William Augustus Muhlenberg
Louis Pasteur

Main Body of Church

Organ loft
Capitals with musicians playing musical instruments. Figures of musicians on top of organ casing

Inscription O PRAISE GOD IN HIS HOLINESS; PRAISE HIM IN THE FIRMAMENT OF HIS POWER . . . PRAISE HIM IN THE SOUND OF THE TRUMPET: PRAISE HIM UPON THE LUTE AND HARP . . . LET EVERYTHING THAT HATH BREATH PRAISE THE LORD *(Psalm 150)*

Capitals in nave
Scenes from Old Testament (north) and New Testament (south)

Creation / Nativity
Temptation and Fall of Man / Temptation of Christ
Flood / Christ Walking on the Water
Abraham Sacrificing Isaac / Raising of Lazarus
Joseph and His Brothers / Christ and His Disciples
Moses and the Burning Bush / Transfiguration
Crossing the Red Sea / Resurrection
Moses Giving the Law / Christ on the Mount

Relief panels in crossing piers
(from northeast, counter-clockwise)
Jesus Calls Bartholomew
Philip Tells Bartholomew of Jesus
Bartholomew Acknowledges Christ
Betrayal of Jesus
Resurrected Christ Appears to the Disciples
Pentecost
Vision of Bartholomew
Preaching of the Apostles

Pulpit

Capitals
Symbols of the Evangelists
John Chrysostom / Athanasius / Jerome / Augustine
Scroll / Open book / Shell / Palm

Figures
Moses
Inscription THE TRUTH SHALL MAKE YOU FREE

John the Baptist
Inscription THE GOODLY FELLOWSHIP OF THE PROPHETS PRAISE THEE

Isaiah
Inscription IN THY LIGHT SHALL WE SEE LIGHT

Lectern

Capital
Symbols of the Evangelists

Above the capital
Eagle standing on a sphere

Apse

Pavement
Marble inlays representing Hagia Sophia, Canterbury Cathedral, and St. Peter's Basilica

Conch
Mosaic of the Transfiguration
Christ flanked by Moses and Elijah; Peter, James, and John witness the event

Inscription HIS EST FILIUS MEUS CARISSIMUS; AUDITE ILLUM

CHAPEL

West Façade
Inscription ALL THY CHILDREN SHALL BE TAUGHT OF THE LORD; AND GREAT SHALL BE THE PEACE OF THY CHILDREN *(Isaiah 54:12)*

Door jambs
Christopher, Cyril, Nicholas, Pancreas, Kenlem, Simon, Holy Innocents

Bronze doors
Young John the Baptist and Jesus; symbols of the Evangelists

Interior

Capitals
Old and New Testament cycle (west to east)
Moses / Nativity and Flight into Egypt

Joseph / Youth of Jesus
Samuel / John the Baptist
David / Christ's Ministry
Naaman / Peter
Tobias / Paul
Children Making Music / Timothy

Apse

Pavement
Mosaic inlays

Center
Ship (the church) / Stag and unicorn (Christ) /
Peacock (eternal life) / Pelican (atonement)

North
Serpent encircling cross (Moses) / Sacrifice of Isaac

South
Goat (Old Testament sacrifice) / Agnus Dei

Fresco over altar
Adoration of the Magi

NOTES

CHAPTER 1

1. For the history of the parish, see E. C. Chorley, *The Centennial History of St. Bartholomew's Church, 1835–1935* (New York, 1935), and L. Young, *A Short History of St. Bartholomew's Church in the City of New York, 1835–1960* (New York, 1960).

2. R. Krautheimer, *Rome: Profile of a City: 312–1308* (Princeton, N.J., 1980), pp. 76–78.

3. W. K. Jordan, *The Charities of London, 1480–1660* (Hamden, Conn., 1974).

4. For a discussion of this term, see J. T. Addison, *The Episcopal Church in the United States, 1789–1931* (New York, 1951), p. 285.

5. Quoted in ibid., p. 288.

6. Julius Kaftan, a follower of Albrecht Ritschl, a nineteenth-century proponent of the Liberal Protestant movement, quoted in B. Reardon, *Liberal Protestantism* (Stanford, Calif., 1968), p. 42.

7. This is one of the main themes of A. Ritschl, *The Christian Doctrine of Justification and Reconciliation; The Positive Development of the Doctrine,* 2nd ed. (Edinburgh, 1900).

8. Quoted in Addison, *Episcopal Church,* p. 322.

9. Chorley, *Centennial History of St. Bartholomew's Church,* p. xiii.

10. Ibid.

11. L. Parks, *The Winning of the Soul and Other Sermons* (New York, 1895), p. 262.

12. Addison, *Episcopal Church,* p. 316.

13. This was expressed very beautifully by the Ritschlian theologian Adolf Harnack: "Either the gospel is in all points identical with its first form, in which case it is a transient phenomenon, appearing in time only to pass away again, or else it presents eternal truth in historically changing forms" (*What Is Christianity?* 2nd ed. rev., trans. T. B. Saunders [New York and London, 1901], p. 46).

14. Parks, *Winning of the Soul,* p. 262.

15. L. Parks, "Protestantism and Democracy. A Present-Day Problem," in *Sermons by Leighton Parks* (New York, 1912), 2:22. The close relationship between Protestantism and patriotism had been a traditional claim. In a sermon of 1820, commemorating the landing of the Pil-

grims in New England, John Chester pronounced that "he who cultivates personal religion and obeys the gospel, is the best friend to his country. Christian piety is practical patriotism." And the Annual Report of the Board of Missions of the Presbyterian Church for 1849 states that "the Christian citizen of an evangelized nation may regard his country as an abode of the church, and love his country the more without loving the kingdom of Christ the less; the more he is a patriot, the more he is a Christian" (quoted in J. Bodo, *The Protestant Clergy and Public Issues, 1812–1848* [Philadelphia, 1954], pp. 8–9, 190).

16. J. F. Bethune-Baker, quoted in Reardon, *Liberal Protestantism,* p. 212.

17. L. Parks, "At the Commandment of the Lord" (Appendix of Texts).

18. L. Parks, "The Spiritual Significance of the Romanesque" (Appendix of Texts). Donald Drew Egbert remarked that since H. H. Richardson's Trinity Church, Boston, was Romanesque and Low Church and St. George's was the same, there may have been a tendency among Low Church Episcopalians to distinguish themselves by stylistic choice from High Church Episcopalians, who, like Roman Catholics, favored Gothic Revival for their churches ("Religious Expression in American Architecture," in *Religious Perspectives in American Culture,* ed. J. W. Smith and A. L. Jamieson [Princeton, N.J., 1961], p. 329).

19. Parks, "At the Commandment of the Lord."

20. Chorley, *Centennial History of St. Bartholomew's Church,* p. 164.

21. Other explanations are worth considering as well. The Vanderbilt family mausoleum in the Moravian cemetery on Staten Island purported to copy St. Gilles-du-Gard; thus that model had a special significance for the donor and an association with the funerary customs of the family. Further, Richardson had used the same model for the portal of his famous Trinity Church, Boston. Links between their rectors and a shared outlook on the nature of Christian ministry might have influenced Greer to consider that example, while the fact that Richardsonian Romanesque was currently fashionable may have spurred Stanford White to emulate Richardson's classic work.

However it came into being, the prized portal had fundamental importance for the present St. Bartholomew's.

22. L. Parks, Sermon, November 9, 1919, in *Sermons by Leighton Parks* (New York, 1919), 7:15. The rector's remarks reveal the influence of a movement within Protestantism to invest ritual, architecture, and decoration with a more sensuous appeal as a stimulus to spiritual experience. The popularity of this trend is suggested by a poem published in *Atlantic Monthly* in November 1899 that begins: "The city's burning heart beats far outside this dim cathedral, / where the mystic air vibrates with voices of impassioned prayer" (Katharine Coolidge, "In the Cathedral," quoted in J. Lear, *No Place of Grace: Antimodernism and the Transformation of American Culture, 1880–1920* [New York, 1981], pp. 192–93).

23. L. Parks, "The House of Martha and Mary" (Appendix of Texts).

24. Ibid.

25. Quoted in Chorley, *Centennial History of St. Bartholomew's Church,* p. 156.

26. Parks, "The Spiritual Significance of the Romanesque."

27. L. Parks, "The Reformation," in *Sermons by Leighton Parks* (New York, 1917), 5:4.

28. Ibid., p.3.

29. Quoted in Chorley, *Centennial History of St. Bartholomew's Church,* p. 258. As early as 1883, E. A. Freeman had recommended Italian Romanesque as the true style for American architecture, praising Richardson's design for the State Capitol in Albany, New York (J. Burchard and A. Bush-Brown, *The Architecture of America: A Social and Cultural History* [Boston and Toronto, 1961], p. 175).

30. For example, David Mck. Williams, Harold Friedell, and Jack Ossewaarde.

31. The altar is not, however, visible from the transepts.

32. Parks, "At the Commandment of the Lord."

33. The figures are from Chorley, *Centennial History of St. Bartholomew's Church,* and the annual *Year Book of St. Bartholomew's Parish.* They should be considered as approximations, since the sources differ in their reports of costs. The cost of the portal designed by Stanford White for the Vanderbilts is not recorded in the church archives.

34. L. Mumford, *Roots of Contemporary American Architecture* (New York, 1959), p. 16.

35. T. W. Higginson, "A Word to the Rich," *Atlantic Monthly,* vol. 107, p. 301.

36. A curious aside is in a letter from Goodhue to Edward Goodhue, June 7, 1917, in which the architect reports that he has received a commission for a house in California (Avery Library Archive, Columbia University). He was informed of this by Mrs. William K. Vanderbilt, "a woman that I don't even remember to have met." Is this indirect evidence of the Vanderbilt family's approval of his work?

CHAPTER 2

1. The most important source for Goodhue's life and work has been C. H. Whitaker, ed., *Bertram Grosvenor Goodhue, Architect and Master of Many Arts* (1925; reprint, with Introduction by Paul Goldberger, New York, 1976). See also R. Oliver, *Bertram Grosvenor Goodhue* (Cambridge, Mass., and London, 1983); R. A. Cram, *My Life in Architecture* (Boston, 1936); A. Johnson and D. Malone, eds., *Dictionary of American Biography* (New York, 1931), s.v. F. Kimball, "Goodhue, Bertram Grosvenor"; and T. Tallmadge, *The Story of Architecture in America* (New York, 1936), p. 261.

2. Quoted in A. Colton, review of *Bertram Grosvenor Goodhue, Architect and Master of Many Arts,* by C. H. Whitaker, *Architectural Record* 59 (1926): 95, and in Whitaker, *Bertram Grosvenor Goodhue,* p. 14.

3. B. G. Goodhue, "Church Architecture in the United States Thirty Years Ago and Today," *Architectural Review* 5 (1917): 251.

4. Quoted in Whitaker, *Bertram Grosvenor Goodhue,* p. 15.

5. This list, which is in Whitaker, may have been drawn up in the early 1920s for the benefit of Goodhue's nephew, Wright Goodhue, who was beginning his architectural training (ibid).

6. The competition is discussed in chapter 4. Goodhue considered it one of his "ambitious and silly designs for a number of competitions which were far beyond my reach in every way" and "that I wouldn't let anyone see for anything in the world" (quoted in ibid., p. 14).

7. Quoted in ibid., p. 13.

8. Quoted in ibid.

9. Letter, Bertram Goodhue to Oswald Villard, January 23, 1909, Avery Library Archive, Columbia University (hereafter ALA). These remarks betray the influence of John Ruskin and Eugène Viollet-le-Duc (and, through them, Hegel) on Goodhue. For example, according to Viollet-le-Duc, "the first law of art . . . is to conform to the needs and customs of the times" (quoted in P. Collins, *Changing Ideals in Modern Architecture, 1750–1950* [London, 1965], p. 131).

10. "Religious matters had no particular interest for him; he saw the problem from a purely aesthetic point of view" (Cram, *My Life in Architecture,* p. 78); see also Tallmadge, *Story of Architecture,* p. 262.

11. Letter, Goodhue to Paul Cret, 1918, quoted in Whitaker, *Bertram Grosvenor Goodhue,* p. 27.

12. Cram, *My Life in Architecture,* p. 277.

13. Quoted in Whitaker, *Bertram Grosvenor Goodhue,* p. 24.

14. Letter, from Goodhue, October 29, 1913, ALA.

15. Quoted in Whitaker, *Bertram Grosvenor Goodhue,* p. 22.

16. B. G. Goodhue, "The Villa Fosca," in *A Book of Architectural and Decorative Drawings by Bertram Grosvenor Goodhue* (New York, 1914). The nineteenth-century sources for this notion were Ruskin and Viollet-le-Duc.

17. Quoted in Whitaker, *Bertram Grosvenor Goodhue*, p. 25.

18. Letter, Goodhue to Ruth Baldwin, August 30, 1916, ALA. For a different interpretation of "The Villa Fosca," see R. Oliver, Modernism that Did Not Exclude Nostalgia: *B.G.G., Architect and Master of Many Arts," Architectural Record* 162 (1977): 41–43.

19. According to Cram, Goodhue possessed "a creative imagination, exquisite in the beauty of its manifestations, sometimes elflike in its fantasy, that actually left one breathless," and "historic data . . . might serve as a basis, but what issued from his fertile imagination and deft fingers had suffered a sea-change into something rich and strange" (*My Life in Architecture*, pp. 76, 78). According to Tallmadge, "He was an architect's architect, the god of designers, the darling of the draughting-room." (*Story of Architecture*, p. 259).

20. R. A. Cram, tribute to Goodhue at the American Institute of Architects Convention, *Proceedings of the Fifty-seventh Annual Convention of the AIA* (Washington, D.C., 1924), p. 24.

21. Letter, Goodhue to Peake Anderson, April 23, 1917, ALA.

22. Letter, Goodhue to Harry Eldredge Goodhue, November 3, 1916, ALA.

23. Goodhue refers to himself as an "ex-theosophist" in a letter to C. F. Bragdon, May 2, 1916, ALA.

24. Letter, Goodhue to Reverend Samuel Drury, February 8, 1922, ALA.

25. Letter, Goodhue to Mrs. R. Rojers, November 19, 1915, ALA.

26. Letter, Goodhue to Reverend Marcus Carroll, December 10, 1917, ALA.

27. Letter, Goodhue to Theodore Price, April 11, 1922, ALA. This was one of the tenets of Theosophy.

28. Quoted in Whitaker, *Bertram Grosvenor Goodhue*, p. 45.

29. "It [St. Bartholomew's] will look more like Arabian Nights or the last act of Parsifal than any Christian Church" (letter, Goodhue to George Horsfield, February 16, 1919, ALA). Oliver suggested, rightly I think, that Goodhue considered architecture and music to be the two greatest arts because they are essentially abstract—that is, pure acts of human creation—whereas painting, sculpture, and literature depend on the imitation of nature.

30. Quoted in Whitaker, *Bertram Grosvenor Goodhue*, p. 45.

31. These events are referred to frequently in the letters that Goodhue wrote during the summer and autumn of 1913 (ALA).

32. Letter, Goodhue to H. C. Henderson, December 10, 1910, ALA.

33. Goodhue says that Royal Cortissoz has been his friend for more than thirty years in a letter, June 18, 1920, ALA.

34. Recommendation of the Art Committee to the vestry, June 4, 1914, Vestry Minutes, St. Bartholomew's Archive (hereafter SBA).

35. Letter, Goodhue to Arthur C. Jackson, April 29, 1914, ALA.

36. Vestry Minutes, December 14, 1914, June 15, 1915, and April 4, 1929, SBA; letter, Goodhue to Charles Mathews, March 6, 1916, ALA; report of the Art Committee to the vestry, October 20, 1927, Vestry Minutes, SBA.

37. "After talk with Goodhue went to talk to Dr. Parks to advocate Goodhue's design. Also telegraphed W. Field [a member of the vestry] to say that Goodhue had made a bulls-eye" (letter, Charles Mathews to Goodhue, January 11, 1916, ALA).

38. Letter, Goodhue to Charles Mathews, December 21, 1915, ALA.

39. First consultation recorded December 14, 1914, Vestry Minutes, SBA.

40. Letter, Wallace Sabine to Goodhue, August 23, 1913, ALA.

41. Letter, Goodhue to Wells Goodhue, September 29, 1914, ALA. The commissions are also described in a letter to Edward Goodhue, November 6, 1914, ALA.

42. Goodhue gives the prices and the price estimates for a number of his works in a letter to J. C. M. Keith, February 3, 1915, ALA:

Chapel, West Point	$350,000
St. Thomas	$1.1 million
Chapel of the Intercession	$550,000
St. Bartholomew's	$600,000 to 700,000
St. Vincent Ferrer	$600,000
First Congregational Church, Montclair	$300,000

43. "I have no head draughtsman; my system does not permit of such; but if I had and if it did, Mr. Stein in all probability would be it" (letter, Goodhue to S. Keeney, October 11, 1916, ALA).

44. Letter, Goodhue to Constance Grosvenor Alexander, November 27, 1914, ALA.

45. Letter, Goodhue to George Horsfield, April 26, 1917, ALA.

46. Letter, Goodhue to Reverend Marcus Carroll, September 26, 1919, ALA.

47. L. Parks, Preface, *Year Book of St. Bartholomew's Parish*, 1915, p. xiv.

48. Cram confirmed (rather than suggested) this interpretation of Goodhue's development as an architect. He noted that Goodhue gradually lost interest in Gothic "and indeed in all the other historic styles. The modern theme

appealed more and more to his exuberant and inventive spirit. He had proved himself in Gothic, Spanish Renaissance, Byzantine, Romanesque, Colonial; and in time he was through. From there, he went on as a purely creative genius until, at last, and working independently, he crowned his life and his labours with the Nebraska State Capitol, perhaps the greatest example of vital, modern architecture in the United States" (*My Life in Architecture*, p. 79).

49. Vestry Minutes, December 14, 1914, SBA.

50. Letter, Goodhue to Harry Eldredge Goodhue, November 3, 1916, ALA.

51. Quoted in Whitaker, *Bertram Grosvenor Goodhue,* p. 23.

52. See, for example, the events of September to November 1916 (Appendix of Documents).

53. Letter, Goodhue to Edward Goodhue, November 6, 1914, ALA; letter, Goodhue to E. D. Robb, November 9, 1914, ALA; letter, Goodhue to Edward Goodhue, January 7, 1915, ALA; Vestry Minutes, January 22, 1917, SBA; letter, Goodhue to Henry Hardenbergh, January 30, 1917, ALA; letter, Goodhue to Robert Brewster, July 17, 1918, SBA.

54. Letter, Goodhue to Leighton Parks, April 14, 1916, SBA.

55. See the events of April 14 to April 29, 1916 (Appendix of Documents).

56. "I hold that while architecture should represent a decent reverence for the historic past of the art, that we should only ignore our rightful heritage for the most compelling reasons, and that one of these compelling reasons is the modern invention of the steel frame, or reinforced concrete, construction: that this form of construction does abrogate practically all known forms—at least definite constructive forms such as columns or arches: that it is not enough that a building should be beautiful, it must also be logical" (letter, Goodhue to Paul Cret, 1918, quoted in Whitaker, *Bertram Grosvenor Goodhue,* p. 27, and in F. Kimball, "Goodhue's Architecture: A Critical Estimate," *Architectural Record* 62 [1927]: 538).

57. Quoted in Whitaker, *Bertram Grosvenor Goodhue,* p. 24.

58. Letter, Goodhue to Paul Cret, 1918, quoted in ibid., p. 27.

59. Marble revetment and extensive use of planar surfaces conceals or denies the weight-support dynamic in the kinds of Byzantine and Romanesque buildings that served Goodhue as models. At St. Bartholomew's, these devices, instead, express the static character of its constructional system.

60. Quoted in Whitaker, *Bertram Grosvenor Goodhue,* p. 19.

61. B. G. Goodhue, "The Modern Architectural Problem Discussed from a Professional Point of View," *Craftsman* 8 (1905): 332–33.

62. This was noted, for example, by C. Howard Walker:

"His very facility became antipathetic to him, and the restraint of reasoned simplicity was making his latest work more serene. . . . His latest conceptions had a nobility transcending detail and the pendulum had swung so far with him that he expressed his idea of architecture as of justly proportioned solids devoid even of mouldings, speaking not with detail but with associated sculpture only" (tribute to Goodhue at the American Institute of Architects convention, *Proceedings of the Fifty-seventh Annual Convention of the AIA* [Washington, D.C., 1924], p. 23).

63. Quoted in Colton, review of Whitaker, *Bertram Grosvenor Goodhue,* pp. 97, 28.

64. These architectural values are not new, and their historical affinities are with certain classes of Romanesque and Early Renaissance structures. The aesthetic has little in common with most Gothic and Classical architecture. This needs to be kept in mind in interpreting Kimball's claim that "paradoxically, yet naturally enough, as Goodhue moved towards 'modernism' he moved also towards classicism—the classicism of calm and ordered masses and spaces" (Johnson and Malone, *Dictionary of American Biography*). Kimball did not mean that Goodhue's choice of historical models changed in the late work (although this is also true), but that his work began to display those timeless virtues of harmony and balance, which are classic.

65. Goodhue's drawing for this detail, with a list of the stones to be used, is preserved at St. Bartholomew's.

66. This, for some critics, produced a false impression of modernity: "As Bertram Goodhue's reputation for originality was enhanced by his dexterity in combining such a variety of eclecticisms as to hamper easy stylistic identification, so lack of any real knowledge of Eliel Saarinen's Finnish beginnings fostered the use of the stop-gap term, 'Modern,' in connection with his Chicago Tribune Contest design of 1922" (W. L. Creese, "Saarinen's *Tribune* Design," *Journal of the Society of Architectural Historians* 6 [1947]: 1–5).

67. I cannot agree with H. R. Hitchcock's claim that the model for the tower of the Nebraska State Capitol was Lars Sonck's tower for the Kallio church in Helsinki, designed in 1910 (H. R. Hitchcock and W. Seale, "How Nebraska Acquired a State Capitol Like No Other," *AIA Journal,* October 1976, pp. 57–61). Not only the measurements of height and width, but also the double-staged (low cupola, high tower), double-shell construction are closely related between St. Bartholomew's and the Nebraska State Capitol. The latter is but the concrete realization of a scheme first envisioned for St. Bartholomew's in 1915 and 1916, improved and enlarged during the following years.

68. Cram, *My Life in Architecture,* p. 169.

69. Assessments of Goodhue's architectural success differ. Although he was posthumously awarded the gold medal by the American Institute of Architects in recogni-

tion of his achievement, most of his contemporaries seem to have felt that, at his death, he was on the threshold of an unrealized excellence. Tallmadge, for example, felt that his late work, prophetic and revolutionary, came close to creating the "long-sought American style," succeeding where Sullivan had failed, but that he died too young (*Story of Architecture,* p. 263). Kimball was less impressed: "In the final estimate of Goodhue's work there must be taken into account, beside the intrinsic quality of his works, the question of leadership. We must recognize that in the great movements on the stage of the world he made but a dilatory entrance, and that his steps were halting and uncertain. . . . Whether the future held for him a new unity, a more vitally creative modernity, we cannot know" ("Goodhue's Architecture," p. 538, and Johnson and Malone, *Dictionary of American Biography*). Even Cram was not sure that Goodhue had "arrived": "Bertram Goodhue did indeed reach maturity, both in years and in power, creating and revealing what was almost a new and potentially national style of architecture. If he had but lived another ten years, the vitality of his design and the dynamic force of his personality might well have wrought an architectural revolution that would have averted the debacle of contemporary modernistic art" (*My Life in Architecture,* p. 17).

While it is understandable that contemporaries would assess Goodhue's work with the yardstick of their concern—the creation of a modern, national style—such judgments have only relative value. Another criterion, the architect's success in giving form to an inner vision or ideal, suggests that Goodhue died at the height of his creativity. His style, moreover, was too personal ever to have constituted an idiom for general use, and it would never have been widely imitated. Although his plans, functional arrangements, structure, and elevations might be copied with some success, his unique sensitivity to color, light, texture, and pattern could not. This is why his works make a much weaker impression when seen in photographs than when actually experienced. At its best, his work is highly abstract and extraordinarily sensual, the product of his temperament and artistic judgment.

CHAPTER 3

1. Letter, Bertram Goodhue to Arthur C. Jackson, April 29, 1914, Avery Library Archive, Columbia University (hereafter ALA); letter, Goodhue to Edward Goodhue, May 15, 1914, ALA.

2. Recommendation of the Art Committee to the vestry, June 4, 1914, Vestry Minutes, St. Bartholomew's Archive (hereafter SBA).

3. Letter, Goodhue to C. Matlock Price, June 30, 1914, ALA.

4. Letter, Goodhue to Mrs. Leo Pierson, June 21, 1922, ALA. Goodhue reveals that he had never been to Sicily in a letter to Constance Grosvenor Alexander, January 25, 1923, ALA.

5. Letter, Goodhue to Robert Brewster, July 17, 1918, SBA.

6. B. G. Goodhue, "The Proposed New St. Bartholomew's Church" (Appendix of Texts). Akoustolith is a molded tile in which tiny pumice particles, which resist compression, leave air spaces that give the tile its acoustic quality. For a discussion of the material and its uses, see G. Collins, "The Transfer of Thin Masonry Vaulting from Spain to America," *Journal of the Society of Architectural Historians* 27 (1968): 176–201.

7. Goodhue, "The Proposed New St. Bartholomew's Church."

8. Contract with the R. Guastavino Company, for timbrel tile vaulting, December 12, 1916, SBA.

9. The timbrel tile vaults that support the pavement are visible as the ceiling of the basement.

10. Letter, Goodhue to Edward Goodhue, November 6, 1914, ALA.

11. Letter, Goodhue to E. D. Robb, November 19, 1914, ALA.

12. Vestry Minutes, January 22, 1915, SBA.

13. Letter, Goodhue to Leighton Parks, June 10, 1915, SBA.

14. Letter, Goodhue to Arthur Molesworth, May 17, 1915, ALA.

15. Goodhue, to Leighton Parks, October 27, 1915, SBA. The sun would be blocked, presumably, by the fifteen-story Ambassador Hotel, on Park Avenue and Fifty-first Street.

16. Ibid.

17. Vestry Minutes, January 11, 1916, SBA.

18. Recommendation of the Building Committee to the vestry, February 14, 1916, Vestry Minutes, SBA.

19. This maximum included 225 folding chairs in the aisles and nave galleries. Thus the pew-seating capacity of scheme A was 1,075—only 50 seats more than that of St. Bartholomew's II. Since scheme A did not provide the larger church that Parks wished, he naturally favored placing the church on the deeper, northern, side of the lot.

20. Vestry Minutes, February 14, 1916, SBA.

21. Letter, Goodhue to Leighton Parks, April 14, 1916, SBA.

22. Letter, James Lane to Albert Milbank, May 8, 1916, SBA.

23. Goodhue, to Leighton Parks, wardens, and vestry, June 16, 1916, SBA.

24. Letter, Goodhue to John D. Moore, July 3, 1916, ALA.

25. Letter, Goodhue to James Lane, November 1, 1916, SBA.

26. Timbrel tile vaulting: contract with the R. Guastavino Company, December 12, 1916; structural steel: contract with Post and McCord, January 5, 1917; rubble masonry: contract with Charles P. Galardi, January 26, 1917; modeling and carving: contract with Piccirilli Brothers, January 26, 1917; setting cast and cut stone: contract with William Angus, Inc., February 3, 1917; cutting cut stone and marble: contract with the George Brown Company, February 8, 1917; brick: contract with O. W. Ketcham, February 15, 1917; roofing tile: contract with the Gladding, McBean Company, February 16, 1917.

27. Letter, Goodhue to James Lane, March 28, 1917, SBA.

28. Letter, Goodhue to Peake Anderson, April 23, 1917, ALA.

29. Letter, Goodhue to George Horsfield, April 26, 1917, ALA.

30. This significance is further suggested by Parks's statement that "even our stores rival in their towers the cathedrals of old! . . . If the Church . . . falls below the artistic demand of the community it will fail to do the work that it desires to do" ("The House of Martha and Mary" [Appendix of Texts]).

31. Some of the imagery, particularly the coat of arms of St. Bartholomew's Church, was devised by Pierre de Chaignon La Rose, a retired professor from Harvard University (Vestry Minutes, April 26, 1917, and payment to La Rose, September 20, 1917, SBA).

32. Letter, Goodhue to Robert Brewster, March 14, 1922, SBA.

33. L. Parks, Preface, *Year Book of St. Bartholomew's Parish*, 1925 (Appendix of Texts).

34. R. Norwood, Preface, *Year Book of St. Bartholomew's Parish*, 1927.

35. See documents for January 11, 1918, January 16, 1918, and January 29, 1918, SBA; letter, Goodhue to Leighton Parks, October 15, 1918, SBA. Wallace Sabine had advised hanging a heavy fabric in the apse, but the vestry decided that a marble revetment such as that in St. Bartholomew's II would make a better sounding board. There was not enough time to install it before the opening of the church.

36. Report of the Art Committee to the vestry, Vestry Minutes, SBA.

37. See Chapter 4.

38. Report of the Art Committee to the vestry, October 20, 1927, Vestry Minutes, SBA.

39. R. Norwood, Preface, *Year Book of St. Bartholomew's Parish*, 1930.

CHAPTER 4

1. B. G. Goodhue, "The Proposed New St. Bartholomew's Church" (Appendix of Texts).

2. Letter, Bertram Goodhue to Leighton Parks, August 12, 1914, St. Bartholomew's Archive (hereafter SBA).

3. Letter, Goodhue to C. Matlock Price, June 30, 1914, Avery Library Archive, Columbia University (hereafter ALA).

4. Almost every reference to the style of St. Bartholomew's Church in the *New York Times* between 1980 and 1985, for example, refers to it as Byzantine: "Byzantine-style interior" (September 11, 1980); "modified Byzantine eclectic architecture" (September 19, 1980); "a medley of the Romanesque and Byzantine" (September 22, 1980); "Byzantine style church" (October 10, 1980); "fake Byzantine eyesore" (October 11, 1980); "Byzantine-style church" (October 15, 1980); "graceful Byzantine church" (October 20, 1980); "Byzantine-inspired complex" (October 26, 1980); "Byzantine-style domed church" (December 14, 1980); "domed, Byzantine-style structure" (June 4, 1981); "inspired by Byzantine architecture" (October 4, 1981); "designed in the Byzantine style" (October 29, 1981); "the Byzantine church" (October 30, 1981); "the Byzantine walls of Bertram G. Goodhue's landmark church" (November 10, 1981); "the Byzantine sanctuary" (November 14, 1981); "the beautiful, stately Byzantine edifice" (January 19, 1982); "the Byzantine-style church" (February 14, 1982); "stately Byzantine church" (January 3, 1983); "the Byzantine grandeurs of the 62-year-old church" (April 12, 1983); "the Byzantine complex" (March 23, 1985).

5. Letter, Goodhue to George Horsfield, February 16, 1919, ALA.

6. Such an impression is suggested in R. Oliver, "Modernism that Did Not Exclude Nostalgia: *B.G.G., Architect and Master of Many Arts,*" *Architectural Record* 162 (1977): 41–43. Oliver also recognizes the professional side of Goodhue's mentality.

7. A. Burnham, ed., *New York Landmarks: A Study and Index of Architecturally Notable Structures in Greater New York* (Middletown, Conn., 1963), p. 366. A similar point is made by Richard Longstreth: "When virtually all the context and most of the architectural fabric are ignored, 'style' is left a lonely and trivial thing" ("The Problem with 'Style,' " *Bulletin of the Committee on Preservation of the Society of Architectural Historians* 6 [1984]: 3).

8. ". . . the two essential things that the Vestry had in mind, in the construction of this building, I hope are entirely successful. We believe that the acoustic conditions of the church are favorable to an intelligent participation in the services of the church and that the seating of the congregation is such that each worshipper has an unobstructed view of the lectern and pulpit" (L. Parks, "Remarks of the Rector" [Appendix of Texts]).

9. A. J. B. Beresford Hope, *The English Cathedral of the Nineteenth Century* (London, 1861), p. 29.

10. M. Schuyler, "The Cathedral of St. John the Divine, New York City," *Architectural Record* 30 (1911): 186.

11. F. M. Simpson, "The New Cathedral for Liverpool,

Its Site and Style," *Architectural Review* 10 (1901): 138–43. An interesting later development of this thesis is discussed in H. Sedlmayr, *Das erste mittelalterliche Architektursystem* (Berlin, 1933). By separating structural systems from stylistic models, Sedlmayr was able to consider Byzantine, Romanesque, and Gothic architecture as belonging to one group, different from all earlier and later architectural systems.

12. R. F. Bach, "Church Planning in the United States," *Architectural Record* 40 (1916): 15–29.

13. Commenting on Heins and La Farge's design for the interior of St. John the Divine, Ralph Adams Cram explained that it focused on a big central "preaching space," which was "at that time, before the sacramental aspect of the Christian Faith had recovered its position of primacy, held by the authorities to be a desideratum" (*My Life in Architecture* [Boston, 1936], p. 169). He also recounted how difficult it was to incorporate the enormous crossing into a Gothic scheme.

14. L. Parks, "The Spiritual Significance of the Romanesque" (Appendix of Texts).

15. B. G. Goodhue, "Church Architecture in the United States Thirty Years Ago and Today," *Architectural Review* 5 (1917): 251–53.

16. Schuyler, "Cathedral of St. John the Divine," p. 190.

17. C. G. La Farge, "The Cathedral of St. John the Divine," *Scribner's Magazine* 41 (1907): 390.

18. "The Cathedral of St. John the Divine," *Architectural Record* 2 (1892): 49.

19. Quoted in H. R. Hitchcock, *Richardson as a Victorian Architect* (Baltimore, 1966), p. 5. Schuyler recognized the influence of Trinity Church on the competition entries for St. John the Divine ("Cathedral of St. John the Divine," p. 190).

20. La Farge, "Cathedral of St. John the Divine," pp. 388, 389. Schuyler noted that the four final entries "had taken the one isolated and sporadic example which English Gothic supplied in the octagon of Ely" ("Cathedral of St. John the Divine," p. 190).

21. "Its artistic value cannot be estimated until it is completed. But even now in it the soul may hear an echo of the great words of John: 'The tabernacle of God is with men, and he will dwell with them, and they shall be his people, and God himself shall be with them, and be their God.'" (Parks, "Spiritual Significance of the Romanesque").

22. Goodhue, "The Proposed New St. Bartholomew's Church"; letter, Goodhue to Wallace Sabine, December 13, 1916, ALA; letter, Goodhue to Henry Hardenbergh, January 30, 1917, ALA; letter, Goodhue to Peake Anderson, November 12, 1918, ALA; letter, Goodhue to Robert Brewster, March 14, 1922, SBA.

23. Letter, Goodhue to Leighton Parks, August 12, 1914, SBA.

24. W. De L'Hôpital explained that the exceptionally wide nave and clear view of the sanctuary characteristic of Byzantine architecture was best suited to the congregational needs of a metropolitan cathedral, enabling the worshippers to see and hear the liturgy (*Westminster Cathedral and Its Architect* [London, n.d.], 1: 25–26).

25. W. R. Lethaby, "Westminster Cathedral," *Architectural Review* 11 (1902): 3.

26. La Farge, "Cathedral of St. John the Divine," p. 395. La Farge's designation of Albi Cathedral as Romanesque followed that of Eugène Viollet-le-Duc.

27. Letter, Goodhue to Peake Anderson, November 12, 1918, ALA.

28. Ibid.

29. Letter, Goodhue to Percy Newton, May 1, 1913, ALA.

30. For a summary of the controversy and a bibliography, see J. Thomas, "The Style Shall Be Gothic," *Architectural Review* 158 (1975): 155–63.

31. "Fifty Years of Building Liverpool Cathedral" [interview with Giles Gilbert Scott], *Royal Institute of British Architects Journal* 60 (1952–53): 222.

32. Letter, from Goodhue, February 28, 1913, ALA; letter, Goodhue to J. C. M. Keith, February 1, 1915, ALA.

33. M. Schuyler, "The Romanesque Revival in New York," *Architectural Record* 1 (1891): 18.

34. See the summary of Romanesque Revival architecture in the United States in M. Whiffen, *American Architecture Since 1780: A Guide to the Styles* (Cambridge, Mass., and London, 1969), pp. 61–67, and H. R. Hitchcock, *The Architecture of H. H. Richardson and His Times* (1936; reprint, Hamden, Conn., 1961), p. 164.

35. The key is John Ruskin's discussion of the importance of "individual religion" in Venetian life, opposed to the Church of Rome (*The Stones of Venice*, in *The Works of John Ruskin*, ed. E. T. Cook and A. Wedderburn [London, 1904], 2:27). That Byzantine was considered to be an international style, as shown by its appearance in Venice as well as in the Byzantine Empire, may have further recommended it for the pluralistic United States (L'Hôpital, *Westminster Cathedral*, 1:26).

36. Goodhue refers to himself as "strongly anti-Catholic" in a letter to Harry Eldredge Goodhue, November 3, 1916, ALA.

37. R. A. Cram, *American Churches* (New York, 1915), 1:intro.

38. Quoted in J. Burchard and A. Bush-Brown, *The Architecture of America: A Social and Cultural History* (Boston and Toronto, 1961), p. 283.

39. Cram, *My Life in Architecture*, p. 126. H. R. Hitchcock disparagingly characterized the result as "Byzantinoid" (*Architecture: Nineteenth and Twentieth Centuries* [1958; reprint, Harmondsworth and New York, 1977], p. 546).

40. Cram, *My Life in Architecture*, pp. 246–47. Aitchison also considered Byzantine to be a non-Catholic style:

"Byzantine architecture may be said to be pre-eminently Christian, just as Gothic may be called Roman Catholic architecture" ("Byzantine Architecture," *Architectural Record* 1 [1891]: 85).

41. Cram, *My Life in Architecture*, p. 66.

42. Beresford Hope simply assumed that some phase of Gothic would be used for new cathedrals (*English Cathedral*, p. 30). Schuyler prefaced his discussion of St. John the Divine by acknowledging that all things being equal, Gothic was the correct style for a cathedral ("Cathedral of St. John the Divine," p. 186). The competition for the design of Liverpool Cathedral further emphasizes this point. Although George Edmund Street thought that Spanish Gothic architecture was interesting, "inasmuch as they [the Spanish churches] help to show what could be done, and ought to be done, among ourselves for providing for our crowded towns large churches in which everyone can see the altar and hear the preacher," his suggestion was not generally accepted (review of *Some Account of Gothic Architecture in Spain*, by G. E. Street, *Ecclesiologist* 23 [1865]: 142).

43. Cram, *My Life in Architecture*, p. 126.

44. "Fifty Years of Building Liverpool Cathedral," p. 222.

45. Cram, *My Life in Architecture*, p. 12.

46. Letter, Goodhue to Dr. Bruce Keator, June 21, 1917, ALA.

47. The church is referred to as "Lombard Romanesque" in L. E. Smith and N. Warren, "The First Methodist Episcopal Church of Asbury Park, New Jersey," *Architectural Record* 50 (1921): 472–80.

48. According to R. Dixon and S. Muthesius, "the basis of High Victorian style is the emphasis on the surface properties of each material" (*Victorian Architecture* [London, 1978], p. 205). Beresford Hope wrote that although Italian Gothic architecture was unsuited to the English climate, its polychromy might be borrowed (*English Cathedral*, p. 34). It is worth noting the connection between Italian Gothic and High Church Anglican patronage and the Ecclesiological Society, which undoubtedly led to the adoption of Italian Gothic as the style for St. Bartholomew's II and thus its incorporation into the parish identity.

49. The most recent publications on Street are H. A. Millon, "G. E. Street and the Church of St. Paul's in Rome," in *In Search of Modern Architecture*, ed. H. Searing (Cambridge, Mass., and London, 1982), and D. Brownlee, *The Law Courts: The Architecture of George Edmund Street* (Cambridge, Mass., and London, 1984).

50. St. Bartholomew's is a good illustration of Ruskin's definition of Gothic architecture, whose formal idea is "considerable size, exhibited by simple terminal lines. Projection towards the top. Breadth of flat surface. Square compartments of that surface. Varied and visible masonry. Vigorous depth of shadow, exhibited especially by pierced

traceries. Varied proportion in ascent. Lateral symmetry. Sculpture abstract in inferior ornaments and mouldings, complete in animal forms. Both to be executed in white marble. Vivid color introduced in flat geometrical patterns, and obtained by the use of naturally colored stone" (*The Seven Lamps of Architecture*, in *The Works of John Ruskin*, ed. E. T. Cook and A. Wedderburn [London, 1903], 8: 187).

51. Ruskin, *Stones of Venice*, p. 93. Ruskin went even further in *The Seven Lamps of Architecture*, asserting that "the only admiration worth having, attached itself *wholly* to the meaning of the sculpture and color of the building" and that sculpture and painting "were in fact the entire masters of the architecture; and that the architect who was not a sculptor or a painter was nothing better than a framemaker on a large scale" (p. 10).

52. Goodhue, "The Proposed New St. Bartholomew's Church."

53. Ruskin, *Seven Lamps of Architecture*, p. 126.

54. Letter, Goodhue to Leighton Parks, August 12, 1914, SBA. It might be thought that Goodhue's design for a domed narthex derived from his design for the Villa Fosca, which has a portico with five domes. But the portico is an open loggia of Renaissance type, reminiscent of Brunelleschi's early-fifteenth-century Ospedale degli Innocenti and the garden façade of Giulio Romano's Palazzo del Te (B. G. Goodhue, "The Villa Fosca," in *A Book of Architectural and Decorative Drawings by Bertram Grosvenor Goodhue* [New York, 1914], p. 34).

55. That St. Bartholomew's was to have occupied the southern half of the lot, not the northern, matters little, since the principal of two main views—one straight-on, and the other on a long diagonal—remains unchanged. A third, subsidiary view of St. Mark's is from the Piazzetta dei Leoncini, to the northwest. This is partially reproduced at St. Bartholomew's with the landscaped ramp area along the north flank.

56. Richardson had included galleries in the transepts in Trinity Church, Boston, in order to accommodate as many people as possible close to the preacher. Goodhue picked this up, in slightly different form, at St. Thomas Church, where it was noticed as a modern feature (that is, a response to the modern requirement that the congregation both see and hear the service) by Schuyler ("The New St. Thomas' Church, New York," in *American Architecture and Other Writings*, ed. W. Jordy and R. Coe [Cambridge, Mass., 1961]). What Goodhue realized, however, was that San Marco provided gallery space in the transepts and west end, as well as along the nave and choir. This maximization of gallery seating results in a church that accommodates almost as many people in the gallery as on the main level.

57. Interesting is the report of a parishioner who is said to have recalled "that everybody [in 1918 or so] . . . was very critical of the new church's Byzantine style, which

did not match the architecture of the old facade" (quoted in Michael Oreskes, "Vision of St. Bart's Rector Pushes Tower Deal Ahead," *New York Times*, 10 November, 1981, p. B1). That the church did not match the portal in style was therefore noticed, but it is difficult to believe that if the parishioners had considered the style to be Byzantine before about 1924, Parks would have consistently referred to it as Romanesque in his sermon.

58. ". . . the Romanesque, which arose out of the Byzantine, also crowned its temples with the dome" (Parks, "The Spiritual Significance of the Romanesque"), and "the congregation had an opportunity to reveal to the people that a Romanesque, or Byzantine architecture, was well adapted to this cosmopolitan city" (quoted in E. C. Chorley, *The Centennial History of St. Bartholomew's Church, 1835–1935* [New York, 1935], p. 258).

59. Still unsurpassed for the historiography of medieval architecture is P. Frankl, *The Gothic: Literary Sources and Interpretations Through Eight Centuries* (Princeton, N.J., 1960). The term *Romanesque* is thought to have been coined in 1818 by Charles Alexis de Gerville (M. F. Gidon, "L'invention de l'expression d'architecture romane par Gerville," *Bulletin de la Société des Antiquaires de Normandie* 42 [1934]: 285).

60. Richardson owned C. F. M. Texier and R. P. Pullan, *L'Architecture byzantine; ou, recueil de monuments des premiers temps du christianisme en orient, précédé de recherches historiques et archéologiques* (London, 1864); F. de Dartein, *Etude sur l'architecture lombarde et sur les origines de l'architecture romano-byzantine* (Paris, 1865–82); H. Hübsch, *Monuments de l'architecture chrétienne depuis Constantin jusqu'à Charlemagne* (Paris, 1866); M. G. Rohault de Fleury, *Les Monuments de Pise au Moyen Age*, 2 vols. (Paris, 1866) and *La Toscane au Moyen Age*, 2 vols. (Paris, 1874); J. Gailhabaud, *L'Architecture du Vᵉ au XVIIᵉ siècle*, 4 vols. (Paris, 1869–72); T. H. King, *The Study-Book of Mediaeval Architecture and Art; Being a Series of Working Drawings of the Principle Monuments of the Middle Ages, Whereof the Plans, Sections, & Details Are Drawn to Uniform Scales*, 4 vols. (London, 1858–68); G. E. Street, *Brick and Marble in the Middle Ages: Notes of Tours in the North of Italy* (London, 1855); and the first volume of the monograph on San Marco published by the Archaeological Institute of America in 1881. Richardson characterized the central tower of Auvergnate Romanesque churches as "a reminiscence, perhaps, of the domes of Venice and Constantinople . . . here fully developed" (quoted in Hitchcock, *Richardson as a Victorian Architect*, p. 5).

61. John Ruskin, *Val d'Arno*, in *The Works of John Ruskin*, ed. E. T. Cook and A. Wedderburn (London, 1906), 23:17; *Seven Lamps of Architecture*, pp. 200–01; and *Stones of Venice*, pp. 40, 401.

62. C. W. David, "American Historiography of the Middle Ages, 1884–1934," *Speculum* 10 (1935): 125–37; F.

G. Gentry and C. Kleinhenz, eds., *Medieval Studies in North America: Past, Present, and Future* (Kalamazoo, Mich., 1982).

63. It is not known how Goodhue and Norton met, but one possible occasion could have been the dinner held in New York in 1893 to celebrate the completion of work for the Chicago Exposition. Alternatively, Cram could have introduced them in Boston while Goodhue was working in the Boston office of their firm. Goodhue refers to Norton as "my old friend" in a letter, June 24, 1914, ALA.

64. Goodhue knew Moore's *Development and Character of Gothic Architecture* (London and New York, 1890), since he referred to it (C. H. Whitaker, ed., *Bertram Grosvenor Goodhue, Architect and Master of Many Arts* [1925; reprint, New York, 1976], p. 20).

65. C. E. Norton, *Historical Studies of Church Building in the Middle Ages*, 2nd ed. (New York, 1902), pp. 29, 22, 53. He also described the unusual four-footed piers of San Marco: "Through the piers ran archways in both directions, so as to open a narrow aisle on each side of the nave and transept" (p. 53).

66. Schuyler, "Romanesque Revival," pp. 7–38. Aitchison defined Romanesque as "that round-arched architecture of the Dark and Middle Ages in use before Gothic" ("Byzantine Architecture," p. 85).

67. Cram, *My Life in Architecture*, p. 181.

68. Letter, Goodhue to J. C. M. Keith, February 1, 1915, ALA; letter, Goodhue to A. B. Horne, November 12, 1920 [1922], ALA; letter, Goodhue to Mrs. Arthur Molesworth, March 10, 1922, ALA. Goodhue praises Lethaby in letters to J. C. M. Keith, February 1, 1915, and to Mrs. H. M. Fletcher, August 27, 1919, ALA. Goodhue's assessment of Lethaby has been challenged by D. Watkin, who describes Lethaby's views on architecture as "romantic, anti-intellectual populism" (*Morality and Architecture* [Oxford, 1977], p. 35). But a more sympathetic evaluation is given by David Talbot Rice; for example, "he was one of the first in Europe, let alone in this country, to realize why the change of the Dark Ages did not necessarily represent a catastrophic flood which washed away all but barbarism, but was, rather, akin to the confluence of a series of independent streams, whose merging was to create the great river of medieval church art and thought" (Introduction to W. R. Lethaby, *Medieval Art: From the Peace of the Church to the Eve of the Renaissance, 312–1350*, rev. ed. [New York, 1950], p. xiii). Goodhue refers to himself as a disciple of Lethaby in a letter to W. R. Lethaby, March 7, 1924, ALA.

69. ". . . of the causes which produced the phenomena of Medieval Art, a large share is . . . to be assigned to Eastern forces acting on the West. A thousand years of receptivity seems to have come to a close with the Renaissance" (Lethaby, *Medieval Art*, p. 119).

70. Ibid., pp. 28, 48.

71. Ibid., pp. 108, 297.

72. Quoted in Whitaker, *Bertram Grosvenor Goodhue*, p. 18.

73. The works in English were paralleled by important contributions in foreign languages, such as C. Enlart, *Manuel d'archéologie française* (1902); F. Cabrol, *Dictionnarie d'archéologie chrétienne* (begun 1903); R. de Lasteyrie, *L'architecture religieuse en France* (1912); A. Michel, *Histoire de l'art* (1905–29); E. Male, *L'art religieux en France,* 3 vols. (1898–1922); E. Bertaux, *L'art dans l'Italie méridionale* (1904); R. Wilpert, *Die römischen Mosaiken und Malereien der kirchlichen Bauten von IV bis XIII Jahrhunderts* (1917); J. Strzygowski, *Kleinasien, ein Neuland von Kunstgeschichte* (1903), *Orient oder Rom* (1901), and *Die Baukunst der Armenier und Europa* (1918); and J. Puig y Cadafalch, *L'arquitectura románica a Catalunya* (1909–18).

74. The books that Goodhue considered to be most valuable for professional use included W. R. Lethaby, *Architecture: An Introduction to the History and Theory of the Art of Building* (London, 1911) and *Architecture, Mysticism and Myth* (New York, 1892); T. G. Jackson, *Byzantine and Romanesque Architecture* (Cambridge, 1913) and *Gothic Architecture in France, England, and Italy* (London, 1915); A. K. Porter, *Lombard Architecture,* 4 vols. (New Haven, Conn., 1915–17), which was published too late to have influenced Goodhue in his design of St. Bartholomew's; King, *Study-Book of Mediaeval Architecture and Art;* A. Venturi, *Storia dell'Arte Italiana,* 5 vols. (Milan, 1901–37); and Eugène Viollet-le-Duc, *Dictionnaire raisonné de l'architecture française du xie au xvie siècle,* 10 vols. (Paris, 1858–68). The list suggests that Goodhue read French and Italian, but perhaps not German.

75. Letter, Goodhue to Dr. Bruce Keator, June 21, 1917, ALA.

76. Letter, Goodhue to Peake Anderson, August 13, 1917, ALA.

77. Letter, Goodhue to Mrs. Leo Pierson, June 21, 1922, ALA; letter, Goodhue to Constance Grosvenor Alexander, January 25, 1923, ALA.

78. The standard monograph on San Marco is O. Demus, *The Church of San Marco* (Washington, D.C., 1960). R. Krautheimer considers San Marco as "breathing much of the spirit of Justinian's art," despite the presence of elements from Middle Byzantine and Western Romanesque architecture (*Early Christian and Byzantine Architecture* [Harmondsworth and New York, 1979], p. 433). San Marco is presented as an example of the specifically byzantinizing character of Venetian Romanesque art in K. T. Conant, *Carolingian and Romanesque Architecture* (Harmondsworth and Baltimore, 1966). In the most recent series of architectural history texts, the volume on Romanesque architecture includes a discussion of San Marco (H. E. Kubach, *Architettura Romanica* [Milan, n.d.]). And the author of the volume on Byzantine architecture claims the basilica for his style: "La chiesa di San Marco a Venezia è giustamente considerata un monumento bizantino" (C. Mango, *Architettura Bizantina* [Milan, 1978]). The most recently published consideration of San Marco is V. Herzner, "Die Baugeschichte von San Marco und der Aufstieg Venedigs zur Grossmacht," *Wiener Jahrbuch für Kunstgeschichte* 38 (1985): 1–58.

CHAPTER 5

1. L. Parks, "At the Commandment of the Lord" (Appendix of Texts).

2. These objects are noted in the *Year Book of St. Bartholomew's Parish,* 1892. The Art Committee was empowered to decide with Goodhue where to place the furnishings from St. Bartholomew's II (Vestry Minutes, March 22, 1918, St. Bartholomew's Archive [hereafter SBA]).

3. D. Lowe, *Three St. Bartholomew's: An Architectural History of the Church* (New York, 1983), p. 7.

4. *Year Book of St. Bartholomew's Parish,* 1892.

5. The window in the west façade was replaced in the 1960s.

6. The Vestry Minutes of March 22, 1918, mentions "chancel furniture" but gives no details (SBA).

7. Contract with Piccirilli Brothers, for modeling and carving, January 26, 1917, SBA; contract with Piccirilli Brothers, for carving the interior stonework, March 30, 1917, Avery Library Archive, Columbia University (hereafter ALA). Only one payment is recorded (November 19, 1917, SBA).

8. Goodhue suggested that Parks visit some of the Romanesque churches of Apulia ("the churches of Bari and Bitonto are also of interest, but difficult of access") in a letter to Parks, August 12, 1914, SBA. Thus Goodhue acknowledged the possibility that Apulian architecture could be a model for St. Bartholomew's.

9. Letter, Goodhue to Paul Cret, 1918, quoted in C. H. Whitaker, ed., *Bertram Grosvenor Goodhue, Architect and Master of Many Arts* (1925; reprint, New York, 1976), p. 27.

10. Whitaker, *Bertram Grosvenor Goodhue*, p. 33.

11. Ralph Cram wrote that his firm discovered Lee Lawrie while working on the chapel at West Point (*My Life in Architecture* [Boston, 1936], p. 188). However, R. Oliver dates Goodhue's first association with Lawrie to 1898 to 1902, in connection with the Cook Sayles Public Library in Pawtucket, Rhode Island (Whitaker, *Bertram Grosvenor Goodhue*, pp. 22–23).

12. On November 19, 1917, Lawrie was paid for constructing models of the grotesques (SBA).

13. Goodhue submitted an estimate of $2,300 for the cost of the lectern and the pulpit in 1919 (Vestry Minutes,

June 27, 1919, SBA), but the lectern was not installed until 1923 (Vestry Minutes, December 5, 1923, SBA) and the pulpit until 1925.

14. L. Parks, *Year Book of St. Bartholomew's Parish*, 1926, p. 7.

15. Report of the Art Committee to the vestry, October 20, 1927, Vestry Minutes, SBA.

16. Cram, *My Life in Architecture*, p. 196.

17. C. R. Morey, *Lost Mosaics and Frescoes of Rome of the Medieval Period* (1915); C. R. Morey and W. Dennison, *Studies in East Christian and Roman Art* (1918); and O. M. Dalton, *East Christian Art* (1925). Kretch also read French and German, so he may have known R. Wilpert, *Die römischen Mosaiken und Malereien der kirchlichen Bauten von IV bis XIII Jahrhunderts* (1917); J. Ebersolt, *Les Arts sumptuaires de Byzance* (1923); M. van Berchem and E. Clouzot, *Mosaïques chrétiennes du IVe au Xe siècle* (1924); and A. Uhli, *Die Mosaiken von Ravenna* (1924).

Church, which was built in 1930 and thus after the mosaics at St. Bartholomew's had been executed.

19. S. Baxter, "The National Shrine of the Immaculate Conception, Washington, D.C.," *Architectural Record* 52 (1922): 2–15.

20. T. Addison, *The Episcopal Church in the United States, 1798–1931* (New York, 1931), p. 227.

21. The collect is, "O God, who on the mount didst reveal to chosen witnesses thine only-begotten Son wonderfully transfigured, in raiment white and glistening; mercifully grant that we, being delivered from the disquietude of this world, may be permitted to behold the King in his beauty, who with thee, O Father, and thee, O Holy Ghost, liveth and reigneth one God, world without end."

22. The lost fresco of San Lorenzo was illustrated by a drawing in Morey, *Lost Mosaics and Frescoes of Rome*. Thus it may have been known to the patrons of St. Bartholomew's.

23. Goodhue may have intended to decorate the domes in the narthex with mosaics. In one of his "Voyages Imaginaires," he drew a portico with five mosaic-covered domes that seem, at first glance, to anticipate St. Bartholomew's narthex (*A Book of Architectural and Decorative Drawings by Bertram Grosvenor Goodhue* [New York, 1914], pp. 34, 36). However, this open, Renaissance-style portico is closer to Brunelleschi's Ospedale degli Innocenti in Florence than to San Marco. That Goodhue conflated Brunelleschi's loggia with the vestibule of San Marco is in itself interesting, since architectural historians have only recently recognized their similarity (I. Hyman, "The Venice Connection: Questions About Brunelleschi and the East," in *Florence and Venice: Comparisons and Relations*, ed. S. Bertelli, N. Rubinstein, and C. H. Smyth [Florence, 1979], pp. 193–209).

24. R. Krautheimer, *Early Christian and Byzantine Architecture* (Harmondsworth and New York, 1979), pt. 4.

25. Correspondence, Goodhue and Harry Eldredge Goodhue, ALA.

26. That is, in the church. Glass from St. Bartholomew's II had been installed in the north transept vestibule and in the mortuary chapel.

27. "There is something lacking in the Romanesque churches which from an artistic point of view makes them seem essentially inferior to the Gothic, and that is the absence of the gorgeous glass which is the glory of Rheims and Chartres and Yorkminster." He then argued that to fill the building "with pictures and mosaics and then obscure the light by painted glass is an anachronism" (L. Parks, "The Spiritual Significance of the Romanesque" [Appendix of Texts]). Thus Parks, at least publicly, shared Goodhue's conception of the decoration of the church, which was subverted after Goodhue's death and Parks's retirement.

28. Report of the Art Committee to the vestry, December 16, 1929, Vestry Minutes, SBA. The mention of the completion of the walls and windows of the narthex refers to marble sheathing and marble window grilles, not stained glass.

29. Only the windows in the apse were not stained glass. The vestry had authorized Parks to have these windows darkened (Vestry Minutes, August 3, 1920, SBA). Perhaps as a result of that decision, they received their panes and grilles of amber onyx.

30. Goodhue failed by his own standards, as so expressed: "It is a strange and wonderful thing, but the final and definitive pronouncement of the great masses of people upon all the difficult, almost esoteric questions dealing with art, is invariably the correct one" (quoted in Whitaker, *Bertram Grosvenor Goodhue*, p. 23).

ICONOGRAPHY

1. These recommendations are preserved on several sheets with proposals, annotations, and corrections in the St. Bartholomew's Archive.

2. The scheme is described in greater detail in *Architectural and Decorative Features of St. Bartholomew's Church in the City of New York* (New York, 1956).

BIBLIOGRAPHY

Addison, T. *The Episcopal Church in the United States, 1789–1931*. New York, 1951.

Addleshaw, G. W. O., and F. Etchells. *The Architectural Setting of Anglican Worship*. London, 1948.

Aitchison, [no first initial]. "Byzantine Architecture." *Architectural Record* 1 (1891): 83–95.

American Institute of Architects. *Proceedings of the Fifty-seventh Annual Convention of the AIA*. Washington, D.C., 1924.

Andrews, R. D. "The Broadest Use of Precedent." *Architectural Review* 2 (1893): 31–36.

Andrews, W. *Architecture in New York: A Photographic History*. New York, 1969.

Architectural and Decorative Features of St. Bartholomew's Church in the City of New York. New York, 1956.

Bach, R. F. "Church Planning in the United States." *Architectural Record* 40 (1916): 15–29.

Barber, D. Obituary for B. G. Goodhue. *Architectural Record* 55 (1924): 469–70.

Baxter, S. "The National Shrine of the Immaculate Conception, Washington, D.C.." *Architectural Record* 52 (1922): 2–15.

Behrendt, W. C. *Modern Building: Its Nature, Problems and Forms*. New York, 1937.

Beresford Hope, A. J. B. *The English Cathedral of the Nineteenth Century*. London, 1861.

Bodo, J. *The Protestant Clergy and Public Issues, 1812–1848*. Philadelphia, 1954.

Brooklyn Museum. *The American Renaissance, 1876–1917*. New York, 1979.

Brown, E. L. *Architectural Wonder of the World: Nebraska's State Capitol Building*. Ceresco, Neb., 1965.

Brownlee, D. *The Law Courts: The Architecture of George Edmund Street*. Cambridge, Mass., and London, 1984.

Burchard, J., and A. Bush-Brown. *The Architecture of America: A Social and Cultural History*. Boston and Toronto, 1961.

Burnham, A., ed. *New York Landmarks: A Study and Index of Architecturally Notable Structures in Greater New York*. Middletown, Conn., 1963.

Carrott, R. *The Egyptian Revival: Its Sources, Monuments and Meaning, 1808–1858*. Berkeley, Calif., 1978.

"The Cathedral of St. John the Divine." *Architectural Record* 2 (1892): 45–53.

"The Cathedral of St. John the Divine, New York City." *Architectural Record* 30 (1911): 185–92.

Chorley, E. C. *The Centennial History of St. Bartholomew's Church, 1835–1935*. New York, 1935.

Clark, B. F. L. *Anglican Cathedrals Outside the British Isles*. London, 1958.

Collins, G. "The Transfer of Thin Masonry Vaulting from Spain to America." *Journal of the Society of Architectural Historians* 27 (1968): 176–201.

Collins, P. *Changing Ideals in Modern Architecture, 1750–1950*. London, 1965.

Colton, A. Review of *Bertram Grosvenor Goodhue, Architect and Master of Many Arts*, by C. H. Whitaker. *Architectural Record* 59 (1926): 95–98.

Cram, R. A. *American Churches*. 2 vols. New York, 1915.

———. *The Substance of Gothic: Six Lectures on the Development of Architecture from Charlemagne to Henry VIII*. Boston, 1917.

———. *My Life in Architecture*. Boston, 1936.

Creese, W. L. "Saarinen's Tribune Design." *Journal of the Society of Architectural Historians* 6 (1946): 1–5.

David, C. W. "American Historiography of the Middle Ages, 1884–1934." *Speculum* 10 (1935): 125–37.

De Mille, G. E. *Pioneer Cathedral: A Brief History of the Cathedral of All Saints, Albany*. Albany, N.Y., 1967.

Dixon, R., and S. Muthesius. *Victorian Architecture*. London, 1978.

Dohmer, K. *"In welchem Style sollen wir bauen?" Architekturtheorie zwischen klassizismus und Jugendstil*. Munich, 1976.

Drake, D. *America Faces the Future*. New York, 1922.

Dynes, W. "Historiography of Medieval Art." In *Medieval Studies: An Introduction*, edited by J. Powell. Syracuse, N.Y., 1976.

Edgell, G. H. *The American Architecture of Today*. New York and London, 1928.

Egbert, D. D. "Religious Expression in American Architecture." In *Religious Perspectives in American Culture,* edited by J. W. Smith and A. L. Jamison. Princeton, N.J., 1961.

Frankl, P. *The Gothic: Literary Sources and Interpretations Through Eight Centuries.* Princeton, N.J., 1960.

Freeman, E. "Choice in Architectural Styles." *Architectural Record* 1 (1892): 391–400.

Gentry, F. G., and C. Kleinhenz, eds. *Medieval Studies in North America: Past, Present, and Future.* Kalamazoo, Mich., 1982.

Germann, G. *Gothic Revival in Europe and Britain: Sources, Influences and Ideas.* Translated by G. Onn. London, 1972.

Goodhue, B. G. "The Modern Architectural Problem Discussed from a Professional Point of View." *Craftsman* 8 (1905): 332–33.

———. *A Book of Architectural and Decorative Drawings by Bertram Grosvenor Goodhue.* New York, 1914.

———. "Church Architecture in the United States Thirty Years Ago and Today." *Architectural Review* 5 (1917): 251–53.

———. Introduction to C. M. Winslow, *The Architecture and Gardens of the San Diego Exposition.* San Francisco, 1919.

Hersey, G. *High Victorian Gothic: A Study in Associationism.* Baltimore and London, 1972.

Higginson, T. W. "A Word to the Rich." *Atlantic Monthly,* vol. 107, p. 301.

Hitchcock, H. R. *The Architecture of H. H. Richardson and His Times.* 1936. Reprint. Hamden, Conn., 1961.

———. *Architecture: Nineteenth and Twentieth Centuries.* 1958. Reprint. Harmondsworth and New York, 1977.

———. "G. E. Street in the 1850's." *Journal of the Society of Architectural Historians* 19 (1960): 145–72.

———. *Richardson as a Victorian Architect.* Baltimore, 1966.

———. "Ruskin and American Architecture, or Regeneration Long Delayed." In *Concerning Architecture: Essays on Architectural Writers and Writing Presented to Nikolaus Pevsner.* Edited by John Summerson. London, 1968.

Hitchcock, H. R., and W. Seale. "How Nebraska Acquired a State Capitol Like No Other." *AIA Journal,* October 1976, pp. 57–61.

Hofmann, W. *The Earthly Paradise: Art in the Nineteenth Century.* Munich, 1961.

Honour, H. *Romanticism.* London, 1981.

Jackson, T. G. *Byzantine and Romanesque Architecture.* Cambridge, 1913.

Johnson, A., and D. Malone, eds. *Dictionary of American Biography.* New York, 1931.

Kidson, P., P. Murray, and P. Thompson. *A History of English Architecture.* Harmondsworth, 1979.

Kimball, F. "Goodhue's Architecture: A Critical Estimate." *Architectural Record* 62 (1927): 537–39.

Kouwenhoven, J. A. *Made in America: The Arts in Modern Civilization.* New York, 1948.

La Farge, C. G. "The Cathedral of St. John the Divine." *Scribner's Magazine* 41 (1907): 385–401.

La Follette, S. *Art in America.* New York and London, 1929.

Lear, J., ed. *No Place of Grace: Antimodernism and the Transformation of American Culture, 1880–1920.* New York, 1981.

Lethaby, W. R. *Architecture, Mysticism and Myth.* New York, 1892.

———. "Westminister Cathedral." *Architectural Review* 11 (1902): 3–19.

———. *Medieval Art: From the Peace of the Church to the Eve of the Renaissance, 312–1350.* London and New York, 1904. Rev. ed. New York, 1950.

———. *Architecture: An Introduction to the History and Theory of the Art of Building.* London, 1911.

Levine, N. "Architectural Reasoning in the Age of Positivism: The Neo-Grec Idea of Henri Labrouste's Bibliothèque Sainte-Geneviève." Ph.D. diss., Yale University, 1975.

L'Hôpital, W. de. *Westminster Cathedral and Its Architect.* Introduction by W. R. Lethaby. 2 vols. London, n.d.

Longstreth, R. "Academic Eclecticism in American Architecture." *Winterthur Portfolio* 17 (1982): 55–82.

Lowe, D. *Three St. Bartholomew's: An Architectural History of the Church.* New York, 1983.

Lowenthal, D., and M. Binney, eds. *Our Past Before Us: Why Do We Save It?* London, 1981.

Meeks, C. "Creative Eclecticism." *Journal of the Society of Architectural Historians* 12 (1953): 15–18.

———. "Romanesque Before Richardson." *Art Bulletin* 35 (1953): 17–33.

———. "Wright's Eastern-Seaboard Contemporaries: Creative Eclecticism in the United States Around 1900." *Problems of the 19th and 20th Centuries. Studies in Western Art. Acts of the Twentieth International Congress of the History of Art.* Vol. 4. Princeton, N.J., 1963.

Middleton, R. "Vive L'Ecole." AD Profiles 17, *The Beaux Arts,* pp. 38–48.

Millon, H. A., "G. E. Street and the Church of St. Paul's in Rome." In *In Search of Modern Architecture,* edited by H. Searing. Cambridge, Mass., and London, 1982.

Millon, J. R. *St. Paul's Within the Walls: A Building History and Guide, 1870–1980.* Dublin, N.H., 1982.

Morey, C. R. *Lost Mosaics and Frescoes of Rome of the Mediaeval Period.* Princeton, N.J., 1915.

Morey, C. R., and W. Dennison. *Studies in East Christian and Roman Art.* New York, 1918.

Mumford, L. *Roots of Contemporary American Architecture.* New York, 1952, 1959.

Norton, C. E. *Historical Studies of Church Building in the Middle Ages.* New York, 1888.

Oliver, R. "Modernism that Did Not Exclude Nostalgia: B. G. G., Architect and Master of Many Arts." *Architectural Record* 162 (1977): 41–43.

———. *Bertram Grosvenor Goodhue.* Cambridge, Mass., and London, 1983.

Parks, L. *The Winning of the Soul and Other Sermons.* New York, 1895.

———. *Sermons by Leighton Parks.* 10 vols. New York, 1905–25.

Patetta, L. *L'Architettura dell'Eclettismo: Fonti, teorie, modelli, 1750–1900.* Milan, 1975.

Perrine, G. "The Construction of the Temporary Dome Over the Crossing of the Cathedral Church of St. John the Divine." *New York Architect* 5 (1911): 56–61.

Pevsner, N. "Canons of Criticism." *Architectural Review* 104 (1951): 3–6.

Porter, A. K. *Medieval Architecture: Its Origins and Development.* New York, 1908.

Reardon, B. *Liberal Protestantism.* Stanford, Calif., 1968.

Rivoira, G. T. *Lombardic Architecture: Its Origin, Development and Derivatives.* Rome, 1901, 1907; London, 1910.

Rowe, C., and F. Koetter. *Collage City.* Cambridge, Mass., and London, 1978.

Ruskin, J. *The Works of John Ruskin.* Edited by E. T. Cook and A. Wedderburn. 39 vols. London, 1903–12.

Schuyler, M. "The New St. Thomas' Church, New York." In *American Architecture and Other Writings,* edited by W. Jordy and R. Coe. Cambridge, Mass., 1961.

———. "The Romanesque Revival in New York." *Architectural Record* 1 (1891): 7–38.

———. "The Cathedral of St. John the Divine, New York." *Architectural Record* 30 (1911): 185–92.

Scott, G. G. [interview]. "Fifty Years of Building Liverpool Cathedral." *Royal Institute of British Architects Journal* 60 (1952–53): 220–26.

Scott, L. *The Cathedral Builders: The Story of a Great Masonic Guild.* London, 1899.

Searing, H., ed. *In Search of Modern Architecture.* New York and London, 1982.

Service, A. *Edwardian Architecture.* London, 1977.

Simpson, F. M. "The New Cathedral for Liverpool, Its Site and Style." *Architectural Review* 10 (1901): 138–43.

Smith, L. E., and N. Warren. "The First Methodist Episcopal Church of Asbury Park, N.J." *Architectural Record* 50 (1921): 472–80.

Summerson, J. *Heavenly Mansions and Other Essays on Architecture.* New York, 1963.

———, ed. *Concerning Architecture: Essays on Architectural Writers and Writing Presented to Nikolaus Pevsner.* London, 1968.

Swales, F. "Bertram Grosvenor Goodhue: Architect, Designer and Draftsman." *Pencil Points* 5 (1924): 42–56.

Tallmadge, T. *The Story of Architecture in America.* New York, 1936.

Taylor, H. O. *The Medieval Mind: A History of the Development of Thought and Emotion in the Middle Ages.* London, 1911.

Thomas, J. "The Style Shall Be Gothic." *Architectural Review* 158 (1975): 155–63.

Vanderbilt, K. *Charles Eliot Norton: Apostle of Culture in a Democracy.* Cambridge, Mass., 1959.

Van Pelt, J. "The Church of St. John of Nepumuk, New York." *Architectural Record* 58 (1925): 517–29.

Watkin, D. *Morality and Architecture.* Oxford, 1977.

Whiffen, M. *American Architecture Since 1780: A Guide to the Styles.* Cambridge, Mass., and London, 1969.

Whitaker, C. H., ed. *Bertram Grosvenor Goodhue, Architect and Master of Many Arts.* New York, 1925. Reprint, with Introduction by Paul Goldberger. New York, 1976.

Withey, H., and E. Withey. *Biographical Dictionary of American Archtitects.* Los Angeles, 1956.

Winks, R. "Conservatism in America: National Character as Revealed by Preservation." In *The Future of the Past: Attitudes to Conservation, 1174–1974,* edited by J. Fawcett. London, Fakenham, and Reading, 1976.

Young, L. *A Short History of St. Bartholomew's Church in the City of New York, 1835–1960.* New York, 1960.

INDEX

Numbers in italics refer to pages on which illustrations appear.